D1526976

HERACLITEAN FRAGMENTS

HERACLITEAN FRAGMENTS

A Companion Volume to the Heidegger/Fink Seminar on Heraclitus

Edited by
JOHN SALLIS
and
KENNETH MALY

The University of Alabama Press
University, Alabama

Library of Congress Cataloging in Publication Data

Main entry under title:

Heraclitean fragments.

 Bibliography: p.
 Includes index.
 1. Heraclitus, of Ephesus—Addresses, essays,
lectures. I. Sallis, John, 1938– II. Maly,
Kenneth.
B223.H47   182′.4   79-17048
ISBN 0-8173-0027-9

CONTENTS

INTRODUCTION

During the Winter Semester of 1966/67 a seminar on Heraclitus was held at the University of Freiburg. It was an exceptional event. For it was codirected by a philosopher who, more than any other in our century, has opened up a new, more original dimension of dialogue with Greek thought. The book *Heraclitus* presents the edited transcript of this seminar.[1]

Heidegger's directing of the seminar consists partly in the fact that its general context is provided by Heidegger's writings on early Greek thinking, especially his two essays on Heraclitus.[2] On the other hand, the specific interpretation that is put at issue in the seminar and that determines, for instance, the order in which the fragments are taken up is the "cosmological" interpretation of the other codirector, Heidegger's long-time associate Eugen Fink. In the course of the seminar Heidegger's contributions are of two general kinds: he poses a series of penetrating questions that lead Fink to clarify his reading of the individual fragments; and he raises again and again the hermeneutical problems with which any philosophically rigorous attempt to interpret early Greek thinking must especially concern itself.

One of the results of the discussion between Heidegger and Fink is that it brings to light within the same general dimension two different directions in which the Heraclitean fragments can be thought through: Heidegger's way proceeds from the fragments dealing with λόγος to those concerning fire, Fink's way in the opposite direction. It is the rhythm of conflict and accord between Heidegger's "logical" reading of the fragments and Fink's "pyrological" or "cosmological" reading that gives the seminar its momentum and makes it a testimony to the concrete practice of thinking.

The entire seminar is devoted to meticulous reading of various individual fragments of Heraclitus. Repeatedly Heidegger introduces a restraint against taking up larger issues except as they arise from the reading of the fragments; even the apparent digressions, for example, the discussions of Hegel, are for the most part not really digressions at all but rather belong as hermeneutical reflections to the reflective side of the readings themselves.

Why is there here such dedication to the seemingly meager fragments of writings set down twenty-five hundred years ago? How is it that Heidegger and Fink engage in the delicate work of interpreting these fragments, not merely as doxographers, nor even as historians, but as philosophers? How is it that the interpretation of these fragments can assume the urgency and dignity of a task integral to that of contemporary philosophical thought as such? Why is it that the Greeks remain an issue for thinking today? Why the fragments of Heraclitus?

Of Heraclitus the man we know little. He was of Ephesus (on the coast of Asia Minor) and was probably in his prime toward the end of the sixth century B.C. A third-century B.C. satirist, Timon of Phlius, called him αἰνικτής ("riddler"), and this gave rise to the later epithet σκοτεινός, *obscurus* in Cicero's Latin; yet we lack all but the most superficial indication of what this epithet really meant, and to that extent the epithet is itself obscure to us. The only substantial ancient biography of Heraclitus that is extant is by Diogenes Laertius. Written in the third century A.D., it is based on handbooks and summaries that we no longer possess but that had been compiled, revised, and often corrupted from the early third century B.C. on. From these sources, Diogenes took over a number of stories about Heraclitus—stories of how he once refused to establish laws for the city of Ephesus; how he would retire to the temple of Artemis and play knucklebones with the children; how he finally became a misanthrope, withdrew from the world, and lived in the mountains feeding on grasses and plants; and how he died attempting to cure his dropsy by burying himself in manure.

These stories are not reliable. In fact, it can be shown that they and nearly all the others handed down almost certainly developed out of sayings of Heraclitus that were well known in later antiquity. Thus, his refusal to make laws for the Ephesians is probably based on his references to law (Frr. 44, 114) together with his severe criticism of his city (Fr. 121); the story of his playing games with children is probably based in part on Fr. 52 ("Time is a child playing a game of draughts. . . ."); his misanthropy most likely is derived from some of the sayings that he directed against the "many"; the fatal dropsy transcribes into biography what Heraclitus says in Fr. 36 ("It is death for souls to become water"); his burying himself in manure reflects the association of corpses with manure in Fr. 96. So, there is considerable reason to believe that the "biography" of Heraclitus handed down by later antiquity is little more than a translation of Heraclitus' sayings into deeds.[3] The historical case of Heraclitus is ironic testimony to the need to understand a thinker through his works rather than indulging in the psychologistic attempt to reduce the work of thought to biographical details. In the case of Heraclitus we have no choice but to attend to what remains of his writings.

Yet there is also much that is obscure to us as regards his writings. Diogenes Laertius tells us that Heraclitus wrote a book entitled "On Nature"; but there is reason to be suspicious of this report, and we cannot be certain whether Heraclitus wrote a book or whether his sayings were perhaps originally oral and only later written down.[4] In any case all that we have of his sayings are *fragments,* that is, sayings that lack their original sense-giving context. That context may have been a further written discourse (a "book"), a further spoken discourse, or merely a situation in which the saying was uttered. Lacking it, the Heraclitean fragments have come down to us transposed into alien contexts, that is, as they were incorporated as quotations into the writings of Aristotle, Theophrastus, and various later authors dependent upon them (Sextus Empiricus, Plutarch, and Church Fathers such as Hippolytus, Clement of Alexandria, and Origen). Any attempt to interpret Heraclitus' sayings must attend carefully to the fragmentary character that these sayings have for us. If it is to be a hermeneutically reflective attempt, it must let its own procedure be prescribed by the fragmentary character of the Heraclitean fragments.

The Heidegger/Fink seminar is such an attempt, and as such it is itself fragmentary in a threefold sense. The first sense is indicated in Fink's prefatory note: "Since it was planned to continue the interpretation over a series of semesters and since this plan could not, however, be realized, the present publication is a torso, a fragment about fragments." Within the seminar itself this torso-character is evident in the fact that the discussion does not go the full way laid out by Fink's projected cosmological interpretation, the way from the fragments regarding fire to those regarding λόγος; and since Heidegger's way through the fragments only properly begins with the λόγος-fragments, the seminar in a sense never even reaches the beginning of Heidegger's "logical" interpretation.

The interpretation attempted in the seminar is also fragmentary in a second sense. This second fragmentary character arises from the fragmentary character of the fragments themselves. Because the Heraclitean sayings are fragmentary for us, because they lack the original context that would serve to reflect their sense and to light up their unity, the attempt to interpret these fragments requires a peculiar interplay of violence and reticence. Such interpretation must attend to the phenomena of which Heraclitus speaks and seeks in reference to the phenomena to reawaken the insight buried in the fragment and to carry it up to its proper level. Granted the remoteness of the fragments, such an effort is necessarily plagued with unbridgeable gaps, unanswerable questions, unjustified leaps. One of the most important things that the Heidegger/Fink seminar teaches is the reticence to tolerate such fragmentation.

The seminar is also fragmentary in still another sense: It constitutes a part of Heidegger's work as a whole yet for the most part leaves out of account precisely its belongingness to this whole. Granted that the fragmentary character of Heidegger's treatment of Heraclitus in the seminar can be largely repaired by having recourse to his two articles on Heraclitus, that the latter allow us to fill out the often cryptic remarks in the seminar, the fact still remains that Heidegger's work of interpreting Heraclitus in all these texts has the appearance of being something fragmentary, something disconnected from his principal work; and there is thus posed for us the task of repairing this fragmentation. Yet, it is already, in general fashion, repaired by Heidegger himself: the alleged gap between Heidegger's own "systematic" thought and his interpretations of the history of philosophy was already in effect closed from the beginning, i.e., in Heidegger's projection of the unity of the two major parts of *Being and Time*.[5] Furthermore, he leaves no doubt in *Being and Time* that his entire effort is to resume at a more fundamental level the issue that stood at the center of Plato's and Aristotle's thought and that they thought more profoundly than any subsequent thinker. It is not to be overlooked that *Being and Time* begins with a passage from Plato's *Sophist*. The relation of *Being and Time* to Greek thought is made even clearer in Heidegger's letter to Richardson.[6] Here he notes that three insights were especially decisive for *Being and Time*. The first was the insight into phenomenology, which came primarily through his contact with Husserl; but even here the Greeks were involved, for, as Heidegger says, a normative role was played by reference back to the Greek words from which "phenomenology" is composed, λόγος and φαίνεσθαι.[7] The other two decisive insights came from his study of Aristotle. There was the insight into the basic feature of οὐσία as presence (*Anwesenheit*), the insight through which Heidegger was led to question Being in terms of its time-character. And then there was also in relation to Aristotle the insight into ἀλήθεια as unconcealment (*Unverborgenheit*). In this connection the peculiar movement of Heidegger's thought from phenomenology back to the Greeks is especially evident. That is, we see here how phenomenology opened up Greek thought for him so that he was, in turn, able to uncover in Greek thought the same issue as that of phenomenology but at a more primordial level. Heidegger speaks openly of this regress in "My Way to Phenomenology":

> What occurs for the phenomenology of the acts of consciousness as the self-manifestation of phenomena is thought more primordially by Aristotle and in all Greek thinking and Dasein as ἀλήθεια, as the unconcealment of what is present, its being revealed, its showing itself. That which phenomenological investigations rediscovered as the supporting attitude of thought proves to be the fundamental trait of Greek thinking, if not indeed of philosophy as such.[8]

In *Being and Time* the question, the method, and the basic insights by which that method is engaged with the question are fundamentally dependent on Heidegger's dialogue with the thought of Plato and Aristotle.

In turn, the dialogue with Heraclitus remains engaged with the issue of phenomenology, of *Being and Time;* it is no accident that at several crucial junctures in the seminar reference is made to Heidegger's major work, and once even to Husserl.[9] What is the engagement that holds together phenomenology and dialogue with Heraclitus? It is primarily an engagement in the same issue that originally led Heidegger from phenomenology to the Greeks: the issue of ἀλήθεια.

Near the end of the seminar Heidegger makes a decisive proposal.[10] The proposal is made in view of an understanding of the task of interpretation as one of retrieving that which, while supporting what gets thought by the thinker being intepreted, remains unthought. Heidegger's proposal is that the unthought in Greek thought is ἀλήθεια *as such*—in distinction from what was thought on the basis of ἀλήθεια. 'Αλήθεια *as* ἀλήθεια is what is to be retrieved in dialogue with the Greeks. Why do the Greeks remain an issue for thinking today? Why turn especially toward the earliest Greek thinkers? Because in the sayings of early Greek thinking the unthought may lie nearer what is thought than in any subsequent thinking. Why Heraclitus? Because in his sayings there is perhaps a primary imaging of this nearness of unthought and thought. In what those sayings make manifest, thoughtful dialogue needs, then, to seek the measure of that distance.

The studies in this volume are intended to aid the Heideggerian dialogue with the Heraclitean fragments. Taken together, they are meant to provide an introduction to the Heidegger/Fink seminar in the sense of laying out certain major issues that are crucial to it. The individual studies set about this task in different ways and with varying degrees of attachment to the actual discussions in the seminar. Their variety should be indicative of the richness and, at the same time, of the fragmentary character of the Heideggerian dialogue with the Heraclitean fragments. Most of all, these introductory fragments, attendant to Heidegger's fragmentary dialogue with the Heraclitean fragments, are intended to rejoin the effort of the seminar itself and to repair, with proper reticence, its fragmentation.

KENNETH MALY   JOHN SALLIS
University of Wisconsin, LaCrosse   *Duquesne University*

FRAGMENTS AND
TRANSLATIONS

We give here all the fragments of Heraclitus for which Heidegger has offered translations into German. For each of these fragments we give Heidegger's various translations. English translations are also given. It is to be emphasized that the English versions are intended to serve as transla*ions of Heidegger's German versions, *not* as new English renderings of the fragments themselves! This distinction is especially significant in view of the peculiar character of Heidegger's translations, which, in turn, is based on Heidegger's way of understanding the philosophical task of translation and thus on the peculiar directive that is operative in his efforts at translation. Not only does he regard a translation of a fragment as already constituting its interpretation, but furthermore he regards a genuinely philosophical attempt at translating a fragment of Greek thought as standing under the demand that our thinking first be translated to the matter at issue in that fragment—that we venture this "leap over an abyss." Heidegger's translations are thus not intended as contributions to philology; rather, they are rooted in a thoughtful experience of the tradition and in the dialogue belonging to that experience. Only if this context and intention are kept in view can the significance of Heidegger's translations of the Heraclitean fragments be genuinely grasped.

The fragments are given here according to Diels except in those cases where Heidegger translates only part of a particular fragment; in such cases only the part translated is given (along with a notation indicating the incompleteness). Heidegger's translations are given exactly as they appear in the various works in which they are offered. In some cases they stand in quotation marks, in other cases not; this difference has been retained in our presentation of the translations and carried over to the English versions.

In some cases where quotation marks are lacking in Heidegger's text it is difficult to determine whether a particular rendering of a fragment is to be regarded as a translation or as a more expansive, specifically interpretive reading. In nearly every case Heidegger's translation is situated in a text that serves to explain it and that especially lays out the context from which the translation issues—the context of thoughtful dialogue and of self-translation into the matter itself. Thus are indicated the limits that belong to any presentation of the translations alone.

The following abbreviations are used in referring to Heidegger's works:

EM   *Einführung in die Metaphysik*. Tübingen: Max Niemeyer Verlag, 1953.
G   *Gelassenheit*. Pfullingen: Verlag Günther Neske, 1959.
H   *Heraklit*. Frankfurt am Main: Vittorio Klostermann, 1970. English translation by Charles Seibert, *Heraclitus Seminar 1966/67*. University: The University of Alabama Press, 1979.

HB   *Über den Humanismus*. Frankfurt am Main: Vittorio Klostermann, (aus
      Platons Lehre von der Wahrheit, Bern: Francke AG., 1947).
HW   *Holzwege*. Frankfurt am Main: Vittorio Klostermann, 1950.
J   *Erinnerung an Hans Jantzen: Wort der Freunde zum Freund in die
      Abgeschiedenheit*. Gesprochen bei der Totenfeier am 20. Februar 1967,
      zusammengestellt und herausgegeben von der Universitätsbuchhandlung
      Eberhard Albert, Freiburg i. Br.
N   *Nietzsche*. Pfullingen: Verlag Günther Neske, 1961. 2 Bände.
SG   *Der Satz vom Grund*. Pfullingen: Verlag Günther Neske, 1957.
VA   *Vorträge und Aufsätze*. Pfullingen: Verlag Günther Neske, 1954. (Ref-
      erences are given, first, to the 3-volume edition and then, in parentheses,
      to the 1-volume edition).
W   *Wegmarken*. Frankfurt am Main: Vittorio Klostermann, 1967.
WG   *Vom Wesen des Grundes*. Halle: Max Niemeyer Verlag, 1929. (Refer-
      ences are given to the fourth edition, Frankfurt am Main: Vittorio Kloster-
      mann, 1955).

B 1
τοῦ δὲ λόγου τοῦδ᾽ ἐόντος ἀεὶ ἀξύνετοι γίνονται ἄνθρωποι καὶ πρόσθεν ἢ
ἀκοῦσαι καὶ ἀκούσαντες τὸ πρῶτον· γινομένων γὰρ πάντων κατὰ τὸν
λόγον τόνδε ἀπείροισιν ἐοίκασι, πειρώμενοι καὶ ἐπέων καὶ ἔργων
τοιούτων, ὁκοίων ἐγὼ διηγεῦμαι κατὰ φύσιν διαιρέων ἕκαστον καὶ
φράζων ὅκως ἔχει. τοὺς δὲ ἄλλους ἀνθρώπους λανθάνει ὁκόσα ἐγερθέν-
τες ποιοῦσιν, ὅκωσπερ ὁκόσα εὕδοντες ἐπιλανθάνονται.

EM 97
"Während aber der λόγος ständig dieser bleibt, gebärden sich die Menschen als
die Nichtbegreifenden (ἀξύνετοι), sowohl ehe sie gehört haben, als auch
nachdem sie erst gehört haben. Zu Seiendem wird nämlich alles κατὰ τὸν λόγον
τόνδε, gemäß und zufolge diesem λόγος*; indes gleichen sie (die Menschen)
jenen, die nie erfahrend etwas gewagt haben, obzwar sie sich versuchen sowohl
an solchen Worten als auch an solchen Werken, dergleichen ich durchführe,
indem ich jegliches auseinanderlege κατὰ φύσιν, nach dem Sein, und erläutere,
wie es sich verhält. Den anderen Menschen aber (die anderen Menschen, wie sie
alle sind, οἱ πολλοί) bleibt verborgen, was sie eigentlich wachend tun, wie
auch, was sie im Schlafe getan, nachher sich ihnen wieder verbirgt."
[*Denn obwohl alles nach diesem λόγος geschieht (H 15 f.)]

"But whereas the λόγος remains ever λόγος, men act as though they do not
comprehend it, both before they have heard it as well as afterwards. For everything comes to be κατὰ τὸν λόγον τόνδε, in accordance with and owing to this
λόγος*; however, men are like those who venture something without experience, even though they have a go at those same words and deeds that I carry out

by unfolding each thing κατὰ φύσιν, according to Being, and by explaining how it is. But from the other men (the other men as they all are, οἱ πολλοί) it remains concealed what they really do while awake, just as what they have done while asleep is afterwards concealed from them again.''

[*For although everything happens according to this λόγος]

B 2

διὸ δεῖ ἕπεσθαι τῶι ⟨ξυνῶι, τουτέστι τῶι⟩ κοινῶι · ξυνὸς γὰρ ὁ κοινός.
τοῦ λόγου δ᾿ ἐόντος ξυνοῦ ζώουσιν οἱ πολλοὶ ὡς ἰδίαν ἔχοντες φρόνησιν.

EM 97

''Darum tut es not, zu folgen dem, d.h. sich zu halten an das Zusammen im Seienden; während aber der λόγος als dieses Zusammen im Seienden west, lebt die Menge dahin, als hätte je jeder seinen eigenen Verstand (Sinn).''

''Therefore it is necessary to follow, i.e., to adhere to, what is common to beings; but whereas the λόγος essentially unfolds as what is common to beings, the masses go on living as if every individual had his own understanding (sense).''

B 7

εἰ πάντα τὰ ὄντα καπνὸς γένοιτο, ῥῖνες ἂν διαγνοῖεν.

EM 101

''Wenn alles Seiende in Rauch aufginge, so wären die Nasen es, die es unterschieden und faßten.''

VA III 16 (220)

''Wenn Alles (nämlich) das Anwesende....''

H 52

Wenn alles das Seiende als Rauch hervorkäme...
hätten die Nasen die Möglichkeit, es zu durchgehen.

''If all beings went up in smoke, then it would be noses that would distinguish and grasp them.''

''If everything, i.e., that which comes to presence....''

If all beings were to emerge as smoke...
the nose would have the possibility of penetrating them.

B 8*

τὸ ἀντίξουν συμφέρον καὶ ἐκ τῶν διαφερόντων καλλίστην ἁρμονίαν

*Only the first of the two parts of this fragment is cited, since only this part is translated by Heidegger.

EM 100

"Das Gegeneinanderstehende trägt sich, das eine zum anderen, hinüber und herüber, es sammelt sich aus sich."

"Things in opposition bear one another, the one to the other, from each to the other, they are gathered from out of themselves."

B 9

ὄνους σύρματ' ἂν ἑλέσθαι μᾶλλον ἢ χρυσόν·

EM 101

"Esel mögen Spreu lieber als Gold."

VA III 77 (281)

"Esel holen sich Spreu eher als Gold."

"Donkeys prefer straw to gold."

"Donkeys get for themselves straw rather than gold."

B 10

συνάψιες ὅλα καὶ οὐχ ὅλα, συμφερόμενον διαφερόμενον, συνᾷδον διᾷδον, καὶ ἐκ πάντων ἓν καὶ ἐξ ἑνὸς πάντα.

H 215, 217

"Zusammengehörenlassen:" . . . in der Allheit aus der Allheit her das Einigende des ἕν sichtbar wird.

"Letting belong together:" . . . the unifying of the ἕν becomes visible in the totality from out of the totality.

B 16

τὸ μὴ δῦνόν ποτε πῶς ἄν τις λάθοι;

VA III 61 (265)*

"wie denn könnte irgendwer verborgen bleiben?"

*Because of the character of the essay in which the translations of this fragment occur it is difficult to separate translations from interpretive (expansive) readings of the fragment.

—63 (267)
"die niemals Untergehenden"

— 65 (269); repeated 72 (276)
das doch ja nicht Untergehen je

— 68 (272)
"das niemals Eingehen in die Verbergung"

— 72 (276)
"Wie könnte dem, der Lichtung nämlich, irgendwer verborgen bleiben?"

"how then could anyone remain concealed?"

"the never-setting"

the not setting ever

"the never going into concealment"

"How could anyone remain hidden before it, that is, before the clearing?"

B 19
ἀκοῦσαι οὐκ ἐπιστάμενοι οὐδ᾽ εἰπεῖν.

EM 101
"Sind zu hören nicht imstande und auch nicht zu sagen."

"Incapable of hearing and of speaking."

B 28*
δοκέοντα γὰρ ὁ δοκιμώτατος γινώσκει, φυλάσσει·

*Only the first of the two parts of the fragment (as given by Diels) is cited, since only this part is translated by Heidegger.

N I 504
"eine umschreibend-erläuternde Übersetzung":
"Jeweils Sichzeigendes—je nur Einem Erscheinendes ist es, was auch der Berühmteste (der am meisten in das Ansehen und den Ruhm Hinausgestellte) erkennt; und sein Erkennen ist: das Bewachen dieses je nur Erscheinenden—das Sichfesthalten an diesem als dem Festen und Haltgebenden."

"Knapper und dem griechischen Wortlaut gemäßer":
"Ansichten haben ist nämlich/ auch nur/ des Angesehensten Erkennen, das Überwachen/ Festhalten einer Ansicht."

"a paraphrasing-explanatory translation":
"What shows itself in each instance—what only appears to one is that which even the most renowned (the one most held in honor and esteem) recognizes (knows); and his knowing is: watching over what merely appears in each case—to hold onto this as the steadfast which gives support."

"More briefly and closer to the Greek wording":
"Even for the most esteemed knowing is having views, is the watching over or holding fast to a view."

B 30*
κόσμον τόνδε, τὸν αὐτὸν ἁπάντων, <u>οὔτε τις θεῶν οὔτε ἀνθρώπων</u> ἐποίησεν, ἀλλ᾽ ἦν ἀεὶ καὶ ἔστιν καὶ ἔσται πῦρ <u>ἀείζωον</u>, ἁπτόμενον μέτρα καὶ ἀποσβεννύμενον μέτρα.

*Heidegger translates only the words underlined.

VA III 71 (275)
"was weder irgendwer der Götter noch der Menschen her-vor-brachte"

— 69 (273)
immerwährend lebend

"that which neither any god nor any man brought-forth"

always enduring and living (ever-lasting living)

B 32
ἓν τὸ σοφὸν μοῦνον λέγεσθαι οὐκ ἐθέλει καὶ ἐθέλει Ζηνὸς ὄνομα.

VA III 17 (221)
"Das Einzig-Eine Alles Einende ist das Geschickliche allein."

— 19 (223)
"Das Einzig-Eine-Einende, die lesende Lege, ist nicht bereit" [und ist bereit] versammelt zu werden unter dem Namen "Zeus."

"the unique One unifying all is alone the fateful."

"The unique-unifying-One, the laying that gathers, is not ready" [and is ready] to be gathered under the name "Zeus."

B 34
ἀξύνετοι ἀκούσαντες κωφοῖσιν ἐοίκασι· φάτις αὐτοῖσιν μαρτυρεῖ
παρεόντας ἀπεῖναι.

EM 99
"die, die das ständige Zusammen nicht zusammenbringen, sind Hörende, die
den Tauben gleichen."
Das Sprichwort bezeugt ihnen, was sie sind: Anwesende abwesend. Sie sind
dabei und doch weg.

"those who do not bring together what is ever together are hearers who are like
the deaf."
The proverb bears witness to them what they are: though present, (yet) absent.
They are there and yet gone.

B 43
ὕβριν χρὴ σβεννύναι μᾶλλον ἢ πυρκαϊήν.

VA III 22 (226)
"Vermessenheit braucht es zu löschen eher denn Feuersbrunst."

"It is more important to extinguish hubris than to extinguish a conflagration."

B 47
μὴ εἰκῆ περὶ τῶν μεγίστων συμβαλλώμεθα.

H 27
daß wir nicht ins Blaue hinein, d.h. unbedacht über die höchsten Dinge unsere
Worte zusammenbringen.

that we not thoughtlessly, i.e., unreflectively, put together our words regarding
the highest things.

B 50*
οὐκ ἐμοῦ, ἀλλὰ τοῦ λόγου ἀκούσαντας ὁμολογεῖν σοφόν ἐστιν ἓν πάντα
[εἶναι].

*Heidegger omits the final εἶναι of the text as given by Diels. This omission is explained in VA III
14 (218).

EM 98
"Habt ihr nicht mich, sondern den λόγος gehört, dann ist es weise, demgemäß
zu sagen: *Eines* ist alles."

VA III 13 (217)
"Wenn ihr nicht mich (den Redenden) bloß angehört habt, sondern wenn ihr
euch im horchsamen Gehören aufhaltet, dann ist eigentliches Hören."

VA III 21 f. (225 f.)
"Nicht mich, den sterblichen Sprecher, hört an; aber seid horchsam der lesenden
Lege; gehört ihr erst dieser, dann hört ihr damit eigentlich; solches Hören *ist,*
insofern ein beisammen-vor-liegen-Lassen geschieht, dem das Gesamt, das ver-
sammelnde liegen-Lassen, die lesende Lege vorliegt; wenn ein liegen-Lassen
geschieht des vor-liegen-Lassens, ereignet sich Geschickliches; denn das
eigentlich Geschickliche, das Geschick allein, ist: das Einzig-Eine einend Alles."
[Stellen wir die Erläuterung, ohne sie zu vergessen, auf die Seite, versuchen wir
das Gesprochene Heraklits in unsere Sprache herüberzusetzen, dann dürfte sein
Spruch lauten:] "Nicht mir, aber der lesenden Lege gehörig: Selbes liegen las-
sen: Geschickliches west (die lesende Lege): Eines einend Alles."

"If you have heard not me but rather the λόγος, then it is wise to say accordingly: all is *one.*"

"When you have listened, not merely to me (the speaker), but rather when you
maintain yourselves in hearkening attunement, then there is proper hearing."

"Do not listen to me, the mortal speaker, but be in hearkening to the laying that
gathers; first belong to this and then you hear properly; such hearing *is* when a
letting-lie-together-before occurs before which the gathering letting-lie, the laying that gathers, lies as gathered; when a letting-lie of the letting-lie-before
occurs, the fateful comes to pass; then the truly fateful, i.e., destiny alone, is: the
unique one unifying all."
[If we set aside the commentary, though not forgetting it, and try to translate into
our language what Heraclitus said, his saying reads:] "Attuned not to me but to
the laying that gathers, letting the same lie: the fateful occurs (the laying that
gathers): one unifying all."

B 52
αἰὼν παῖς ἐστι παίζων, πεσσεύων· παιδὸς ἡ βασιληίη.

N I 333
"Der Aeon ist ein Kind beim Spiel, spielend das Brettspiel; eines Kindes ist die
Herrschaft" (nämlich über das Seiende im Ganzen).

SG 188
Seinsgeschick, ein Kind ist es, spielend, spielend das Brettspiel; eines Kindes ist das Königtum—d.h. die ἀρχή, das stiftend verwaltende Gründen, das Sein dem Seienden.

HW 258
"Weltzeit, Kind ist sie spielendes das Brettspiel; eines kindlichen Spiels ist die Herrschaft."

"The Aion is a child at play, playing the board game; to a child belongs dominion" (namely over beings as a whole).

What grants Being is a child, playing the board game; to a child belongs the kingship—i.e., the ἀρχή, the grounding which establishes and rules, the Being for beings.

"World-time is a child playing the board game; to childlike play belongs dominion."

B 53
Πόλεμος πάντων μὲν πατήρ ἐστι, πάντων δὲ βασιλεύς, καὶ τοὺς μὲν θεοὺς ἔδειξε τοὺς δὲ ἀνθρώπους, τοὺς μὲν δούλους ἐποίησε τοὺς δὲ ἐλευθέρους.

EM 47
Auseinandersetzung ist allem (Anwesenden) zwar Erzeuger (der aufgehen läßt), allem aber (auch) waltender Bewahrer. Sie läßt nämlich die einen als Götter erscheinen, die anderen als Menschen, die einen stellt sie her(aus) als Knechte, die anderen aber als Freie.

VA III 73 (277)
[Indirect discourse:] πόλεμος, die Aus-einander-setzung (die Lichtung), zeige die einen der Anwesenden als Götter, die anderen als Menschen, sie bringe die einen als Knechte, die anderen als Freie hervor—zum Vorschein.

Contention is indeed the begetter (who lets emerge) of all (that comes to presence), but (also) the dominant preserver of all. For it lets some appear as gods, others as men; it sets some forth as servants, others as free.

πόλεμος, contention (the clearing) shows some of those present to be gods, others to be men; it brings some to appearance as servants, others as free.

B 54

ἁρμονίη ἀφανὴς φανερῆς κρείττων.

EM 102

"der nicht (unmittelbar und ohne weiteres) sich zeigende Einklang ist mächtiger denn der (allemal) offenkundige."

"the accord which does not (immediately and without further ado) show itself is more powerful than the (always) manifest."

B 55

ὅσων ὄψις ἀκοὴ μάθησις, ταῦτα ἐγὼ προτιμέω.

H 225

Alles, wovon Gesicht und Gehör Kunde gibt, das ziehe ich vor.

I give preference to everything of which sight and hearing give knowledge.

B 64

τὰ δὲ πάντα οἰακίζει Κεραυνός.

VA III 18 (222)

"Das Alles jedoch (des Anwesenden) steuert (ins Anwesen) der Blitz."

"But the lightning steers (into presencing) everything (which comes to presence)."

B 72*

ὧι μάλιστα διηνεκῶς ὁμιλοῦσι λόγωι [τῶι τὰ ὅλα διοικοῦντι], τούτωι διαφέρονται, καὶ οἷς καθ᾽ ἡμέραν ἐγκυροῦσι, ταῦτα αὐτοῖς ξένα φαίνεται.

*Bracketed phrase omitted by Heidegger.

EM 99

"denn, womit sie am meisten fortwährend verkehren, dem λόγος, dem kehren sie den Rücken, und worauf sie täglich stoßen, das erscheint ihnen fremd."

VA III 76 (280)

"Dem sie am meisten, von ihm durchgängig getragen, zugekehrt sind, dem Λόγος, mit dem bringen sie sich auseinander; und so zeigt sich denn: das, worauf sie täglich treffen, dies bleibt ihnen (in seinem Anwesen) fremd."

"For they turn their backs to that with which they have to deal continually and most of all, the λόγος; and that which they encounter daily appears strange to them."

"From that to which for the most part they are bound and by which they are thoroughly sustained, the λόγος, from that they separate themselves; and it becomes manifest: whatever they daily encounter remains foreign (in its presencing) to them."

B 73*

οὐ δεῖ ὥσπερ καθεύδοντας ποιεῖν καὶ λέγειν·

*Only the first of the two parts of this fragment is cited, since only this part is translated by Heidegger.

EM 98

"nicht soll man wie im Schlaf tun und reden."

"one should not act or speak as if asleep."

B 80*

εἰδέναι δὲ χρὴ τὸν πόλεμον ἐόντα ξυνόν, καὶ δίκην ἔριν, . . .

*Only the first part of this fragment is cited, since only this part is translated by Heidegger.

EM 127

"im Blick aber zu behalten, not ist, die Aus-einander-setzung wesend als zusammenbringend/und Fug als Gegenwendiges. . . ."

"but it is necessary to keep in view both the setting forth (contention) as essentially gathering-together and the faying as diverging. . . ."

B 89

τοῖς ἐγρηγορόσιν ἕνα καὶ κοινὸν κόσμον εἶναι, τῶν δὲ κοιμωμένων ἕκαστον εἰς ἴδιον ἀποστρέφεσθαι.

WG 23 (in W 39)
Den Wachen gehört eine und daher gemeinsame Welt, jeder Schlafende dagegen wendet sich seiner eigenen Welt zu.

The world is one and therefore common to those who are awake; but each one who is asleep turns to a world all his own.

B 93

ὁ ἄναξ, οὗ τὸ μαντεῖόν ἐστι τὸ ἐν Δελφοῖς, οὔτε λέγει οὔτε κρύπτει ἀλλὰ σημαίνει.

EM 130

"Der Herrscher, dessen Wahrsagung zu Delphi geschieht, οὔτε λέγει οὔτε κρύπτει, er sammelt weder, noch verbirgt er, ἀλλὰ σημαίνει, sondern er gibt Winke."

J 20

"Der Hohe, dessen Orakelsitz der ist in Delphi, weder entbirgt er noch verbirgt er, sondern er winkt."

"The lord whose prophecy occurs at Delphi οὔτε λέγει οὔτε κρύπτει, neither gathers nor conceals, ἀλλὰ σημαίνει, but gives signs."

"The one on high whose oracle is the one in Delphi neither discloses nor conceals but gives signs."

B 97

κύνες γὰρ καταβαΰζουσιν ὧν ἂν μὴ γινώσκωσι.

EM 101

"denn die Hunde bellen auch jeden an, den sie nicht kennen."

"for dogs too bark at everyone whom they do not know."

B 103

ξυνὸν γὰρ ἀρχὴ καὶ πέρας ἐπὶ κύκλου περιφερείας.

EM 100

"in sich gesammelt, dasselbe ist der Ausgang und das Ende auf der Kreislinie"

"gathered in itself, as are the beginning and the end of the circle"

B 119

ἦ θος ἀνθρώπωι δαίμων.

HB 41 (in W 187)

"Der (geheure) Aufenthalt ist dem Menschen das Offene für die Anwesung des Gottes (des Un-geheuren)."

"Man's (familiar) abode is the region open to the coming of god (the unfamiliar) to presence."

B 122
ἀγχιβασίην.

G 72
"In-die-Nähe-gehen."

"Going into the nearness."

B 123
φύσις κρύπτεσθαι φιλεῖ.

VA III 67 (271)
"Das Aufgehen (aus dem Sichverbergen) dem Sichverbergen schenkt's die Gunst."

SG 122
"Zum Sichentbergen gehört ein Sichverbergen."

W 370
Das Sein liebt es, sich zu verbergen.

"Rising (out of self-concealing) bestows favor upon self-concealing."

"To self-disclosing belongs a self-concealing."

Being loves to conceal itself.

B 124
ἀλλ' ὥσπερ σάρμα εἰκῆ κεχυμένων ὁ κάλλιστος κόσμος.

EM 102
"wie ein Misthaufen, wüst hingeschüttet, ist die schönste Welt."

"the most beautiful world is like a dungheap, rudely dumped."

STUDIES

1
REMARKS ON THE DIFFERENCE BETWEEN FINK'S AND HEIDEGGER'S APPROACHES TO HERACLITUS

FRIEDRICH-WILHELM VON HERRMANN

In the seminar on Heraclitus held during the winter semester of 1966/67 at the University of Freiburg the dialogue between Martin Heidegger and Eugen Fink was governed, sometimes explicitly and at other times implicitly, by the difference between their respective approaches to the interpretation of Heraclitus. This difference of approach may be expressed in terms of the difference between the problem of man's relation to the disclosure of Being and the problem of the relation of world, which lets beings appear, to beings within the world. The book *Heraklit* renders word for word this highly significant dialogue. Now for the first time, in addition to the numerous Heidegger lectures that have been published, a complete text of a Heidegger seminar is at hand; it shows an intensified immediacy and vitality in Heidegger's reflections and discussions, carried out in his role as intellectual leader in the dialogue with a philosopher congenial to him.

Bracketing the strictly philological problematic, both thinkers ponder over what Heraclitus has already thought in order to break through to the issue for thinking caught sight of therein. The roles of the partners in dialogue are distinct. Fink offers an interpretation in which the fragments appear as having an inner coherence of meaning. Heidegger on the other hand lays major importance on critically and questioningly clarifying the pathway of this interpretation in regard to the issue that is thematic therein. The phenomenological seeing is decisive for the thinking of both thinkers, but the manner of seeing takes diverging paths. Heidegger thinks along the way of language. For him the phenomena reveal themselves in language and its junctures. Heidegger's returning to the roots of language has nothing to do with etymology, but rather is phenomenology grounded on language.

With Fink the situation is different. His phenomenological seeing—the most important fruits of his daily philosophical association over the period of a decade with the founder of modern phenomenology, Edmund Husserl—is directed toward the things as they show themselves within the manifold ways of our perceiving, without directing his gaze—as Heidegger does—primarily at the junctures in language, within which the phenomena become understood. The path of phenomenological seeing leads to a true liberation in the interpreting of the fragments of Heraclitus, which are not easily accessible. It sets Heraclitus

free from the often abstruse sounding explanations which the history of philological and philosophical research up to the present has superimposed upon the
coherence of meaning that Heraclitus had seen running through everything,
sometimes distorting that meaning. At the same time it also frees our relationship
to Heraclitus, which is now mediated solely by means of the issue to be thought.
In the phenomenological manner of seeing, even the most obscure fragments
gain a clarity and simplicity of thought which allows an insight into the meaning
of this early Greek thinker that is removed from all fantastic doctrines, as for
example the doctrine of world conflagration.

When Heidegger, in his earlier publications, puts Fr. 16 at the beginning of his
own interpretation of Heraclitus ("How can one hide himself in the face of that
which never goes under?"), then the relation of man to the disclosure of Being is
thereby placed at the center of his own thinking as well. Likewise, Fink's
divergent starting point (Fr. 64: "The lightning flash steers all beings.") is
indicative of his philosophical approach. He sees the all-encompassing and pervasive fundamental coherence in the totality of world in its relation to the things
that it lets appear within it. At one time Fink himself defined his philosophical
task to be that of thinking the cosmological horizon of Heidegger's question of
Being; this says that, along with the unique difference, made visible by Heidegger, between Being and beings [Sein und Seiendes] in its reference to the essence
of man, we must also think the totality in Being: the world in its difference from
all that comes to appear within it. But where is man's place within the relation of
world to all that is within the world? Does man have the same essential place in it
as every other living organism or thing in the world? Or can the relation of
all-disclosing Being to what is disclosed be thought in proper measure only in
terms of the relation of Being to the essence of man, which would then be seen as
primary? Does not the proper character of man's essence show itself in his being
"needed" [gebraucht] for the appearing of beings from out of the unconcealment of Being? Does man belong among beings only because he belongs above
all to Being? With that Heidegger's question as well as his answer are brought
into words.

For Fink the compelling question is whether the relation of world to what is
within the world does not overwhelm man in spite of his relation of understanding to Being. Man is indeed man only in terms of his understanding of Being and
world. But is he thereby a participant in the universal process of letting what is
within the world appear? Does world in its universal letting-appear have domi-
nance over man's relation to world? Indeed, there are ways of appearing that
things within the world have only as objects of man's ways of knowing. But is it
not the case that things can appear as objects of knowing only insofar as they and
man have, within that process in which world lets things appear, first of all come
to appear within the world? Is man the disclosing one only in a reduced manner?
Does world also hold sway without man's relation to world, or does the coming
to appear of everything finite have a necessary relation to human knowing?

Questions of this kind cannot be decided at random, but rather only in an unpretentious thinking toward the issue to be thought.

By means of his cosmological problematic—formulated in a series of publications—Fink has elaborated a question that allowed him, as a former student of Heidegger's, to become Heidegger's partner in dialogue. Therefore Heidegger ends the dialogue on Heraclitus with two quotations from one of the Seven Sages of Greece. The first sentence: μελέτα τὸ πᾶν—"take into care the whole as whole"—applies to Fink's effort in thinking. The second sentence: φύσεως κατηγορία—"making φύσις visible"—refers to his own thinking. The concluding juxtaposition of these two ancient Greek sayings indicates that what is named in them belongs together and could become a task for future thinking.

2

HEGEL
HEIDEGGER
HERACLITUS

DAVID FARRELL KRELL

A seminar is what the word itself suggests: a place and an opportunity to scatter seed, seeds of reflection that someday may flourish and bear fruit in their own way.

M. Heidegger

Professors Heidegger and Fink raise the issue of Hegel's philosophy a dozen times in the Heraclitus seminar. Why they do so is not obvious. At the outset we may suppose that the principal reason has to do with Hegel's incomparable importance for contemporary philosophy and history of philosophy: Heidegger's and Fink's efforts to encounter Heraclitus beyond the pale of traditional philosophy, "no longer metaphysically," cannot attain Heraclitus' own "not yet metaphysical" standpoint; they can rediscover forgotten or concealed significance in the fragments only if they recollect what metaphysics has persistently found there. Since in Heidegger's view Hegel is "the only Western thinker who has thoughtfully experienced the history of thought,"[1] Heidegger's attempt to envision Heraclitus on a new horizon requires exploration of the old, which everywhere is dominated by Hegel and shades of Hegel. Even if for contemporary philosophy some monstrous sponge has obliterated *all* horizons (Nietzsche), Hegel still looms ubiquitous. If only for reasons of what Fink calls the *via negationis*, Hegel's understanding of Heraclitus must be remembered.

There may be more positive reasons. These may emerge when we (1) examine the context of the major references to Hegel in the Heraclitus seminar, observing the movement of the issues in play there, (2) turn to Hegel's lectures on the history of philosophy and philosophy of history in order to assess the importance Heraclitus and the Greeks in general held for him, and (3) bring into focus the conflict of interpretations resulting from Heidegger's *hermeneutical project* and Hegel's *ontotheological perspective*. This we will do by examining several of Heidegger's texts on Hegel. Heidegger's essays on Heraclitus we will not consider. In order to pursue the matter of the conflict between hermeneutics and ontotheology we will insert (4) a digression on the problem of *death* in Hegel's philosophy. Finally, (5) we will return to the seminar itself in order to express provisionally the *Sache des Denkens* concealed in that euphonious title—which actually encompasses several epochs of Being—*Hegel Heidegger Heraclitus*.

1. Hegel in the Heraclitus Seminar

Although Fink cedes "intellectual leadership" to Heidegger during the first moments of the seminar, it gradually becomes clear that his own "cosmological" interpretation of the fragments will guide the discussion throughout. Heidegger's covert leadership works in two ways. First, his published work on Heraclitus helps to shape the cosmological interpretation—which nevertheless cannot be identified with the Heideggerian. Second, Heidegger's participation in the seminar, which most often takes the form of daimonic no-saying, serves to bring the cosmological interpretation into sharper outline, so that it can be seen *as* an interpretation and in this way confront its limits. The discussion itself rises on the tide of two related matters, the relation of ἕν and πάντα, where the One is interpreted as lightning, fire, sun, or luminous bringing-to-appearance (hours I–VII), and the relation of ἀθάνατοι and θνητοί, immortals and mortals, gods and men (hours VIII–XIII). Professor Fink's greatest effort in the seminar is to bring these two matters together, to relate the two relations. Heidegger's greatest effort is to thematize the hermeneutical problem implicit in Fink's—or anyone's—preoccupations with the Heraclitean fragments. Essential to such thematization is the matter of Hegel's response to Greek philosophy and his peculiar adoption of Heraclitus.

Even the relatively minor references to Hegel merit attention,[2] but here we will consider only the five major, extensive references, all of which, being instigated by Heidegger, center on the problem of a *speculative interpretation* of Heraclitus. This problem is broached in the fifth, seventh, tenth, eleventh, and thirteenth hours (82–83, 124–29, 180–86, 195–99, and 257–60). While referring to Fink's efforts to interpret πᾶν ἑρπετόν cosmologically, Heidegger speaks of a "speculative leap" by which Fink tries to advance beyond the initial, "tactically naïve" way of reading the fragments to the *lectio difficilior*, "the more difficult reading" (11, 69, 106). Heidegger does not object in principle to such a leap, since thinking always makes such leaps and is itself always a risk, but he finds himself throughout the seminar compelled to urge restraint. "The twenty-five hundred years that separate us from Heraclitus are a dangerous affair. In order for us to see anything here in our interpretation of the Heraclitean fragments we need the most stringent self-criticism" (62). Precisely for this reason Heidegger proposes that Heraclitus B 47 serve as a "motto" for the seminar: μὴ εἰκῆ περὶ τῶν μεγίστων συμβαλλώμεθα, which might translate colloquially as, "When you try to speak about the most important things, don't go off into the blue." Perhaps not until the final hours of the seminar, with the meandering but sober discussion of sleep, death, and man's body, is the motto in force. Not for want of persistent trying on Heidegger's part. He several times laments the fact that Karl

Reinhardt's plan to provide a critical history of the fragments in their contexts never materialized, and often expresses doubts about whether the fragments in their present form, as citations whose original and adopted contexts have both been obliterated, can supply a basis solid enough for any leap at all.[3] He raises this suspicion most forcefully at the very end: "The poverty of all Heraclitus interpretation is in my opinion to be seen in the fact that what we call 'fragments' are not fragments at all but quotations taken from a text where they do not belong" (242). Such textual difficulties plague Heidegger from beginning to end, and he takes great pains to apprise Fink of them, not always successfully. Heidegger takes such pains because these philological problems lead to the very serious hermeneutical stumbling block that unless the cosmological interpretation remains acutely aware of its own λόγος, its own way of gathering and letting lie before it what shows itself, or seems to show itself, as a phenomenon, it fails to perceive its own limitations. It incorrigibly says "too much" (35, 88). Most of that "too much" takes the form of modes of thought and language indigenous to metaphysics, which project onto Heraclitus what—for all we know—was never there.

It is against the background of these difficulties that Heidegger first invokes the problem of "speculation" (82 ff.). For medieval philosophy the *existimatio speculativa* is theoretical observation of species and categories. For Kant it is the application of reason to areas where no possible object can be experienced. But for Hegel "speculation" is something quite different, and Heidegger now begins to ask about the Hegelian sense. He will not stop asking about it for the remainder of the seminar. Admittedly, his primary purpose is "only to make clear that here, in our own attempt to reflect on Heraclitus, it is not a matter of the speculative in Hegel's fully developed sense." But what about their own attempt? How does Fink venture a "speculative leap"? Fink describes his interpretive method as a phenomenological "presentifying" of the phenomenal material in each fragment "as though it lay immediately before our eyes." Then follows an attempt at "clarification," which, to be sure, is "selectively guided." By what? By an effort to surpass the "sensuous phenomena" portrayed in the fragments in the direction of a "nonsensuous realm." But not a "supersensuous" one, Fink hastens to add: any two-world theory and all metaphysical paths of thought must be avoided in such an advance. Heidegger rejoins that they must also avoid confusion between, "on the one hand, our attempt to reflect on the fragments of Heraclitus and, on the other, the way Heraclitus himself thought." But such confusion arose in the very first hour of the seminar, on the first printed page of its protocol, when Fink voiced his intention to "press on to the matter itself," which he then defined, with some misgivings, as "the matter that must have stood before the intellectual vision of Heraclitus" (9). Heidegger's final question to Fink (256) touches on this dubious "matter" and even there, as we shall see, remains profoundly involved in the issue of Hegel's philosophy.

During the seventh hour the question of interpretation again becomes thematic. It opens with a reference to the previous hour (107 ff.), when Heidegger affirmed

Fink's search for a "philosophical" way to read the fragments that is nevertheless not "metaphysical," but asked, "From what sort of hermeneutical position are you attempting that?" Fink wishes to approach Heraclitus *nicht mehr metaphysisch,* "no longer metaphysically." Heraclitus himself thinks *noch nicht metaphysisch,* "not yet metaphysically." "Does this involve the identical situation for thinking?" asks Heidegger. "Presumably not," Fink replies. Heidegger now (124 ff.) explains that "no longer metaphysically" in any case cannot really mean that contemporary thought has left metaphysics behind, like discharged freight, and insists that in fact metaphysics "still clings to us, we are not free of it." At that moment he asks about the thinker who has "in the most decisive way" specified the relation of various epochs in the history of metaphysics to one another, namely, Hegel. He refers to the famous words of the Preface to the *Phenomenology of Spirit*—better, to the Preface of the entire *System of Science*—that the true is to be grasped and expressed not only as *substance* but also as *Subject.*[4] By directing a series of questions to the participants, Heidegger now recounts the transformation of ὑποκείμενον (substance), which according to Hegel is the sole essential thought of the Greeks, into the modern *subiectum.* According to Hegel, the relation of thought to the thinking subject himself does not become thematic in and for Greek thought, and this is its decisive limitation. "For Hegel, their thought was attendance upon what lay before them, at the base of things, which he calls thought of the unmediated. . . . Hegel characterizes all Greek thought as the stage of unmediatedness" (127). The Greek Odyssey does not arrive home at the "firm ground" of the *ego cogito me cogitare.* In response to an observation by a participant who mentions Socrates as symptomatic of a "tendency toward subjectivity" in Greek philosophy, Heidegger concedes that the threefold schematic of unmediatedness–mediation–unity can be *applied to itself* in such a way that each stage of the history of philosophy somehow always reflects or foreshadows the others. Yet the schematic itself remains rooted in the understanding of truth as "the absolute certitude of absolute Spirit." Heidegger rejects the schematic, insisting that Greek thought must once again become *questionable;* yet he continues to inquire about the "speculative" as a determination of "the logical." He advises that the participants turn to Hegel's *Encyclopedia of Philosophical Sciences* [§§ 79–83] in order to consider the three moments of the logical: (1) the abstract, one-sided moment, corresponding to the unmediated content, (2) the dialectical moment, corresponding to mediation, and (3) the speculative moment, which acknowledges the unity of the first two. Heidegger concludes by noting that a determination of the meaning of "the speculative" is important for the divergent starting-points of Fink (lightning, Fr. 64) and himself (the never-setting, Fr. 16, related to ἀλήθεια).

During the tenth hour (180 ff.), as the discussion takes up the second theme— the openness to beings shared ostensibly by gods and men—the talk again turns to Hegel, mediated this time however by Hölderlin's poetic speculations in "Mnemosyne" and "Der Rhein" on the need of immortals for mortals. The Hegelian text which offers promise of insight here is the one that reverses the first, from *History of Philosophy* to *Philosophy of History*. Here the interpretation of Greek civilization revolves on the axis of *beauty*. But once more, through a series of questions aimed at the participants, Heidegger tries to establish the meaning of "the speculative moment" for Hegel's history of philosophy. He notes the curious circumstance that the *second* moment receives the name "dialectical," although one would expect from the identification of matter and method that this name would have to be reserved for the *third*. The dialectical moment is "negative-rational." On the basis of the clue contained in the word *vernünftig* (rational), Heidegger pursues the question of Hegelian dialectic by asking about Hegel's critique of Kant, especially Kant's understanding of *Vernunft* (reason), expressed for instance in the appendix to the Transcendental Dialectic, "On the Regulative Use of the Ideas of Pure Reason," KrV, B 670. For Hegel the "*positive*-rational" moment is the speculative. It grasps the unity of the abstract and dialectical moments in their differentiation. Hegel's criticism of Heraclitus parallels somewhat his criticism of Kant: while Kant fails to advance from a logic of the categories of the understanding to a positive-rational, speculative philosophy, Heraclitus and all Greek philosophy remain at the level of an unmediated logic that has not yet made the turn from substance to Subject.

This discussion continues at the next meeting (195 ff.), when Heidegger urges the participants to read the second part of Hegel's lectures on world history, where they will get "a different idea of Hegel" with respect to the Greeks. At the same time he wishes to correct an oversight: for all their attention during the last hour to the moments of logic, the participants and seminar leaders have neglected to ask what "logical" as such means in Hegel's usage. He refers to §19 of the *Encyclopedia,* where logic is defined as "the science *of the pure Idea,* i.e., the Idea in the abstract element of thought." Idea must be understood, not so much as Platonic ἰδέα, but rather as Cartesian *perceptio*, subjective representation *(Vorstellen)*. As clear and distinct representation, Idea now is found to be rooted in truth as certitude.

The final extensive reference to Hegel occurs during the closing minutes of the seminar (257 ff.). Heidegger recalls Fink's statements at the beginning (9) concerning the *challenge* the Greeks pose for contemporary thought and the *Sache des Denkens* for such thought—especially when it presumes to grasp the matter thought by Heraclitus himself. But we should not be in too great a hurry to conclude this brief account of Hegel in the Heraclitus seminar: the final exchange between Heidegger and Fink, where once again Hegel is central, should wait upon an independent inquiry into Hegel's account of the Heraclitean philosophy, a consideration of Heidegger's criticism of the Hegelian point of departure, and a discussion of the resulting conflict of interpretations.

2. Hegel on Heraclitus

We know that for Hegel, as for so many Germans of his generation, and of the preceding and succeeding generations as well, discovery of "the Greek Miracle" was a formative experience second to none.⁵ Even in Hegel's mature philosophy and its understanding of art, religion, politics, history, and logic the significance of "Greece," reflected of course through the prisms of Winckelmann, Goethe, and Schiller, is so profound and many-sided that we can no longer really comprehend it.

For Hegel never simply reflects *on* the Greeks; they are everywhere reflected *in* him. J. Stenzel begins his essay on Hegel's conception of Greek philosophy by citing Hegel's "elective affinity with the free intellectuality of the Greeks," but ends by affirming that Hegel went "bravely on the 'way to the mothers', to the sources of Western thought."⁶ Now, Goethe knew better than anyone that mothers are not elected: Hegel's affinity to the Greeks is an "organically" determined matter, or, in more Heideggerian language, is a matter of the essential destiny of Hegel's thought. It is hardly accidental that Hegel "too" understands *motion* as the basic issue of logico-metaphysical philosophy, that he "also" takes up the guiding question of Aristotelian philosophy. Nor is it accidental that in his lectures on world history Hegel feels immediately "at home" when he arrives at the "Greek world." For him Greek civilization is not only one moment in the development of world history; his encounter with the Greeks "sets in motion the formation of the world-historical categories" in general.⁷ When Hegel defines the Greek as "beautiful individuality," as the mediator between Nature and Spirit, as the plastic artist who makes his own bejeweled and supple body a work of art, each of his gods an individual artwork, and his city an embodiment of his own free individuality, he knows *that it is the Greeks themselves who introduce such forms into the history of Spirit.* Among all such forms "philosophy" is the most perfect synthesis of Spirit's life. And this word, as Diogenes Laertius reminds us (I, 4), resists translation into any barbarian tongue. If at this point we turn to Hegel's account of Greek philosophy, indeed to the philosopher of motion par excellence, it is not because we think we have exhausted the other facets of Hegel's relation to the Greeks that Heidegger urges the participants in the Heraclitus seminar to consider (195–96).

Heraclitus' importance for Hegel can be evaluated only in relation to the figure of Parmenides, whose "chief thought" is the identity of Thinking and Being— the speculative thought as such. "Thinking produces itself, and what is produced is a thought. Thinking is thus identical with its Being; for there is nothing outside of Being, this great affirmation."⁸ But this identity is not yet dialectical: the two halves of Parmenides' poem do not converge, and the identity of Being and Thinking remains abstract rather than concrete. Motion and change remain outside the compass of the Parmenidean system. It is Zeno's contribution to introduce movement into pure thought itself, to father dialectic (XVIII, 295 ff.). But in Zeno's dialectic as well, "the speculative [thought] is that there is no change at all," so that Being and Nothingness do not yet penetrate one another. Although dialectic appears as nascently "objective" in Zeno's thought, for the Eleatic school as a whole dialectic remains "subjective" in the bad sense: motion has found a place in ratiocination but not yet in Being in and for itself (XVIII, 301,

319). "Now, Heraclitus grasps the Absolute itself as this process, as dialectic itself" (XVIII, 319). With him Being and Nothingness interpenetrate radically; their dialectical union produces Becoming. With Heraclitus "we first encounter the philosophical Idea in its speculative form: the reasoning of Parmenides and Zeno is abstract intellect; Heraclitus is universally acknowledged to be a profound philosopher, indeed, his fame has spread widely." Hegel now adds what has become the most famous—but is also the most ambivalent—celebration by one thinker of another: "Here we see land; there is no statement of Heraclitus that I haven't taken up into my Logic" (XVIII, 320). There is of course another occasion in the history of philosophy when Hegel cries "Land!" and that is with the recognition of self-consciousness as an essential moment of truth, in modern philosophy, in Descartes (XX, 120). But these two kinds of "land" are quite different. We may anticipate that the Ionian terrain will resist depiction more stubbornly than the modern.

In Hegel's account of Heraclitus' life (XVIII, 320–23), two aspects are especially stressed: Heraclitus withdraws from political life, departing from the tradition of the Seven Sages and the aristocratic Pythagorean brotherhood, to live in the "total solitude of philosophy" and science; further, his notorious obscurity results principally from the fact that in his cryptic prose "a profound, speculative thought is expressed." "He is the consummation of prior consciousness—a consummation of the Idea underway toward totality, which is the beginning of philosophy or the essence of the Idea, which expresses the infinite that it is." Hegel's account of the work (XVIII, 323–43) proposes three topics, "The Logical Principle," "The Way of Reality," and "Process as Universal, and Its Relation to Consciousness." A close reading of the text bears out what these titles at first glance suggest, to wit, *that Hegel's account of the Heraclitean philosophy conforms to the three major divisions of his* Encyclopedia, "Logic," "Philosophy of Nature," and "Philosophy of Spirit."

The first section, on *das logische Prinzip,* is puzzling: here there is virtually no talk of λόγος as such—for that we must wait until the third section and the introduction of consciousness—or of what we traditionally understand by the discipline of "logic." Hegel begins by elaborating Aristotle's account of the "doctrine of Heraclitus" that "everything is and is not" (*Met.* IV, 7, 1012a 25 ff.). At first such an assertion seems senseless (Aristotle rejects it out of hand), but it must be understood as an affirmation of Becoming, an affirmation that flows from speculative insight into the dialectical nature of Being and Nothingness. "It is a great thought—to go from Being over to Becoming; it is still abstract, but at the same time it is also the first concrete [thought], the first unity of determinations that are opposed to one another" (XVIII, 324–25). Heraclitus' universal principle of Becoming is therefore essential, and Hegel advises that it can be found in his own *Logic,* "at the beginning, right after Being and Nothingness" (XVIII, 325). He means the first part of the *Science of Logic,* "The Doctrine of Being," where the transition from Being to Existence (*Dasein*) is made, via Becoming (*Werden*). There Hegel writes: "The profound Heraclitus raised against that simple and one-sided abstraction [Nothingness, emptiness, as the absolute principle in Buddhism] the higher, total concept of Becoming, and said: *Being is, just as little as Nothingness,* or else, everything *flows,* i.e., everything is *Becoming.*"9 The same essential transition occurs in the "Shorter Logic" of the *Encyclopedia* (§§ 86-88), without direct reference to Heraclitus. (The *Zusatz* to § 88 added by Hegel's earlier editors, rightly eliminated by Friedhelm Nicolin and Otto Pöggeler in their edition for the *Philosophische Bibliothek,* 1959, nevertheless is perfectly in the Hegelian spirit: "Becoming is the first concrete thought, and thereby the first concept [*Begriff*], in comparison with which Being and Nothingness are empty abstractions. In the history of philosophy it is the system of Heraclitus that corresponds to this stage of the logical Idea.'"10

The moment of *negation* involved in such a transition from Being to Becoming is not the external, sterile negation in Zeno: "With Heraclitus the moment of negativity is immanent; in it the concept of philosophy as a whole is involved" (XVIII, 326). For Heraclitean negativity stems from a prevailing unity of real and ideal, objective and subjective, whose truth is in process of becoming. Finally, in the Heraclitean notion of harmony Hegel sees the nascent expression of identity within difference. "To harmony, difference [*Unterschied*] belongs." Not that everything slides into everything else, so that pure otherness rules in the carnival of an existence bereft of definition. Every being has *its* other, a determinate other that constitutes its identity. "This is the great principle of Heraclitus; it may seem obscure, but it is speculative" (XVIII, 327).

Heraclitus expresses himself logically in concepts, Hegel continues in the second part of his exposition, but also in the more "real" form of a philosophy of nature. To be sure, it is no Milesian nature philosophy, not the "speculative water" of Thales, since Heraclitus has grasped the "infinite concept" of the identity of Being and Nothingness. He locates Becoming or process in its primal intuitive form—time—and then in its more physical form—fire (XVIII, 329-30). Hegel elaborates:

> Time is pure Becoming as intuited. Time is pure alteration, it is the pure concept, simple, out of absolute opposites harmonic. Its essence is to be and not to be. . . . Not as though time *is* or *is not*; rather time *is* this, not to be unmediatedly in Being and to be unmediatedly in Nonbeing. . . . In time, what is gone and what is to come are not, only the now is; and the now *is* only not to be; it is forthwith annihilated, gone—and this Nonbeing turns abruptly into Being, for it *is.*11

Time is process. But now Heraclitus' concept of process must "real-ize" itself further, and it does so as fire. "Fire is physical time; it is this absolute unrest, absolute dissolution of subsistence, the perishing of the other, but also of itself" (XVIII, 330). Hegel then pursues the meaning of the interpenetration of opposites in the fragments, the ways up and down, the interplay of πόλεμος and εἰρήνη. Not without criticism, for he finds some of the fragments "too general" and "quite obscure." But what fascinates Hegel is the unity-in-trinity of these oppositions. "Nature is this never-resting, and is the universe of transition from the one into the other, from diremption into unity, from unity into diremption" (XVIII, 332). Furthermore, this objective intuition of fire as process suggests cosmic vitality; it foreshadows the principle of soul, "life in general, the general process of the universe." After digressing awhile on "the speculative observation of nature" in general (XVIII, 334–36), Hegel proceeds in the direction of ψυχή, soul as universal process, which in the further course of Spirit's development will prove to be a "relation of consciousness." But Heraclitus himself does not progress so far.

In the third and final section of his account of the Heraclitean philosophy Hegel shows that the essence of the Idea (the radical interpenetration of opposites, of Being and Nothingness) is not yet grasped as concept in and for itself, i.e., as universality. "*Process* is not yet grasped as *universal*" (XVIII, 337). The unity-in-opposition is not yet *in sich reflektiert* (reflected into itself). This advance must wait for Anaxagoras (if not Cartesius) who will identify the soul as νοῦς or intellect (XVIII, 379 ff.). Heraclitus takes λόγος as his starting point but never advances decisively beyond the forms of natural philosophy. If he looks ahead to a philosophy of Spirit it is indeed through the multicolored dome of nature; if he voices the relation of λόγος to thought it is in a "lovely, ingenuous, childlike way" (XVIII, 338). It is therefore an instance of searching too hard for the sources, of yearning too much for the beginnings, which Hegel criticizes so forcefully in his introductory lectures (XVIII, 58–69), when Hegel himself translates τοῦ λόγου . . . ὁμολογεῖν σοφόν ἐστιν ἓν πάντα εἶναι as "The one is wise—to know reason [*die Vernunft zu erkennen*], which rules throughout everything" (XVIII, 339). Still, however much Heraclitus in his exhortations to wakefulness typifies a kind of "naïve Idealism," he inclines toward genuine recognition of the universal when he advises (Fr. 2) that the λόγος is "common to all" and abhors idiosyncratic interpretation. Originality in thought is deception and error, the vanity of a philosophy that prides itself on novelty and forgets that only consciousness of the universal grasps the truth. In Heraclitus Hegel sees an anticipation of Spinoza, since both withdraw from total absorption in sensuous certainty and find the necessity in thought to be necessity of Being, the essence of thinking to be the essence of the real world. But just as Spinoza needs Schelling, and Schelling Hegel, so does Heraclitus need Anaxagoras, and Anaxagoras Socrates.

Hegel now introduces one last fragment "among the many others" available to him, which the present discussion of consciousness seems to evoke. It is Fr. 62, on the relationship of mortals and immortals, which serves as the second major source of discussion in the Heraclitus seminar. Hegel offers a translation and a succinct commentary:

> "Men are mortal gods and gods are immortal men; living their death and dying their life." The death of gods is life; dying is the life of gods. The divine is

elevation above mere naturalness by means of thought. Naturalness belongs to death (XVIII, 343).

Precisely why this fragment merits remembrance, and precisely why it must be translated and interpreted in this fashion, are questions that should give us pause. In Hegel's presentation Fr. 62 appears as a kind of afterthought. Yet it may be that this fragment, which occasions a four-line summary of Hegel's interpretation of the death of the Logos (as Christ) in his *Lectures on the Philosophy of Religion*, extends to postmetaphysical thought the opportunity for a confrontation with Hegel.

3. Heidegger on Hegel: Hermeneutics and Onto-Theo-Logy

In the expectation that other contributors to this volume will refer to Heidegger's own earlier attempts to think back to Heraclitus,[12] we will instead turn to three texts in which Heidegger confronts Hegel's philosophy. Ignoring for the moment his essay on Hegel's concept of experience (1942-43),[13] we will take up three essays stemming from the period (1956-58) of Heidegger's preoccupation with Hegel's *Science of Logic:* the little-known "Grundsätze des Denkens," the better known "Onto-Theo-Logische Verfassung der Metaphysik," and the essay Heidegger has emphasized recently as most important for his own confrontation with the Greeks—"Hegel und die Griechen."[14]

In "Grundsätze des Denkens" Heidegger portrays the dimension that thinking has entered in our own time as a coarsened form of the dialectical-theoretical-speculative thought of German Idealism and its progeny. He predicts that we still have much of the history of this dimension before us. For intellectual history dialectic, even in the fashionable form of dialectical materialism, is a thing of the past, whereas for a thinking that undertakes to know its own provenance and the forces that determine it dialectic and the speculative-theoretical remain still undiscovered sources. *Die grosse Überlieferung kommt als Zu-kunft auf uns zu:* what is great in our tradition is transmitted to us as what is to come, as future rather than as past. It is for this reason that during the Heraclitus seminar speculative thought must suffer examination—not simply in order to avoid the pitfalls of Hegelian philosophy, as though these had already been mapped out and labeled, but in order to confront the major precursor of Heidegger's own interpretation of the history or destiny of Being. But to bridge the smallest gap—that between Heidegger's *Geschick des Seins* and Hegel's *Geschichte des Geistes*—is most difficult of all. For it requires nothing less than confrontation with metaphysics as a whole, the constitution of which Heidegger designates, with special reference to Hegel, as onto-theo-logical.

In an effort to initiate a dialogue or conversation with Hegel, Heidegger raises three questions: (1) What is the real issue each wants to think; how does each understand the *Sache des Denkens?* (2) What is the *standard* for dialogue with the history of thought in each case? (3) What is the resultant *character* of the dialogue? Each of these questions, of course, recoils on the present situation—Heidegger's conversation with Hegel. To the first Heidegger responds that for Hegel, as for himself, the issue for thinking is thought itself. But whereas for Heidegger thinking is response to a call to remember the difference between Being and beings, for Hegel it is "the developed fullness" of what has been thought as such (*die entwickelte Fülle der Gedachtheit des Gedachten*). Hegel's name for this fullness is reason, *Vernunft,* the one presupposition that philosophy brings to history (XII, 20), because it is the result of the history of philosophy (XVIII, 21). Reason that grasps itself in and for itself, that has differentiated itself into Being and reconciled Being to itself, is absolute or speculative. Being is not merely "indeterminate unmediatedness," not merely the absolute beginning of Hegelian logic, but also the absolute result: Being is subjectivity, absolute reflection, thought thinking itself, the deed of infinite self-knowing divinity. Since the beginning is also *Resultat,* its deed is a "rebound" or "recoil" of completed dialectical, self-thinking thought: Λόγος is the cycle of alienation and reconciliation of θεός and ὄντος: speculative philosophy is onto-theo-logy.

But the deed is historical. As *Resul-tat* it celebrates the ultimate mystery of the interpenetration of infinite and finite realms, of the cyclical and rectilinear. Hegel thinks the Being of beings not only *spekulativ* (speculatively) but also *geschichtlich* (historically). "For Hegel the matter of thinking is Being as self-thinking thought, coming to itself only in the process of its speculative development, whereby it advances through variously developed—and therefore at first necessarily undeveloped—forms."[15] Because thinking is *Resultat,* however, Hegel's relation to the history of thought is first of all *das spekulative* and only in this way *ein geschichtliches.* This establishes the standard for dialogue with the history of philosophy: for Hegel the strength of earlier thought lies in what it *has* thought, insofar as this is underway to the goal of absolute subjectivity. Dialogue with the history of thought accordingly takes on the character of cancellation of this history's externality. It conceptualizes its own development as the completely unfolded and perfectly grounded certainty of self-knowing knowledge.

For Heidegger, on the contrary, the standard by which previous thought is examined is something "unthought" within which what has been thought finds its "essential space." Such a standard cannot serve to subsume the history of thought into a system, but must try to "release" past thought to its own essential destiny. (Whether specification of the "unthought" permits such a release or whether it serves ultimately as a standard for grounding past philosophies as stages in the destined oblivion of Being remains a much disputed question.[16]) For Heidegger the prerequisite for such dialogue must therefore be "a step back," out of philosophy into the essence of philosophy, essence understood verbally, a step back into the heretofore unexplored realm of truth as unconcealment. Such a step remains a more modest undertaking than ontotheological philosophy, which in its drive to the universal risks what Voltaire derided in the name "Pangloss," he who lets his tongue glide over all things, Pan-gloss, who teaches *métaphysico-théologo-cosmolonigologie*! But the Heideggerian step back remains more modest only if it actively remembers the limitations imposed on it by the history of its own genesis and the hermeneutical encirclement expressed in *Being and Time* (§ 32) as *Vorhabe, Vorsicht,* and *Vorgriff.* Since the Greek understanding of ἀλήθεια, never explicitly thought through by the Greeks, remains the principal *Vorgriff* for Heidegger, his view of "Hegel and the Greeks" is of central importance for the whole of his inquiry into the destiny of Being.

The two components of the title "Hegel und die Griechen" appear as the Alpha and Omega of philosophy, the Greeks initiating it, Hegel presiding over its end. However, Hegel is the very first to "think the philosophy of the Greeks as a whole, and [to] think this whole philosophically."[17] One might object that Aristotle is actually the first to do this and that Hegel is beholden to him not only for his view of early Greek philosophy but also for the idea of a history of philosophy in general. But if the history of philosophy is defined as "the intrinsically unified and therefore necessary process of the progress of Spirit toward itself," then Hegel is indeed the first. Between Aristotle and Hegel much transpires, but nothing more essential than the sighting of "firm land" in the *ego cogito* of Descartes. At the peak of the development of reason as subjectivity in modern philosophy Hegel stands as the *synthesis* of what has gone before; at the point of departure for modern philosophy Descartes stands as the *antithesis* of a philosophy of substance or pure objectivity; at the outset of philosophy as such stands the Greek who, not yet grasping the true and substantial as Subject, posits the *thesis* of the abstract universal as pure objectivity. That the Greek thesis is not yet concrete can be demonstrated only at the level of speculative thought, which by advancing through sundry alienations, cancellations, and syntheses, returns to itself, having grown together—*concrescit.* With the Greeks, however, who stay at the level of abstraction and of beauty, thought remains captivated by the immediacy of beings that are beaming and beautiful (*das Scheinen = das Schöne*[18]). With the Greeks philosophy has not yet arrived at its truth, "the absolute certainty of the self-knowing absolute Subject" (W, 267). Hence Hegel's appreciation of the basic words of Greek philosophy, Ἔν, Λόγος, Ἰδέα, Ἐνέργεια, may be summarized as follows: "Being—and thereby whatever those basic words represent—is *not yet* mediated by and in the dialectical movement of absolute subjectivity," dialectic being "the mirroring and uniting of opposites, the process of Spirit's very production" (W, 266, 259). "The philosophy of the Greeks is the stage of this 'Not yet'" (W, 266).

For Heidegger, as we have noted, Heraclitus is to be interpreted "no longer metaphysically" because that is our own closest approximation to Heraclitus' "not yet metaphysical" position in the history of thought. For Hegel, Heraclitus is "not yet metaphysical" because he has not yet achieved the level of speculative thought. To Heidegger, Heraclitus is "not yet" speculative only in the sense that the lightning-bolt of the lighting of Being has not yet vanished from his thought and has not yet been replaced by the *lumen supranaturale.* Again, not-yet-speculative means, to Hegel, not yet properly cognizant of its own essence as thought thinking itself; not-yet-metaphysical means, to Heidegger, not yet deaf to its own essence as finite thought responding to presencing and unconcealing. In these "not yets" the smallest gap, the most difficult to bridge, opens: that between the ontotheological and hermeneutical approaches to, or experiences of, the history of thought. This difference of interpretation, where the "not yet" is taken on the one hand as a symptom of the "poorest and most abstract" philosophies, and on the other as a token of "the unimpaired strength of great beginnings,"[19] becomes gradually clear in the course of Heidegger's most detailed account of Hegel's interpretation of Heraclitus. Because an English version of "Hegel und die Griechen" may not be available, the following passage appears without abridgment:

> For Heraclitus the fundamental word is Λόγος, the gathering which lets everything that is appear and lie before us as a whole, as being. Λόγος is the name Heraclitus gives to the Being of beings. But Hegel's interpretation of the philosophy of Heraclitus does *not* advance in the direction of the Λόγος. That is curious, all the more so since Hegel concludes the foreword to his interpretation of Heraclitus with the words, "There is no statement by Heraclitus that I haven't taken up into my Logic . . . (Hoffmeister ed. XIII, 328). But for this "logic" of Hegel's, Λόγος is reason in the sense of absolute subjectivity, while "logic" itself is speculative dialectic. Through the movement of such dialectic the unmediated universal and the abstract, i.e. Being, is reflected as what is objective, in opposition to the Subject. This reflection is determined as mediation in the sense of Becoming, in which opposites converge, become concrete, and so come to unity. To grasp this unity is the essence of the speculation that evolves as dialectic.
>
> In Hegel's judgment Heraclitus is the first to recognize dialectic as a principle. He thereby surpasses and progresses beyond Parmenides. Hegel explains: "Being (as Parmenides thinks it) is the One, the first; the second is Becoming—with regard to this determination he (Heraclitus) makes an advance. It becomes the first concrete, the absolute as the unity of opposites in itself. Thus with him (Heraclitus) we first encounter the philosophic Idea in its speculative form" (ibid.). Thus Hegel, in his interpretation of Heraclitus, lays the chief emphasis on those statements in which the dialectical, the unity and the unification of contradictions, comes to language (W, 264).

Here our own observations on Hegel's interpretation of Heraclitus receive some corroboration. The "logical" principle has little to do with λόγος as such or with traditional logic, and receives concrete filling only in the third section where it is interpreted as "relation to consciousness" and even *Vernunft*. Logic itself becomes speculative dialectic, the conflict and resolution of oppositions which spawns Becoming. Yet in Heidegger's account of Hegel's interpretation the same ambiguity hovers: the Greeks as a whole do not, in Hegel's eyes, achieve the level of the subjective or of negative dialectic, much less that of the synthesis of Object and Subject, of positive speculative thought; and yet *Heraclitus himself is said to have arrived at the first concrete form of thought and to have grasped the speculative Idea.* Indeed, the Hegelian schematic, when it reduplicates itself or subdivides itself in order to get a closer look at some crucial turn in the history of thought, allows space for an ambiguity that is thought-provoking in the highest degree. We might compare the logic of Hegel's historical analyses to a Chinese box, where the smaller boxes within are decorated more minutely than the larger ones, with greater attention to detail; or to a Russian Babushka whose smaller interior figures do not simply reproduce the expression of their larger sisters but show a marvelous variation of physiognomy. If the larger, more sweeping applications of the Hegelian schematic no longer satisfy, the more minute analyses never fail to stimulate thought. Perhaps that is why Heidegger insists that Hegel is the only Western thinker who has experienced the history of thought thoughtfully and why virtually all his *seinsgeschichtliche* investigations proceed with reference to Hegel.[20]

4. Excursus: Hegel on Death and the Λόγος of Philosophy

For Heidegger the speculative identity of Being and Thought, inasmuch as it rests on the interpretation of truth as certitude of the self-knowing Subject, founders in the wake of the question of the essence of truth. The fate of truth (as certitude) in Nietzsche's philosophy, its exposure as the will to self-deception, compels this question. Here there is no way to relate its history summarily.[21] But in an effort to see more deeply into that gap between ontotheology and hermeneutics we may ask how λόγος differs for Hegel and Heidegger. For Heidegger we may advise close study of *Sein und Zeit*, §§ 7 B, 44 B, 63 and 83, with special regard to the reciprocal relation of interpretation and finitude, a relation we might designate as "thinking within anxiety," or, more topographically, as "descensional reflection." Against the background of *Being and Time* we now venture a digression into the problem of death for ontotheology.

In this darkling century man everywhere goes down to confront his limitations—perhaps nowhere so stark as in anticipations of death and in failures of communication. Thought and speech no longer rescue us from mortality, if they ever did. Nor does literature: with pen in hand we no sooner dream of omnipotence than collide against unbudging obstacles which we must ascribe ultimately to our "facticity" or "finitude." During each session at the writing desk we die a bit, in the manner of Herman Melville's *Pierre,* and in our time reflection is not so much elevating or elevated as it is *descensional*. Often the same appears to have been true for Hegel. In the *Phenomenology of Spirit* (PG, 69) he calls the failure of natural consciousness a kind of death and stresses that phenomenology must dwell in the negativity of its own demise. "Death, if we so wish to name that unreality, is what is most frightful, and to hold onto what is dead requires the greatest force. [The life that endures death] and in death maintains itself is the life of Spirit. Spirit achieves its truth only insofar as it finds itself in absolute abscission" (PG, 29–30). At the same place Hegel insists that Spirit must "dwell with the negative," *bei dem Negativen verweilen.* Yet Heidegger is surely correct when he observes that in Hegel's science of the experience of consciousness the consciousness that has achieved the level of

absolute reflection suffers perpetual death throes only because it *offers itself* up
to death, "in order to achieve through this sacrifice its resurrection unto itself."[22]
The violence of its setbacks is ultimately willed by consciousness itself, as
absolute, and is therefore destined to be quelled by consciousness.

Without pretending to offer an adequate account of Hegel's thoughts on
death,[23] this brief *excursus* argues that Hegel's own philosophical writing, his
λόγος, confronts but circumvents in a violent way the facticity that is bound up
with mortality. It concludes by asserting, in opposition to Hegel, the inevitable
confluence of λόγος and death without resurrection. Its "descensional reflection" bears witness to the inextricability of thought and language, language and
death.

In the very first stage of his phenomenological explication of the ascensional
progress inherent in the experience of consciousness, Hegel demonstrates the
failure of language to grasp the truth of sensuous certainty. But he interprets this
failure straightaway as a prelude to success, writing:

> We utter the sensuous as a universal. What we say is: *this*, i.e., the *universal* this,
> *Being in general*. . . . We simply do not utter what in this particular sensuous
> certainty we *mean*. But language is, as we see, the more truthful. (PG, 82)

In Hegel's view consciousness is under the constraint to speak out and express
(*aussprechen, ausdrücken*) objects apprehended by the senses. But language
overshoots its target since it is unable to grasp the sensuous certainty of the "this
is, here and now." Swept along in the ceaseless rush of time, the present escapes
even as the word "now" is expressed, abducting with itself any "this is, here"
that is meant. Not language, but the character of sensuous certainty itself, which
language and its universals miss, undergoes fundamental change: the moment of
certitude is canceled or negated and the moment of sensuous externality sublimated. The experience of sensuous certainty, in which Spirit wanders into a
foreign exteriority, is transcended by a reversal of consciousness into its proper
experience of *perception*. This early stage in the dialectical progress toward
absolute knowledge, the first reversal of consciousness from exteriority to interiority, is unthinkable without the revelation by language of what it (language)
is. "But language is, as we see," Hegel assures us, "the more truthful." For
language expresses the true as the totality of experience gathered into all that can
be meant in general (*das Allgemeine*), the universal truth of Being. But what sort
of language does Hegel have in mind? What is its relation to the sensuous
world—which compels speech and then flees from it? What kind of universality
does language possess if indeed it fails to grasp sensuous particularity?

By *Sprache* Hegel does not mean the noise of sensuous utterance, "this is,
here and now," but the silent articulations of *Vernunft*, λόγος in the form of
Logik. In his monograph on Hegel's understanding of language, Theodor
Bodammer argues that in the silence of reflection, where thinking thinks itself in
an elevated, superterrestrial autonoesis,

. . . thought is not determined through language but rather determines itself 'in' language. The *determining ground*—if you will—is for Hegel not language but rather infinite reason, 'Spirit' or 'God' Himself.[24]

Thinking determines itself '' 'in' '' language. What does the '' 'in' '' signify, and why the quotation marks? Reason is, "if you will," the determining ground of language. Who wills here, and in what way? Does thinking ever succeed in determining itself beyond the ambiguity of its language, its '' 'in' '' and "if you will"? In Hegel's view λόγος is a power for which words are mere vehicles or instruments. Hegelian autonoesis steers its language through thinking as Helios steers his golden chariot through the sky. In autonoesis language is utterly in service to the mastery of Spirit (subjective genitive). Now, in Hegel's master-and-slave paradigm a dialectical reversal of roles inevitably occurs. How is it that the mastery of Spirit over language—of all things—escapes *dialectical* reversal? Bodammer replies, "Although logic . . . is written in the language of a certain time and socio-cultural orientation, that logic can be claimed on the basis of Hegel's systematic position to be the *categorical presentation of the one, universal, and truly infinite reason.*" Although reason is constrained to speak, its presumed mastery over speech is total. Spirit subjects speech to its will, and speech submits.

The dialectical *Aufhebung* of sensuous certainty, the move to perception, first opens the way for Spirit's return to the ground of all objectivity, i.e., to subjectivity. Along this way certitude of self-consciousness embraces the ontological truth of all otherness and ascends toward a knowledge that is absolutely certain of itself. But the first crucial step of this ascension, the reversal of consciousness from sensuous certainty to perception, proceeds on the ground of an unexpressed confidence in the impact of *das bleibende Jenseits,* the perduring Beyond, on the λόγος of philosophy. The Beyond serves as the immutable ground of that reversal in which the speech of subjectivity, of the *ego cogito,* resonates. Hence this first stage of the dialectical ascension of consciousness brings together God, death, and λόγος, securing its ascension however in the cancellation of the middle term. Such securing occurs less explicitly in the *Phenomenology* (although see PG, 545, lines 14 ff.) than in the third part of the *Lectures on the Philosophy of Religion,* "Absolute Religion."

Absolute religion knows Spirit as the Trinity: (1) God in the eternal Idea in and for itself: the kingdom of the Father; (2) The eternal Idea of God in the element of consciousness and representation, or difference: the kingdom of the Son; (3) The Idea in the element of community, or the kingdom of the Spirit.[25] For the moment we are concerned solely with the science of the experience of *consciousness,* hence with *difference* and with the obscure mediating role of the Logos which is exposed to mortality and yet is preserved in it: the "kingdom of the Son" is therefore of special interest. The Son is Spirit incarnate, alienated from itself in the σῶμα-σῆμα of corporeal existence, and fallen into an already fallen world. But incarnation is merely the preparatory stage of redemption.

"With the death of Christ," however, Hegel now tells us, "the reversal of consciousness begins" (R, 295). *Die Umkehrung des Bewusstseins* is crucial for both religion and science: it expresses the meaning of the death of Christ and the cancellation of sensuous certainty. Here the history of salvation and the science of the experience of consciousness coincide. With the death of God (as the Christ), man's relationships to God, death, and philosophical language alter. God is no longer something "distant" (*ein Drüben*) and "remote" (*ein Fernes*), but something "at hand" (*ein Vorhandenes*) (R, 297). Moreover, the presence of the divine transforms death, thought, and language, in such a way that the death of the Logos institutes the beginning rather than the end of absolute religion, itself under way to reflexive philosophy. To secure this transformation Hegel employs the most violent language: "Death is natural, every man must die. But insofar as this dishonor is brought to supreme honor [in the Crucifixion of Christ], just so are the limitations of human life as a whole attacked at their very base, throttled, and dissolved."[26]

The chalice of the Mount of Olives is more palatable than the bitter cup of Socrates: the "interiority" of the *Christosmysterium* contains "an infinitely greater depth than the interiority of Socrates."[27] For while the jailer's cup brings to an end the words of the wordy Greek, the sweet chalice of Christ, the Word, releases man from his mortal integument. How? "In Christ both the Son of God and the Son of Man are named" (R, 294). In other words, "Christ" is the difference which, upon death, restores the primal unity of Spirit. Logos is the link between God and man, infinite and finite, closing the chain of eternity. The death of the Word reconciles all opposition and equivocation in the language that Spirit as reason speaks: it ushers mortals to the secure ground of the *cogito*. By negating all negation Christian redemption provides the spiritual continuum for the unerring reversal of consciousness: even after the sighting of "land" by Descartes, security-in-certitude remains rooted in security-in-sanctity.[28]

"It is God who has deadened death by resurrecting Himself out of it; finitude, humanity, and deficiency are therewith determined as foreign to Christ" (R, 301). But because *Christos* names the Son of Man as well, it is *man's* finitude and deficiency that Christ has overcome. Christ's death is the death of *man's* death; the death of the Word is the death of sensuous errance; the death of death and of errance introduces man to the absolute Spirit that speaks in and as reflexive philosophy or science in the Hegelian sense.

But what we have just presented is Hegel's conclusion. It is derived from the following passage. (A hiatus divides the passage into two parts.) The first part reads:

Gott ist gestorben, Gott ist tot—dieses ist der fürchterlichste Gedanke, dass alles Ewige, alles Wahre nicht ist, *die Negation selbst in Gott ist;* der höchste Schmerz, das Gefühl der vollkommenen Rettungslosigkeit, das Aufgeben alles Höheren ist damit verbunden.—

God has died, God is dead—this is the most frightful thought, that everything eternal, everything true, is naught; *that negation itself is in God;* the most extreme pain, the feeling of complete abandonment, the surrendering of everything elevated is bound up with that.—

Even Nietzsche might have penned these words but for the fact that they are soon followed by very different ones. Between the words just quoted and the ones we are about to cite a hiatus appears:—. It would be no exaggeration to say that contemporary interpretation, in contrast to ontotheology, wishes to insert itself into that hiatus — whose peculiar silence announces something decisive. The second part of the passage reads:

Der Verlauf bleibt aber nicht hier stehen, sondern es tritt nun die *Umkehrung* ein; Gott nämlich *erhält sich* in diesem Prozess und dieser ist nur der Tod des Todes. Gott steht wieder auf zum Leben: es wendet sich somit zum Gegenteil.

But the advance does not stop here; rather the *reversal* now enters in. For God *maintains Himself* in this process and it is only the death of death. God is resurrected to life: everything thereby turns in the opposite direction.[29]

The first part of the passage consists of two parallel phrases that reiterate the grim tidings by first affirming what is highest and then plunging to its negation:[30]

Now comes the inescapable conclusion, the "most frightful" parallel, which we may express in the form of the equation: Gott = Negation. Several other parallel constructions now reinforce the overwhelming sense of collapse:[31]

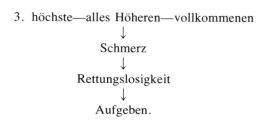

This first half of the passage is broken by eight punctuations: our reading is continually interrupted, brought almost to a standstill. We watch aghast as the language drags itself painfully across jagged rock.

The hiatus occurs. Our reading resumes, now fairly racing through a passage where only four punctuations appear, none of them really indications of pause. All is violent motion: *Verlauf* (advance), *bleibt nicht stehen* (does not stop), *tritt ein* (enters in). The motion itself is the reversal of collapse: *Umkehrung* (reversal), *wendet sich* (turns). It is the negation of negation: *aber nicht* (but not), *sondern* (rather). The equation of God and negation or death is now reduced to an "only": *nur Tod des Todes* (only the death of death). After this reduction the language lifts itself from the abrasive earth and struggles against the air: *erhält sich* (maintains himself), *steht auf* (is resurrected), ↑.

Between the two parts of the passage stands: —. What does this dash signify? Why does Spirit here speak a language that needs this curious runway for its flight? Does Spirit survive all difference in its speech, do its words remain in total servitude? Or does Spirit allude to something of utmost importance, something that smacks of utmost violence, in its dash? If this is the case, then however much Spirit may afford to be contemptuous of the language by which it categorically represents the truth of reason, it can scarcely afford to be contemptuous of its —. For — is not a category, not in Aristotle, not in Kant, not in Hegel. One must wait for what we have called descensional reflection, in Nietzsche's genealogical critique and thought of Eternal Recurrence, as well as in Heidegger's attempt to reawaken the question of the meaning of Being, which alike enter into the unsaid, underground, where — is the only category.[32]

To descensional reflection the Hegelian hiatus seems to be a violent essay to circumvent the confluence of language and finitude, interpretation and mortality. For Hegelian ontotheology the death of God means the murder of death and the vehement seizure of metaphysical ground; for descensional reflection the death of God necessitates *Gelassenheit,* releasement. It means that in our speaking and dying the god of loquacious Greek mortals, Hermes, prevails.

5. Hegel Heidegger Heraclitus

Although we seem to have ranged far from the Heraclitus seminar we have in fact followed at a distance its own movement. Beginning with the problem of a speculative interpretation that wants to be no-longer-metaphysical, we took up the question of Hegel's speculative interpretation of the Greeks as not-yet-speculative; in search of the difference between this and Heidegger's hermeneutical project we asked about the relation between λόγος and death for Hegel. But this is precisely the question raised by Fr. 62, on mortals and immortals, the question that capped Hegel's account of the Heraclitean philosophy and that dominates the latter half of the Heidegger/Fink Heraclitus seminar—to which we now return.

In the closing moments of the seminar (256 ff.), Heidegger refers back to

Fink's opening remarks. He asks what sort of challenge the Greeks pose to contemporary thought and whether *die Sache selbst* (the "real issue") can be identified as Heraclitus' "intellectual vision." Fink agrees that such vision lies beyond our scope. In the course of the seminar it has become clear that the two-and-a-half millennia that separate us from the Greeks fatally combine two elements: (1) all later thought derives from Greek thought, which however (2) undergoes severe modifications. The result is that contemporary thought often projects onto its Greek origins the most vulgar derivatives of Greek thought. We are descendants of the Greeks but inevitably misconstrue our patrimony. As to the first question, Fink replies that the challenge represented by "Heraclitus" consists in a "conscious confrontation" with his thought. "But we find this also in Hegel," Heidegger retorts. As the thinker of the absolute, Hegel is fully conscious of the challenge Heraclitus and all Greek philosophy pose: their not yet mediated thought must be reconciled with absolute, speculative reflection. As unmediated, the thought of the Greeks waits upon such mediation. It depends on this mediation to satisfy and fulfill its own essence as thought. But such dependence is not limited to *Hegel's* conscious confrontation. The problem for phenomenology today, in the form also of Fink's cosmological interpretation of the fragments, is that some sort of mediation always intrudes upon the ostensibly unmediated presentifying of phenomena. For Hegel the challenge is to reconcile the unmediated with what is mediated, i.e., self-knowing thought: such is the need (*Bedürfnis*) of his thought. "Do we too have a need?" asks Heidegger.

We do have a need, Fink replies, but no wherewithal to satisfy it. Prodded by Heidegger's incessant questions concerning the situation for thought in Hegel's time and in our own, Fink achieves eloquent clarity about his own situation. "In the course of the history of thought we have come to an end in which the entire tradition has become worthy of question" (259). The question is whether "with our new experience of Being we can encounter the Greek world." Does that mean that our experience of Being is equal to that of the Greeks? Are we prepared now to mediate? Or are we still too poor for that? With surprising trenchancy Fink now defines the need forged in the crucible of this new experience of Being: "Only as nihilists can we speak with the Greeks." Which is to say: only if we have raised the question of the "essence of the nothing" in which Being is sheltered, such protection and concealment not to be understood dialectically-speculatively, can we clear a space for discourse with the Greeks.[33] But such discourse, Heidegger now remarks, requires above all that we ask how well we understand ourselves, how ably we bring to mind the source and the impetus of all our inquiries. In such asking Hegel remains important, neither as a model nor as a *Sündenbock* (scapegoat), but as an extraordinary participant in the conversation with Heraclitus.

At the close of his final attempt to recapitulate the matter for thinking as he understands it, ἀλήθεια or unconcealment, Heidegger notes, "For Hegel there was a need to satisfy what was thought," which is to say, to reconcile it with what in the course of Spirit's progress thought had shown itself to be; "for us, in contrast, the thrust of the unthought in what is thought prevails'' (260). This *Bedrängnis des Ungedachten im Gedachten* is a dangerous affair—like those twenty-five hundred years that separate us from Heraclitus. Dangerous because *Un-gedachtes* (unthought) resembles *noch nicht Gedachtes* (not yet thought), dangerous because it apparently claims to know well enough what the Greeks did or did not achieve in their thought, dangerous ultimately because of the violence of interpretation. But Heidegger has no other source for the "unthought" than the Greeks themselves, mediated of course by the epoch of metaphysics, a mediation he knows to be an intrusion. Hence his efforts to think the unthought must leave even greater room for variation than the most minute applications of the Hegelian schematic to the history of thought.

This "leaving room for" is the essence of *Gelassenheit* (releasement). Ironically, releasement must continually urge restraint, as it occupies no firm ground. The full title of Melville's book is *Pierre, or the Ambiguities*. For mortals who are taking the first steps toward knowing who they are, steadied by the Greeks, ambiguity is the only possible approach, ἀγχιβασίην,[34] along those paths "where the land—" (Hölderlin, *Griechenland*, third draft).

3

MAN AND
DISCLOSURE

Kenneth Maly

> What if with the Greeks there were something unthought
> that is precisely the decisive element for their thinking and
> for what is thought in the whole history [of thinking]?
>
> (H 259)

At the very end of the seminar on Heraclitus, Heidegger distinguishes between the bearing that Hegel (and all of modern metaphysics[1]) has on the history of thinking and the bearing that we are to take up. "With Hegel there prevailed the need for fulfillment of what was thought. For us, on the other hand, what holds sway is the thrust of the unthought in what is thought" (H 260).

When Hegel carried out thinking, what was thought, what was already on hand for thinking, had taken on the character of a bifurcation (*Entzweiung*) and confronted thinking with an opposition within the thinking subject, man. With Hegel, thinking had to overcome this opposition; thinking had to reestablish a unity. Thinking after Descartes found itself with the subject as center, where for the sake of certainty it thought whatever is in terms of the certainty of the subject who thinks. Thinking that thinks what is in terms of the subject—where the subject grants from out of itself the essential character of what is, where the subject is that by which things are—comes to its extreme when it thinks truth as certainty in the full self-knowing of the absolute subject. What Hegel's thinking images is this momentum of the thinking of subjectivity unto its completion, i.e., unto the unity of absolute knowing knowing itself. Hegel writes early in the movement of his own thinking: "Bifurcation is the origin of the *need for philosophy*."[2] The single most important task that thinking has is to transform the opposition in the bifurcation of what is thought into a new shape, to reestablish a unity from out of the diversity of what is thought.

Whereas Hegel's thinking found itself engaged with what was thought, in order to bring it to fulfillment in a transforming, preserving unifying, Heidegger means for thinking today to take up the demand made on it by the unthought. The issue for thinking today is the unthought, which is decisive for thinking and for what is thought—as well as for what has been thought throughout the history of thinking. It is in the realm of the unthought that what is thought gets decided. What is unthought is not what a thinker "missed" and *thus* would demand our attention now so that we can "make up" for a past thinker's "lack." Rather it is the *unthought as such* that is the issue; and it is the issue as that which *carries* the thought and bears it up. It is within the unthought that the various turns in the history of thinking have been made. Once thinking comes into the extreme of dealing with the thought only from the realm of the thought, by and for the sake of removing therein all bifurcation and reestablishing within itself absolute unity—as in the thinking of modern metaphysics—then, within that movement of thought, the unthought emerges as the issue for thinking.

Thus thinking is not merely a taking possession of what is thought. Thinking has to do not only with what is thought. Rather, thinking is a drawing near to the realm for thinking that is precisely not yet thought; it is a holding to this realm and becoming aware of it.

Heidegger offers the suggestion (as an issue to be worked through) that the unthought is ἀλήθεια, disclosure. This suggestion is not coincidental; rather it is fitting and appropriate to the emergence of the issue of the unthought. For if the issue is the unthought, then the thinking of the thought (precisely our bestowed way of thinking) must understand how it itself comes to be, how it emerges from out of the unthought that gives it its bearing and that holds it (the thought) in its preserve (in the preserve of the unthought). The issue for thinking is that thinking always and fundamentally thinks the thought from out of the unthought: thinking's thought has a fundamental and originary bond to the unthought—even when thinking means to have dealt in thought with everything, when thinking attempts to transform the unthought into something more transparent to the subject, when thinking transcends the unthought in its essential character as unthought, removing the unthought as essentially unthought by taking it up into the thought.

It is at this point that the unthought demands to be heard and dealt with, thrusting itself upon us. In the movement of thinking that attempts to transcend the unthought, thinking, because of the extreme character of that attempt, finds itself facing the staying power of the unthought, with its power to remain unthought. This staying power of the unthought disturbs the thinking that wants to transcend the unthought; it makes that thinking uneasy. The thrust of the unthought is then issue for thinking.

There is a twofold enigma in this issue: (1) what thinking today essentially is, and (2) the call of that thinking to be intently wakeful to the thrust of the unthought upon it—the thrust of that which it precisely is not, but is capable of. Heidegger's naming the issue ἀλήθεια is fitting in that thinking today, when it draws near and is intently wakeful to Heraclitus's thinking, is involved in this twofold issue named in ἀλήθεια, disclosure. First, disclosure is that which lets become manifest to thinking today its own need to overcome the opposition of thought-unthought and to transcend the unthought, transforming it into the thought and reestablishing unity (the fulfillment of the thought). This manifestation becomes an issue for thinking today because it is the disclosure of the essential character of today's age. Secondly, disclosure is that which allows anything at all to be thought or to be. It is in this sense the issue of being: that by which something is. But to give the issue of being the name of "disclosure" is

always already to say that the issue of being is this and only this: the emergence
into presence, the coming to be of what is. The issue of being as disclosure is
disclosure itself, the emergence from out of hiddenness, the unfolding from out
of the withdrawing, the ἀ-λήθεια from out of the λήθη.

Our task in being open to the thrust of the unthought is to follow the unthought
in the thought, i.e. to follow in thinking the way in which thinking (= doing =
being) comes to presence, comes to be; it is to follow the question: How, from
out of where, in terms of what, does thought come to be?

1. The Problem of Retrieving the Thought of Heraclitus

When we approach the fragments of Heraclitus thoughtfully and attempt to lay
them out, to gather their import for him and for us, we can never be sure that the
imaged as it is imaged for our thinking is correct, in the sense that it fits
completely (as would two gears meshed together, a quantitative enmeshing).
Many imagings are possible, depending both on the manner in which a thinker
gathers the several moments and on the ensemble of images as it shows itself,
however obscurely, to a thinker. But beyond that one must raise the question: Is
the thinking of Heraclitus carried out in such a way that it *demands* to be left
uncertain—that the thinking, when properly heeded, requires, as part of its
essential character, not to be quantified, systematized, or fully unfolded—and
thus that any yearning for correctness of interpretation (one that would ''mesh'')
would necessarily come from something *external to* the thinking itself? That is,
does Heraclitus's thinking image itself in such a way as to call upon genuine
thinking to hold back? Does the issue remain for Heraclitus somehow always a
question? Would the enigmatic character of his sayings still remain, even if we
were able to discover the work as a unified text? The sayings are not oracular or
enigmatic because we have lost the coherent context. Rather the issue for Heraclitus's thinking is itself enigmatic. The oracular saying ''neither reveals nor
conceals, but rather grants hints'' (B 93). Heraclitus is ''the Obscure'' because
the issue in his thinking (disclosure) remains essentially—for him and for us—a
question (cf. VA 282, III 78).

Thus the problem of retrieving the thought of Heraclitus is twofold: (1) to gain
access to the barely accessible fragments, misshaped by philological and
philosophical research that has not heeded the questionable character of the issue,
and (2) to pay heed to the questioning character itself of Heraclitus's thinking.
Our bestowed way of thinking is at work in both aspects of the problem. This
(metaphysical) way must be seen for what it is in both of these moments.

Our task in this essay is to think the issue of disclosure (ἀλήθεια) in Heraclitus
as the issue of the unthought for Heidegger's thinking, whereby we must *pay
heed to the care with which Heidegger approaches Heraclitus* (seen above all in
the attitude of his thinking and spoken words in the seminar), and whereby we
must ruminate on the difficulties that Heidegger sees for any laying out of
Heraclitus's thought. Ἀλήθεια, disclosure, is in play in all of Greek thinking;

but because it is never thought by the Greeks as an issue, never becomes *the issue,* it therefore gets covered over and forgotten in its character as that which, although unthought, bears up all of thinking. Thus thinking today can hardly find the issue—and it is generally content with an analysis in terms of personalities or in terms of the consciousness-oriented thinking in which it finds itself,[3] leaving entirely out of focus the issue of disclosure itself. This lack of attention to the issue of disclosure is, in turn, responsible for the nonessential character of such efforts at thinking. Failing to heed the issue of disclosure can reach such convolutions that even the dedicated thinker (who gives himself to the issue) is not able to get at the issue until and unless it is granted to him to do so.

In trying to gain a proper access to the fragments, several difficulties of interpretation emerge. First, the text of Heraclitus that we have is in fact impoverished. Heidegger says: "that which we call fragments are no fragments at all, but rather quotations from a text to which they do not belong" (H 242; cf. also 204). Secondly, given the history and "tradition" of our language and concepts (our own bestowal), we tend to say too much, to interpret *into* the text, to bring *our* perspective to bear unduly on the fragments.[4] Thirdly, once aware of the poverty of the text and of the tendency to let our conceptual and linguistic structures bear too much on our understanding of Heraclitus's fragments—which at his time were not yet loaded down with these structures—still perhaps the most fundamental difficulty for our thinking is the impenetrability of Heraclitus's thinking in his thought. Heraclitus as he lived and thought is closed off to our thinking. We have only *what* he thought (not the thinking itself or the living that lived the question What is philosophy?). This third difficulty is then the leap that our thinking *must* make into the context in which the thought was thought: it is the difficulty of the movement of *our* thinking among the fragments of Heraclitus.

This third issue is not separable from the second one. In our attempt to understand how Heraclitus himself carried out thinking, we must remain aware of *our* attempt to rethink the fragments.

Given the several fundamental difficulties, it becomes clear to our thinking that we cannot retrieve Heraclitus in his thinking nor the thinking in the thought. Thus we are engaged at best in a rethinking that pays heed to the fragments themselves, to the said and the unsaid within them.

(This is the same issue as the issue of the "not yet metaphysical" place of Heraclitus and the "no longer metaphysical" stance that we take [H 108, 123f.]. We can think the not yet metaphysical character of Heraclitus's thinking only from out of our own bearings within metaphysics. The question then is: How can the relationship of Heraclitus's thinking, which comes before metaphysics, be named in terms of metaphysics—as "not yet metaphysical"—even if it should have in some sense prepared the way for metaphysics? On the other hand, how is our thinking "no longer metaphysical," given its rootedness within metaphysics and its necessary bond to metaphysics? The name "not metaphysical" is insufficient in characterizing the "not yet" in Heraclitus's thought and the "no longer" in ours. But the attempt to think these junctures named therein opens up the possibility of thinking beyond metaphysics while being essentially within it. It is to think the possibility of preserving the essential character of the fragments, once thinking again gains an insight into this character, and then to absorb—that is, surpass and preserve—it into the movement of thinking that carries metaphysics along in the direction beyond metaphysics. Such a thinking would be intently wakeful to the issue of disclosure as it is presented for thinking today.)

But if the fragments of Heraclitus are so closed off to our thinking, what do they offer us? What they offer us is named as possibility in the second aspect of the problem of retrieval, mentioned above: paying heed to the *essential character* of Heraclitus's thought, i.e., to its questioning. Our task is not to retrieve Heraclitus's thinking as he carried it out, but rather "through interpretation to get into the dimension which is called for (insisted upon) by Heraclitus's thinking" (H 32). Our task is not to question the reliability of the text of the fragments for the sake of philological correctness; it is rather to become intent upon (draw near to) the *question* of Heraclitus's thinking—and that from out of our bearings within the metaphysical thinking that has closed off the fragments to us.

Any interpretation of Heraclitus today stands within the bestowal. Thus the interpretation is always already a dialogue between Heraclitus and our established and bestowed way of thinking, a going back and forth from Heraclitus to us. The only speaking possible for us is from out of the movement of this "dialogue, which is fundamental for thinking and above all for the pathway on which we are moving [in thought]" (H 186). Our task is to get at the issue for thinking in the context of a dialogue with Heraclitus, hearing him as best we can through language and responding to what is heard from out of our position within the bestowal of thinking. Heidegger's aim in the seminar is our aim: "a determining of the issue for thinking within a dialogue with Heraclitus" (H 122). Our aim is not a secured interpretation, but entry into the movement that can free us unto the issue; it is to get into the dimension demanded from thinking by Heraclitus's thought.

Thinking has to hold to the issue and to hold itself back from interpreting too much, from understanding too quickly and thereby dismissing the issue. Heidegger says: "we know too much and believe too quickly to be able to become at home in a question properly experienced. For that, one needs the ability to wonder at the simple and to take this wonder as one's abode" (VA 259, III 55). In becoming aware of our blindness as being within metaphysical thinking, which has closed off the one issue in Heraclitus, we are suddenly astonished and wondering again. The issue is worthy of question again; we undergo the experience of standing in wonder before that which is wonder-full, but whose astonishing character has long ago ceased to come forth and be seen. From out of this insight into the need to regain the experience of wonder, our thinking sees the appropriateness of thinking Heraclitus in order to get into the dimension of what is to be thought at all. For it is in Heraclitus and early Greek thinking that this wonder and astonishment was still experienced. Thinking through Heidegger's pathway of thought, Walter Biemel writes: "Returning to the early thinkers is returning to the questions in which the questionable first of all flashed up."[5]

Beneath the realm of the thought in Heraclitus's thinking the unthought vibrates in hidden manner. Our thinking must relearn astonishment in the presence of this unthought. Thinking's task is to gather thought, to bring it together, in such a way that the unthought emerges as issue. But the disclosure of the unthought to thinking does not unfold for thinking in order to be transcended or abolished, to be taken up into thought. Rather, when heeded, the unthought as issue manifests its own refusal to yield itself up to thought; and thus it shows its essential character as insisting on continual astonishment. It is the interplay between this withholding and manifesting of the unthought that is the issue for thinking. It is the issue of disclosure and hiddenness: ἀ-λήθεια.

2. Ἀλήθεια

The *one* issue for philosophy, pursued by Western man ever since the early Greeks, was *first* named, in Parmenides, as: ἀλήθεια. This was philosophy's *first* name, which very soon yielded to other names until it became fixedly named as: philosophy, its name in the academic world today. The almost unbreachable gap between philosophy today and ἀλήθεια can be seen in the insistence by academic philosophy that the unthought of ἀλήθεια is *not* an issue for it. In its initial shape, ἀλήθεια, the activity that we now call philosophy was most fittingly named, *for it lacked all designation* and thereby *as name* allowed for all possibility. For us within our bestowed way of thinking, the issue of philosophy is extremely designated. It is almost impossible for our thinking to get any distance from the issue of philosophy as it has become designated. The terminology of the words used in the designation has an almost unbreakable grasp on our thinking.

Our task—that which the careful reading of the Heidegger/Fink seminar on Heraclitus calls for—is to regain the *issue* hidden by the terminology and to try to think the essential character that *indeed is covered over within the word,* but which *remains.* The issue withholds itself, but it is still hidden there. Thus there is the possibility that by thinking the hidden issue without terminology's authoritative hold, by thinking the essential character hidden within, thinking can again attain to the *dimension* in which early Greek thinking gained insight into what lay before it: ἀ-λήθεια.

For Parmenides ἀ-λήθεια still meant the uncovering and was still involved in that which is behind what shows itself, which withholds itself, but which makes all showing possible. Ἀλήθεια was coming forth out of the veiled, a revealing (unveiling). The issue for "philosophy" (not yet thought or present in the form that is suggested by the word) was the emergence into presence, coming forth from hiddenness, the "how" of what is present. And for early Greek thinking this emerging of what is always remained essentially tied to λήθη, to something which was precisely *not* present, to something hidden or withdrawing. Ἀλήθεια was "withdrawing presence." Disclosure was understood as emergence into presence (the coming to be of what is) from out of withdrawing λήθη.

This original and originary sense of ἀ-λήθεια quickly got covered over and reduced to the sense of correctness and became used mostly for *verba dicendi;* ἀληθές was primarily used to indicate whether the spoken statement is "true" or "false" and thus to indicate what is true, real, or actual.[6] The momentum of ἀλήθεια in terms of disclosure, "withdrawing presence," subsided. The word very quickly lost its freshness. Ἀλήθεια no longer carried the necessary meaning, and the *issue* of ἀλήθεια took on a new name; first philosophy, or simply, philosophy.

As Heidegger repeatedly says, the issue of ἀλήθεια, of the disclosure in which what is comes to be at all, remains unthought as such from the time of early Greek thinking onward. Ἀλήθεια was, however, said in the beginning; thinking dealt in terms of ἀλήθεια without making it explicitly an issue. Ἀλήθεια did not become the question or issue for thinking, although early Greek thinking thought in terms of it and even spoke of it.

Parmenides named the issue for thinking: ἀλήθεια. He gave that name to the issue of his own thinking. He says:

ἡ μὲν ὅπως ἔστιν τε καὶ ὡς οὐκ ἔστι μὴ εἶναι
πειθοῦς ἔστι κέλευθος (Ἀληθείηι γὰρ ὀπηδεῖ)

Fr. 2, 3f.

How there is coming to be (at all) and how not coming to be cannot be—
This is the reliable way of going (for it goes the way of ἀλήθεια).

    . . . χρεὼ δέ σε πάντα πυθέσθαι
ἠμὲν Ἀληθείης εὐκυκλέος ἀτρεμὲς ἦτορ
ἠδὲ βροτῶν δόξας, ταῖς οὐκ ἔνι πίστις ἀληθής.

Fr. 1, 28 ff.

    . . . but it is fitting that you come to know everything:
the unwavering heart of well-rounded Ἀλήθεια
as well as the holding of opinions by mortals, in which there is no reliability in
    terms of ἀλήθεια.

It is here in Parmenides's poem that ἀλήθεια, disclosure, is named for the first time in the history of thinking. It is that in terms of which thinking gains insight into coming to be and into the essential character of coming to be: that there is always already a coming to be, an emerging into presence: that not at all coming to be is not possible. Ἀλήθεια, disclosure, is that which guides thinking when it thinks the question of εἶναι: coming to be. Ἀλήθεια is the momentum that bestows to what is its bearing; it holds what comes to presence in its proper place within disclosure.[7]

Thinking has to undergo the experience of the well-rounded disclosure. Thinking is to experience that unwavering heart of the well-rounded disclosure: the λήθη in which all presencing rests, from out of which it emerges, and which holds all presencing. All coming to be and all thinking have their bearing in terms of the disclosure. That is, disclosure is that by which everything (1) is and (2) becomes understood. Thinking is thus bound to this realm of the disclosure.

> Disclosure [*Unverborgenheit*] is, as it were, the element in which there first of all is being as well as thinking and their belonging-together. Ἀλήθεια is indeed named at the beginning of philosophy, but from then on it is not really thought as such by philosophy (ZSD 76).

What is this "difference" between being involved in the thinking (being named) and not being thought as such? How is it that early Greek thinking thought *in terms of disclosure* but did not focus upon and think the issue of disclosure as such? How was disclosure in play in Greek thinking while it remained *unthought*? Can we now understand better how the issue of the unthought is the issue of disclosure?

What was thought and experienced was only that which ἀλήθεια grants: what comes to presence and thus is. Because ἀλήθεια itself remained hidden and unthought, what comes to presence lost its connection to the presencing and became thought only in terms of itself—removed from its essential bearing within disclosure. This essential bearing got covered over and forgotten.

This initial covering over of disclosure as issue has to do with the character of the issue of the unthought. Had disclosure become explicitly the issue for early Greek thinking, then we could imagine another outcome for the history of thinking. But this other possible outcome has no bearing on the issue. For that the issue of disclosure remained hidden to thinking belongs essentially to the disclosure of the issue that we have to deal with. It is not the "fault" of thinking, and neither is it accidental, that disclosure as issue remained hidden and unthought. For the λήθη in ἀλήθεια is at the core (heart) of ἀλήθεια.

As we think the issue, our first attempt to understand the issue is to gain insight into the step back from metaphysics: that what is is not something in terms of itself, but that it is *as having come to be,* as having emerged. Our focus then turns to the emerging, the *coming* to be, the *movement* of disclosure. Our initial bearing to what is is that it is there as something constant; and thinking tends (and has tended throughout all epochs of metaphysics) to assume that its ground or cause is also something constant. Thus "God" or "Being" (capitalized!) have this character for us today. The entire issue is in terms of what is. What is becomes thought as phenomenon—and philosophy today hardly grants anything else to be possible. The phenomenon—be it what shows itself in language or in scientific research—is all that is at issue. In our thinking here this first turn toward disclosure is a turn away from this metaphysical way and toward understanding the coming in the coming to be: that there is an emergence.

But the phenomenon, when heeded carefully, shows itself precisely as that which *shows* itself; thinking must heed the showing.

Heidegger's thinking has not only carefully engaged itself in the phenomenon as it *shows* itself (thus in the showing itself, in *Erschlossenheit*), but it has also verged upon and made several approaches toward the issue of the hidden character of that which grants the showing. (It is essential to keep in mind that fundamental thinking cannot penetrate this hidden realm. It is as unfitting for thinking to penetrate the λήθη as it is for Odysseus actually to *enter* the underworld during his stop *at* the underworld on his journey home to Ithaca. As the shades emerged from out of their realm to meet Odysseus, so does the showing emerge from out of its realm in the hidden.) Heidegger's thinking has dealt with two essential issues that philosophy has not handled before: (1) the issue of the showing of the phenomenon: that whatever is is as disclosed, shown; and (2) the issue of the unthought withdrawing character of the disclosure. This second issue (that of the λήθη in ἀλήθεια) is the issue that is continually left unheeded in Fink's interpretation of the fragments, to which Heidegger, then, must continually return. His return takes the shape of questions raised, hints made, and repeated warnings to hold back in interpretation. That Heidegger's holding onto the issue of the λήθη takes these shapes in the seminar is because of (1) the character of the seminar, in which Fink primarily determines the course of the discussion, even though Heidegger is the "intellectual leader"—stemming from his own being in touch with the *issue*—and (2) the character of the issue of λήθη, which somehow does not let itself be thought. When philosophy brings the issue that is in front of it to its furthermost, then in that extreme something always remains essentially hidden and unthought—something that cannot be thought by philosophy and is no longer the issue for philosophy (ZSD 71), although thinking must always pay heed to that which is hidden therein.

Philosophy's issue remains essentially that which it cannot think; the unthought is that which grants to thinking, although it itself cannot be thought. The unthought in the issue of ἀλήθεια is first of all the issue itself; but more fundamentally the issue is the λήθη in the ἀλήθεια.

3. Λήθη

The issue of ἀλήθεια points initially to what comes to appearance, to what has left the λήθη behind. This is imaged in the character of the α- as an α-privativum. But the juncture in which something comes out of hiddenness calls on genuine thinking precisely to be drawn into the nearness of the λήθη. For *it* is in the end the astonishing issue that transposes us into wonder. How are we capable of this λήθη?

Thus Heidegger begins his interpretation of Heraclitus *and* his own pathway of thinking with Fr. 16 of Heraclitus:

τὸ μὴ δῦνόν ποτε πῶς ἄν τις λάθοι;
How could anyone hide himself from that which never goes under?

This fragment belongs, according to Heidegger, at the outset of any interpretation of the fragments of Heraclitus. It must be thought as the fragment that, when thought, grants to our thinking its entrance into the issue for thinking, then and now and always: withdrawing presencing, *dis*closure, showing from out of hiddenness.[8]

Heidegger's efforts in his dealing with Fr. 16 are solely for the purpose of "bringing us, by means of a dialogue with an early thinker, nearer to the realm of what is to be thought" (VA 261, III 57).

The fragment is in the form of a question and begins with the last word of the saying: λάθοι, from λανθάνω: I remain hidden.[9] Man (i.e., τις, anyone) cannot remain hidden (how could he?) from τὸ μὴ δῦνόν ποτε. In a series of carefully thought out responses to the possible meaning of that phrase—always holding to the fundamental question: what was at issue therein for Heraclitus?—Heidegger works toward an originary way of thinking that *one* realm of disclosure.

Literally and at first glance τὸ μὴ δῦνόν ποτε means: what does not go under. How could anyone remain hidden in the presence of that which does not set? Then Heidegger thinks what δύειν meant for the Greeks: to go into something, to go under (e.g., the setting sun goes into the sea), to go under or behind the clouds. "As the Greeks thought it, going under takes place as a going into hiding" (VA 266, III 63). Thus what does not go under is that which does not go into hiding or disappear.

What does not go into hiddenness or hiding is something that is always in the movement of emerging (Aufgehen). It is the continual coming out of, the continual uncovering or disclosing. Thus the saying has to do with the realm of *dis*closure and not of hiding as such. (There is not some static realm devoid of movement which is hidden and lying at the basis of what comes to be; rather the hidden character of disclosure gets its essential character from out of the momentum of *dis*closure: the *one* realm is the movement of λήθη/ἀ-λήθεια.)

Thus Heidegger thinks the μὴ . . . ποτε as being other than a denial of going into hiding (in which there would be no hiding left)—the meaning it would have if Heraclitus had used οὐκ instead of μὴ.

The μὴ . . . ποτε says the movement whereby there is always a going away from and moving toward the realm of the δῦνόν, λήθη, or hiding. The not going into hiding is a continual distancing from it while essentially tied to it. Thus the τὸ μὴ δῦνόν ποτε is the very not going into hiddenness. It is not about some-*thing* that moves into or out of hiddenness, but is rather about the movement itself. Heraclitus thinks only the emerging, for it alone is movement (the λήθη alone is not movement and is by itself not the *one* issue for thinking). Heraclitus names the hiding in terms of never going into it. It provides an impetus for thinking and being, but is, taken by itself, not the realm. In one word Heraclitus names both the not-going into hiding and the ever-pervading emerging: the never going into λήθη and the ever-pervasive emerging from out of it. The moment of the essential interplay "into" and "out of" is the one realm of disclosure. Thus Fragment 16 says: How could anyone remain hidden from this interplay of δῦνόν, this

movement into and out of λήθη? It is the central issue, the *one* realm for thinking. "It is that [realm] within which . . . every possible 'whither' of a belonging-
to resides" (VA 272, III 68). This realm is the *one* realm named in all of Heraclitus's basic words: φύσις, πῦρ, λόγος, ἁρμονίη, πόλεμος, ἔρις, ἕν. (A future
task for thinking is to think how all these words image this interplay named in
δῦνον.) The realm of τὸ μὴ δῦνόν ποτε is the realm of λήθη/ἀ-λήθεια. It is the
hidden character of this interplay λήθη/ἀ-λήθεια that remained unthought when
early Greek thinking thought *that which* ἀλήθεια granted.[10]

> Only that which Ἀλήθεια as clearing grants is thought [in Greek thinking], not
> what it is as such.
>   This remains hidden. Does that happen by accident? Does it happen only because
> of a negligence of human thinking? Or does it happen because the self-hiding, the
> hidden, the λήθη, belongs to Ἀ-Λήθεια, not as a mere addition, as a shadow
> belongs to light, but as the heart of Ἀλήθεια? And does there reign in this
> self-hiding of the clearing of presence yet another hiding and preserving, from out
> of which disclosure can first of all be granted and what comes to presence can thus
> appear in its presence? (ZSD 78)[11]

The coming together of λήθη and ἀ-λήθεια is not a static unity or an identity
without difference; it is not a hollow oneness. Rather it is an interplay, a movement of a belonging-together. It is a dimension of the between, that juncture *into
which* thinking must penetrate, holding it open as juncture, as interplay. It is the
play of differences, the realm of movement that lays claim to what is (and to
thinking) and into which what comes to be must continually be released.

Thinking responds to the movement of disclosure so that thinking itself can
move, can go the way of disclosure whereby it is ready (readied *in* the response)
for the enabling of disclosure, which enables thinking to recharacterize what is its
issue, to regain a bearing to the unthought.

Disclosure, as the interplay between λήθη and ἀ-λήθεια, is both an issue for
thinking and an issuing: it is that which issues and that from which any matter for
thinking becomes an issue.

The interplay between ἀλήθεια and λήθη is from out of a withdrawing,
holding unto itself. Thus it has a twofold within the onefold that it is: the onefold
of the interplay maintains the twofold of emerging (in the "from out of") and of
withholding. This is its essential character. For if there were only emerging,
coming to be, presencing, that would destroy the interplay (that is what the
reduction of the unthought to the thought does). On the other hand, if there were
only withholding, withdrawing, then the interplay would lose its enabling power.
(This is what took place in the turn into metaphysics, which forgot the issue of
disclosure as such and had to deal only with what was present and to understand
the enabling [that by which] only in terms of what is, resulting in being's having
the character of *a* being, of something that is.) In either case what would take
place is a mere transformation, i.e., transcending (an escape into transcendence).
Rather the interplay must be thought as an ἐνέργεια, a being at work together, a

momentum back and forth, a vibrating within itself. The interplay is always at work and thus is always involved in the being of whatever is. The "being" of anything is, therefore, never separate from the interplay of disclosure. What is in the world is, having gotten its "being" from the ἐνέργεια of the disclosure, from the withholding enabling that is "at work" in the interplay.

The way of thinking has been bestowed to us in which we think everything that is as something in itself, separate from the ἐνέργεια of the disclosure. In our thinking we give a metaphysical import to what is present, what comes to be. Thus that which does not show itself as something that is, *is not*. The unthought is not a part of the issue for thinking. Now, the issue that Heidegger thinks in thinking the interplay of ἀ-λήθεια is nothing that is. Yet it is in some way present for thinking: it has issued for thinking, i.e., has become an issue. (Thus he can speak of a *Nichts* that has nothing to do with nihilism.) To call the issue ἀλήθεια is to let that dimension be seen which enables what is to be and enables any kind of understanding of that. Ἀλήθεια names the issue in a new way: it focuses on that which enables, on the very movement of coming to presence, on disclosure itself. (This focus is less likely when the issue is called "being.")

4. Man and Νόος

The one word in Fr. 16 that we have left unthought up until now is: τις, anyone. With that word our thinking comes to the central question of man's relation to disclosure. For the τις names man. Who is man? What is the essential character of man? In order to handle, i.e., think, this issue of man in terms of the fragment, thinking has first to undergo an experience of how ἀλήθεια is disclosure for the Greeks and then, beyond what the Greeks thought, to think ἀλήθεια as the emerging of the self-withholding, the withdrawing emerging (cf. ZSD 79).

There are two central issues within the *one* issue of man and disclosure. (1) How is man within the interplay of disclosure? How could anyone (man) remain hidden from the interplay of λήθη/ἀ-λήθεια? That is, man has to do with the interplay, is in play in the shaping of the interplay. We must understand how the establishing by the subject in modern metaphysics and how the provocation in modern technology (with whose emergence man has something to do but that in turn provokes man) are themselves moments of disclosure. The provocation and the establishing by the subject are disclosures, are ways of ἀλήθεια. (2) How is man called upon to think, given his own place within disclosure, given that disclosure is not without man but is also not controlled by him? Man's essential character, what he is called upon to be, is to be heedful of, to be awake (wakeful) to the issue. Man has as essential task: wakefulness, νόος.

Disclosure was first named by Parmenides. But whereas for early Greek thinking it was essentially involved in the issue of thinking—though it was itself left unthought—the turn into metaphysics turned to *what* was disclosed and forgot the issue of disclosure as such, i.e., lost sight of the involvement of all thinking and being in the movement of the interplay of disclosure as such.

Given this forgotten character of disclosure, thinking could attain to that shape in which the subject poses its own self. The subject who poses can only be man. Through the establishing of man as subject, objects come to be for the first time, over against the subject as consciousness. Given the fundamental character of disclosure—as an emerging from out of a hiddenness—this establishing of the human subject as the measure in terms of which whatever is is as it is, the disclosure that is subjectivity in consciousness-oriented thinking could not recognize itself as a disclosure. It is only in having undergone the experience of ἀλήθεια that thinking can gain the insight that the subjectivity of the subject and the rational character of consciousness-oriented thinking belong essentially to the disclosure that is modern metaphysics. (The same holds for the provocation of modern technology. From out of itself alone it is blind to its character as emerging from out of disclosure: that it *is* the disclosure in which what is is present as provoked, provoked to fit into the planning and ordering, which is precisely how the essential character of modern technology discloses itself.)

In the disclosure of modern metaphysics, in which thinking follows what is disclosed and takes its measure from out of it, the possibility of thinking (gaining insight into) disclosure as such is closed off. Heidegger's first major (and still most essential) contribution to philosophical thinking is his insight in *Sein und Zeit* into the essential character of man as Dasein, contrasted to the knowing of consciousness-oriented thinking of subjectivity, in which the known is as object of the subject, including the known as the noema of a noesis: every noema is fundamentally object for consciousness. It is this fundamental insight of Heidegger's into man as Dasein that opens up the possibility of thinking disclosure as such.

In the Heraclitus seminar Heidegger remarks: "In *Sein und Zeit* Dasein is written as: Da-sein. The Da is the clearing and openness [*Lichtung* and *Offenheit*] of what is, which man undergoes (passes through)" (H 202). The clearing or open (the realm of the interplay), in which what is comes to be, encounters man. Consciousness is possible only as derived from this momentum of the vibration of the open and man. The interplay is thought only in terms of the emerging that happens within it, i.e., in terms of disclosure. Thus the interplay of the disclosure has significance only in terms of man.

This relation of disclosure to man is, for Heidegger, fundamental to the understanding of how things come to be in the world, or in terms of ἕν and πάντα (cf. the first six sessions of the seminar). That is, the issue of disclosure and man lies at the basis of the issue of the coming to be of world or of what is in it. This brings us to a crucial juncture in understanding the movement that thinking takes in the seminar: Fink's bearing toward Heraclitus is secondary in that it begins with and holds to the issue of world and its coming to be, without first coming to terms with the issue of ἀλήθεια as such.[12] This is necessary because of the possibility that the way of ἀλήθεια has an essential bearing on the essential character of the ἕν, i.e., of that by which world is at all. The danger in Fink's interpretation is that it simply places man within the back and forth movement of the ἕν and πάντα, of world as enabling and what comes to be within that enabling, without thinking man's essential bearing upon it.

For Heidegger the issue of man is always already essentially there in any coming to be, i.e., disclosure, of world. Thus "man and disclosure" is the primary issue; it must be thought before any thinking of ἕν and πάντα in terms of the world. In focusing only on ἕν and πάντα, ἕν gains its essential character from πάντα. In the more primordial issue of man and disclosure, ἕν gains its essential character in terms of disclosure as such. Heidegger's question of man and disclosure reveals the questionableness of Fink's approach in that it shows the issue of disclosure to be more fundamental.

Thus the first question for the thinking of the seminar is: What is the character of the movement underlying Heraclitus's thinking? For Fink it is the coming to be of world; for Heidegger it is man's place in the movement. Thus it is that Fr. 16 is the primary fragment for Heidegger, whereas for Fink it is Fr. 64.

Now, the κεραυνός of Fr. 64 is also named πῦρ in Heraclitus; and the τὸ μή δῦνόν ποτε of Fr. 16 is also named λόγος. Fr. 1 says that (1) everything comes to be in accordance with and owing to λόγος and (2) that men act as though they do not grasp λόγος, i.e., do not remain within the realm of λόγος. The issue of λόγος and the issue of disclosure are the same. Our thinking must be awake to the words λόγος and πῦρ and to their saying the same as τὸ μὴ δῦνόν ποτε and ἀλήθεια, in order to understand Heidegger's weighty remark to Fink in the seminar: "Your way in interpreting Heraclitus proceeds from fire to λόγος; my way in interpreting Heraclitus proceeds from λόγος to fire" (H 179f.). For when λόγος (ἀλήθεια) is not the starting point, then thinking can perhaps understand the coming to be of what is from out of the one (ἐξ ἑνός πάντα) in Fr. 10; but it cannot think the ἐκ πάντων ἕν in that fragment. When λόγος is not the starting point for interpreting Heraclitus, then thinking cannot understand the emergence of the one; that the one emerges from out of the many (or πάντα) is unthinkable *unless* one understands the essential character of the ἕν and then of the πάντα therein. This is possible only when the issue is not in terms of things that are, in terms of what is, but rather in terms of λόγος, of the fundamental gathering or bringing together (λέγειν) from out of the unthought and hidden, i.e., in terms of disclosure. That is, the ἕν does not emerge in terms of πάντα, does not get its determination from *what* is gathered, but rather in terms of λόγος-ἀλήθεια. Everything in Heraclitus, and in early Greek thinking imaged therein, has to do with disclosure: emerging and the hidden reserve.

Genuine thinking rescues man and disclosure, thinks in such a way that their separation is seen for what it is. This insight, in turn, frees each unto the onefold which they are. But what is the character of genuine thinking, if it is to rescue the separation and to think the *one* issue? It is the character of thinking as νόος, or νοῦς.

We now return to the second question raised above: How is man to become heedful of disclosure, to become awake to it? To do this our thinking goes back

again to the τις of Fr. 16. Heidegger appropriately indicates (VA 277, III 73) that
τις does not mean just man, but anyone who has the capability of hiding, in
which characterization the gods are included, too (cf. Fr. 30: "neither of gods or
of men"). That is, the "anyone" involved here is anyone who can have care for
his own essential character—and therefore who is capable of being blind to it.
We cannot call "blind" something that cannot see: a rock is not "blind." Thus
τις is anyone, man or god, whose own essential character is at issue for him. It is
any Dasein, i.e. any existing one for whom his own being is at issue. ("Dasein
existiert als ein Seiendes, dem es in seinem Sein *um* dieses selbst geht"—SZ
406, 12.)

How can anyone remain hidden from λήθη/ἀ-λήθεια? How can man become
or remain blind to disclosure? For us today the clue lies within consciousness-
oriented thinking, which insists on a center unto itself. The absolute certainty of
subject knowing itself cannot think ἀλήθεια in its essential character as emerging from a withdrawal. The ἀλήθεια of Greek thinking cannot be released from
the knowing subject—and thus it becomes determined only in terms of that
subject. In *that* determination its own essential character gets lost, becomes
transcended by the consciousness of subjectivity: the unthought of ἀλήθεια
becomes thought. But whereas all disclosure is for man, it is not established by
man. For man to establish it is to be blind to disclosure as such, i.e., to remain
hidden from the λήθη/ἀλήθεια that is disclosure.

This way of thinking dominates in modern metaphysics. We do not see it for
what it is; we do not see it as a disclosure but rather take it to be the measure
itself. Thus we are measured by ourselves and are blind to all but ourselves. We
can remain hidden before this issue by not heeding our being within disclosure.
"Everything comes to be in accordance with and owing to λόγος," but "men act
as though they do not grasp λόγος (do not have their abode in λόγος)" (Fr. 1).
The impetus for Heraclitus, too, was that man in his time was blind. His thinking
is to show the blindness of the men around him, i.e., who were unthinking, not
"hearing" the λόγος. Men do not understand. Thus the essential character of
genuine thinking is to understand the disclosure in which it is in each epoch *and*
to heed the essential blindness. It is to be intently wakeful to that blindness.

The issue is not to know, but to be awake to. Πολυμαθίη νόον οὐ διδάσκει:
"Learning of many things does not teach wakefulness (νόος)" (Fr. 40). Νοεῖν
is to be awake to, to be aware of, to take into one's care (cf. WHD 124–29), to
take up, hold, have it there for what it is. Νόος is insight or wakefulness to. Man
with νόος is awake, alive to, has his attention directed intently toward. Man is
intently open to. The openness of νόος is not a passive receptivity; it is a being
prepared intently. "Those who gather and say (λέγοντας) with intent wakefulness must persist in (hold strongly to) what is common" (Fr. 114). But:
"Whereas λόγος essentially unfolds as what is common, the masses go on living
as if every individual had an own understanding" (Fr. 2). Man is to have νόος:
to be awake, to be intently ready for taking carefully in. That is the opposite of
blindness. In his essay on Aristotle, Jacob Klein writes: "This state and manner

of being is a state and manner of being in which we are not closed up but *open*. Wakefulness is openness—the very openness of a huge open door. It is not a state of activity, but rather a state of preparedness, of alertness. This state or manner of being is commonly called in Greek νοῦς or νοεῖν.''[13]

Νοῦς or νόος as rational comprehension is somewhere in the vicinity of the issue of νοῦς as intent wakefulness, for rational comprehension has to do with grasping something. But to call the νοῦς "rational" is to impose structures that are present only after thinking has entered the age of subjectivity. Hegel's identification of νοῦς in Anaxagoras with *Denken*, which is identical with *Ich=Ich* (i.e., with *Ich denke*) is such an imposition.[14] For Hegel νοῦς is to be identified with thinking, and thinking is the I think, or the I. Thus νοῦς becomes the self-consciousness of the I. Understood in this way, νοῦς has to do with rational comprehension; but it is no longer the νοῦς of early Greek thinking.

The νόος in Heraclitus's thinking has to do—not with a rational way of dealing with what is, in a rational comprehension—but rather with an intense (intent) wakefulness that is open to the disclosure of what is, to perceive and take it in as it is.[15] Everyday man is "overcome by fatigue, his wakefulness yields to sleep."[16] On the other hand man's proper way is wakefulness, openness (cf. H 224ff.).

Why and how are men and gods (τις), that is, those for whom their own being is an issue, not capable of remaining hidden from the τὸ μὴ δῦνόν ποτε? (We must note that the optative in ἄν τις λάθοι—"how could anyone remain hidden''—has this negating sense and means: "no one really is able to.'') Those beings for whom their own being is an issue are not capable of remaining hidden from the interplay of disclosure because their relation to their own essential character (their being) is nothing other than the interplay itself. That is, man is man only in the interplay, in his intent wakefulness to it. Not all who are biologically determined to be human are men in this essential sense. Being human means precisely being wakeful to (intently aware of) the interplay. This is not possible within the separation that belongs essentially to consciousness-oriented thinking. (Thus man's first and nearest task today, in order to become man, is to become intently wakeful to *this* disclosure of consciousness-oriented thinking and the subject-object separation inherent within it.)

The hidden in the disclosure itself unfolds. Thus when being wakeful, i.e., being *man*, man is open not only to the disclosure, but also in the same essential manner to the hidden that grants what is to be disclosed. Man is within this essential bond to the hidden and to that which emerges only when he is intently wakeful. That means for man today: only when he is intently there to *allow* the limitation of metaphysics to show forth its fundamental character as itself a disclosure.

The phenomenon of the interplay of disclosure, in its various levels of showing, presents to thinking the possibility of a continually new characterization of man in this movement of relation. Properly heeded (in the essential νοεῖν), the phenomenon of the interplay of disclosure presents precisely the vibrating movement itself, the movement necessary for man to remain wakeful, to remain within his element. Thus the τὸ μὴ δῦνόν ποτε is what allows man his wakefulness. In order to be the movement in which man is fundamentally and essentially, the interplay must show itself to have the character of a onefold within it, the character of a whole that somehow encompasses all possibilities and even possibility as such, and to have also the character of a movement that brings about movement.

The λόγος is the gathering that is the measure for the interplay, which measure is the interplay. Man is the one who intently heeds this measuring that is going on in the interplay. This measuring by man, following upon λόγος, becoming aware of it, belongs to man's essential character even when he is not engaged in it. Even when everyday man is blind and unaware, his essential character is to become intently wakeful and to be the place of the measuring of the interplay. Man *has* to be in the gathering of the disclosure, even when something keeps him from it; it is incumbent upon him *as man*.

In Fr. 119 Heraclitus says:

ἦθος ἀνθρώπῳ δαίμων.
Man's familiar abode (there where man belongs most properly) is the region open
    for the daimon.

This most fitting abode for man can be called his ἀρετή, his most proper way to be: in the region open for the daimon, in the region of the interplay.[17]

When man heeds properly his most proper way to be (intently wakeful for the coming of disclosure), then he is held by and is holding to the gathering of λόγος. Perhaps thinking can gain a fresh insight into the realm of ἦθος (ethics) if it thinks man's ἀρετή as essentially tied to the gathering of λόγος. What today is named *ethics* and has little bearing on man's *proper* abode within the open might be renamed *elegance* (from ἐ-λόγος): Elegance is being intently wakeful, is dealing with what is in proper fashion. To be ethical is to follow the norms established by society, having then its measure within itself; to be elegant is to follow the gathering of the λόγος, having its measure within the interplay that bears up the elegance of man.

For Hegel's as well as for Heidegger's thinking the ἀλήθεια at the beginning of Greek philosophy was a "not yet." For Hegel the "not yet" was on the level of immediacy, without mediation, and did "not yet" satisfy (fulfill) the need to unify the thought. For Heidegger ἀλήθεια is also a "not yet." But it "is a 'not yet' of the unthought . . . a 'not yet' for which *we* do not satisfy, to which *we* do not give satisfaction" (W 272). In Hegel's thinking the issue of ἀλήθεια was not yet enough; in Heidegger's thinking it is thinking that is not yet enough for ἀλήθεια. What is not yet thought by Heraclitus is unthinkable, not in the sense of lacking the necessary character by which it could be taken up into thought, but rather in its being the ever-pervasive issue for thinking. The issue for thinking remains essentially unthought.

Man cannot remain hidden (how could he?) from the unthought.

Or, to repeat the quotation at the beginning of this essay—with a turning of the phrase that is, one hopes, *also* appropriate:

If with the Greeks there was something unthought that is precisely the decisive element for their thinking . . . , then how?

4

HADES
Heraclitus, Fragment B 98

JOHN SALLIS

My concern is to engage in a thoughtful reading of a fragment of Heraclitean thinking. Any attempt at such a reading must contend with the distance at which the tradition, in running its course, has placed us. Yet we are prepared for this contention, opened to it in a unique way, insofar as we are thrown out of the tradition through its very ending and freed of that weight which we would otherwise bear to the beginnings of the tradition. In this respect Fink's insight is decisive: "It is only as nihilists that we can speak with the Greeks"[1]—even if, on the other hand, the very self-insight of nihilism proceeds already from a bearing toward beginnings, from dialogue with Greek thinking.

I

Fr. 98 reads: αἱ ψυχαὶ ὀσμῶνται καθ᾽ Ἅιδην. Diels translates: Die Seelen atmen Geruch ein im Hades.[2] Burnet renders it in English: Souls smell in Hades.[3] Freeman eliminates the ambiguity: Souls have the sense of smell in Hades.[4] Cherniss eliminates any suggestion of mere passivity: Souls employ the sense of smell in Hades.

This fragment is handed down only by Plutarch. It is quoted in his dialogue "Concerning the Face which Appears in the Orb of the Moon," specifically, in the course of the myth with which this dialogue concludes. The myth, told by an unnamed stranger, portrays the moon as inhabited by souls that have left their bodies after death on earth or have not yet been incorporated by birth into terrestrial bodies. Among these are certain souls who,

> resembling the ether about the moon, . . . get from it both tension and strength. . . .
> In consequence, they are nourished by any exhalation that reaches them, and Heraclitus was right in saying: "Souls employ the sense of smell in Hades."[5]

Such is the context in which the fragment is handed down, a context in which it was placed by Plutarch more than five hundred years after the death of Heraclitus. It is a decidedly Hellenistic context, related back probably to Plato's *Timaeus*[6] but foreign to early Greek thinking. The early Greeks did not set Hades in the sky; nor could they have identified Hades with the source of night's illumination.[7] Hades was much too awesome.

We are thus obliged to take up Heraclitus' saying as a fragment in a dual sense: not only does it lack its original context but also it must be wrested from that context in which it has stood since Plutarch. To attempt a thoughtful reading requires, first of all, that we let the fragment be radically fragmentary.

So, we let the context drop away and attend to the isolated fragment. But, then especially, the paradox that the fragment seems to express comes to light. We wonder that souls can be said to have any senses whatever in the realm to which they pass after death, much less a sense so inferior as smell, so coarse and bodily especially in comparison with sight.[8] Is not death precisely the separation of the soul from everything bodily and sensible—hence, from all senses and, most emphatically, from senses as bodily as smell? This teaching regarding death, extracted from the beginning of Plato's *Phaedo,* provided the basis for the traditional understanding of death (if not also of life), and it is only by utmost diligence that we can be so nihilistic as not still to carry this teaching with us. When we let the context drop away, the danger is that we may then merely draw the fragment into that context which we carry along. Little is accomplished if the fragment is freed from the Plutarchian context only to be transposed to the context provided by a sedimented, traditional teaching, especially since the latter context serves only to render the fragment hopelessly paradoxical. It is only as nihilists that we can speak with the Greeks.

So, we grant the fragment its requisite distance from the traditional teaching regarding death and the soul. Instead of drawing it into our context we undertake to set it back within the context of early Greek teachings regarding death and the soul. According to certain of these teachings the soul is breath; when at death the soul is separated from the body, the other senses perish, so that souls in Hades neither see nor hear; but since soul is breath and since smell is inhaled with the breath, even the bodiless souls in Hades retain the sense of smell.[9]

Thus, without being accommodated to something alien, the fragment becomes understandable from this context—even though the puzzle remains as to how the sense of smell could be had by mere breath, i.e., without any organ of smell. However, in this way the fragment becomes understandable *only* as an affirmation and extension of popular opinion regarding the soul. We expect something more and, seeking to read thoughtfully this fragment of thinking, anticipate a dimension in which the fragment would become understandable in that radicalness which distinguishes all genuine thinking from popular opinion. There is reason for our anticipation, not only in the reports about Heraclitus' haughtiness and his disdain for common opinions,[10] but, more significantly, in the various fragments expressing the opposition between a hearkening to the *logos* and the many's mere semblance of understanding.[11]

But how are we to think the fragment back into the dimension anticipated? Perhaps by heeding the warning expressed in another fragment:

You would not find out the limits of soul, even by travelling along every path: so deep is its *logos*. (Fr. 45)

How shall we undertake to think the fragment back into its anticipated dimension? By proceeding not from soul but rather from the word with which Fr. 98 ends, "Hades"—that is, by regressing from the end of the sentence back toward its beginning, by reading the sentence backwards.

II

"Hades" (Άιδης) is not primarily the name of a place; in classical Greek it is rather the name of a god.[12] On the other hand, the god is closely connected with his domain and his character thoroughly determined by that connection. Thus, the extension of the name "Hades" to the domain of the god Hades is not without grounds.

Homer tells of the original assignment of the god's domain. In the *Iliad* he has Poseidon speak of how, when the world was divided into three parts, the three brothers, Zeus, Poseidon himself, and Hades, cast lots and of how each then received his own domain, sky being granted to Zeus, sea to Poseidon, and the dark underworld to Hades.[13] The name "Hades" already anticipates the allotment: it means "unseen." Hades and his domain are withdrawn from the light, from the light of the sun. They are withdrawn, not merely in the way that things are temporarily enclosed in the darkness of night, but rather in such a way that they never admit the light of the sun. This withdrawal is in part retraced by Heraclitus in Fr. 120. He names four directions: the limit of morning, that of evening, the bear, and (opposite the bear) the boundary mark of flashing Zeus. It is thus that the domain of the sun, including both day *and* night, is measured out.[14] Hades is set over against this domain, withdrawn from it into the "nocturnal abyss," into essential concealment. The domain of Hades is a λήθης δόμος, a place of oblivion, an abode of concealment.[15]

For Homer, Hades is not only the "unseen" god withdrawn from the domain of sun and light but also the ruler of the dead; the domain into which he is withdrawn is that to which all are withdrawn after death. It is the domain in which dwell, according to the *Odyssey*, "the unheeding dead, the phantoms [εἴδωλα] of dead men."[16] It is the abode where men, withdrawn by death, live on as εἴδωλα, as phantoms, as images. It is the abode in which men, withdrawn from the open life of the *polis*, reduced to mere images, are enclosed amidst shadows, in obscurity, in concealment.

In Fr. 27 Heraclitus poses death in its concealing power. "There await men after they are dead things which they do not expect nor opine." This says: beyond death are things which in no way reveal themselves to us, which we in no way can foresee, things radically concealed.[17] For living man death is radical concealment, a veil on which shimmer only the faint images cast there by the poets. But how, then, does it happen that Heraclitus says: souls employ the sense of smell in Hades?

Perhaps we should begin to wonder what the fragment says and especially whether it carries the claim of telling how things are *in* Hades. Also we should

again recall that ''Hades'' refers to the god, not the place; and then we rightly
wonder how souls can be said to be *in* Hades. In fact, the fragment does not say
ἐν Ἅιδη but rather καθ᾽ Ἅιδην. What does καθ᾽, i.e., κατά, mean here?
Certainly it may mean ''in'' (for instance, in the sense of ''throughout''). But it
has a wide range of other possible meanings. It may have the sense of direction
toward a thing or purpose, the sense that would be expressed in such statements
as: ''Souls are on the scent of Hades'' or ''Souls employ the sense of smell for
the sake of Hades.'' The preposition may also have the sense of fitness, con-
formity, accord. In this case the fragment would be rendered: Souls employ the
sense of smell in accord with Hades. Thus rendered, the fragment says: In the
specific mode corresponding to the sense of smell, souls comport themselves in
accord with Hades. Now the fragment has ceased being a proclamation of how
things are after death. But what does it mean for souls to comport themselves in
accord with the god Hades? What kind of comportment would this be? Both in
his character as withdrawn from the sun's domain and as ruler of the dead, Hades
is the god whose comportment is determined by concealment—no less than Zeus'
comportment is determined by the unconcealing wrought by the lightning bolt he
wields. Souls comport themselves to Hades precisely insofar as they are engaged
in and by concealment. What is at issue in the fragment is not the state of dead
men but rather living man's engagement in λήθη.

III

But why is that mode of comportment in which man comports himself to
concealment identified as corresponding to the sense of smell? What does smell
have to do with concealment? Does it perhaps serve to make phenomenally
manifest man's comportment to concealment?

Another fragment regarding smell needs to be brought into consideration,
namely Fr. 7 which reads: εἰ πάντα τὰ ὄντα καπνὸς γένοιτο, ῥῖνες ἂν διαγνοῖεν. In translation: ''If all things were to become smoke, distinguishing would
be by means of the nose.''

This fragment has been frequently discussed and variously interpreted.[18] Almost invariably, however, interpretation has come down to a correlating of the
fragment with an abstractly conceived relation between one and many. For
example, the fragment has been regarded as ironical, specifically, as a criticism
of man's tendency to find diversity while ignoring the unity of things. It is thus
regarded as saying: Even if things turned to smoke so that their oneness became
evident, men's noses would still smell out differences and concentrate on the
diversity of things. However, the one (ἕν) of which Heraclitus speaks is not the
mere outcome of a dissolution of all differences between things but is rather that
which gathers all things (τὰ πάντα) and lights them up in their articulated
differences, just as the lightning steers all things (Fr. 64) by flashing out in the
night so as to light up things and let them be seen in their articulation.[19] For
things to turn to smoke would thus hardly suffice to make evident their oneness

but would rather serve to conceal their unity no less than their diversity. Another direction of interpretation regards the fragment as simply putting forward something that in a paradigmatic fashion is both one and many, in the sense that the smoke is one to sight but many to smell; but this interpretation also fails completely to retain the proper tension between one and many, that is, it regards the one as a mere result of dissolution of differences (in this case, differences for sight).

Nevertheless, it is important to bring into play the contrast between sight and smell in relation to the phenomenon of smoke. If all things were to become smoke, then we could not employ the means on which usually we rely primarily for distinguishing between things, namely sight. At least as regards sight, smoke conceals.[20] Not only does it conceal whatever stands behind it, but also, as itself impenetrable to sight, it is peculiarly self-concealing. For all things to become smoke would mean that they become concealed from our sight, not by something else that would come to stand in front of them, but rather by themselves, by their own self-concealing withdrawal from our sight. What the antecedent clause of the fragment poses is concealment.

So, if all things were to become smoke, distinguishing would be by means of the nose, that is, by the sense of smell. Why? Because under this condition sight could not execute that distinguishing usually entrusted primarily to it. But then, the question is: How capable is the nose of taking over the work of the eyes? How capable is smell of laying out things in their distinctness? Later, Aristotle will contend that man's sense of smell is inferior in two respects, "inferior to that of all other living creatures and also inferior to all the other senses we possess";[21] in both respects the inferior position of our sense of smell lies in its inferior capacity for distinguishing things.[22] Heraclitus also attests, though indirectly, to the inferiority of our sense of smell by speaking of the superiority of other senses, the senses that teach us something, the senses to which a teaching and learning (μάθησις) attaches: "I give preference to everything of which sight and hearing give knowledge."[23] But what, most of all, attests to the inferiority of the sense of smell is the phenomenon itself. For man, the sense of smell is hardly at all a matter of teaching and learning (μάθησις). For man, the sense of smell is, least of all the senses, capable of genuinely distinguishing things, of reenacting the lighting-articulation to which so many of the fragments are in one way or another addressed—the lighting–articulation which the one (ἕν) brings to all things (τὰ πάντα). Smell least of all is capable of embracing the distinct contours of things in such a way that they become manifest as they are. In utmost contrast to our sight, our sense of smell lets things remain submerged in indistinctness, sunk in concealment.

Thus, there is a peculiar fittingness of the sense of smell to the smoke of which the fragment speaks. Whereas the antecedent clause poses concealment, the consequent clause poses that way of comportment toward things that is most subjected to the power of concealment, that is least capable of drawing things out of their withdrawal into self-closure and indistinctness. What the fragment poses

as correlative to the concealment (of smoke) is human comportment to concealment.

Let me add, in passing, that another mode of comportment that is intrinsically
linked to concealment is sleep. According to Hesiod, sleep is carried by night,
has its home in the underworld, and, most significantly, is the brother of death.[24]
It is in this connection that—if we accept the testimony handed down by Sextus
Empiricus[25]—we might understand the peculiarly privileged position that Heraclitus assigns to breath in sleep: in sleep, breath (and, hence, smell) is the only
point of attachment that one retains with the surrounding. Within that reposing in
concealment that we undergo in sleep, there is a withdrawal from our waking
comportment with things into a passive retention of the one mode of that comportment that is most fitted to concealment.

IV

We are now in a position to read more thoughtfully the fragment with which
we began: αἱ ψυχαὶ ὀσμῶνται καθ᾽ ῞Αιδην. "Hades" names the god who
withdraws from the domain of the sun and rules over the dead—the god whose
basic comportment is determined by concealment, whose mythic deeds trace, as
it were, the direction and movement of concealment. The fragment speaks of
comportment in accord with Hades—that is, of comportment which accords with
that of Hades by being itself a reenactment of the god's comportment, by being
itself an engagement in the movement of concealment. This engagement Heraclitus makes phenomenally manifest by the reference to smell, that manner of
comportment in which man is pre-eminently engaged by, drawn into, held
within, the movement of concealment.

Thus read, the fragment is a tautology—that is, a sentence (λόγος) which says
the same thing (τὸ αὐτό) over again. What it says is: engagement in concealment. But it says it in two quite different ways: phenomenally in the reference to
smell, mythically in the reference to Hades.

Let me, then, displace the literal translation—the translation: souls employ the
sense of smell in Hades. Or rather, let me expand it in such a way as to install
within it the reading we have attempted. Then it might be rendered: Souls,
employing the sense of smell, are engaged in the movement of concealment. Or,
still more expandedly: The soul's employment of the sense of smell exemplifies
and makes phenomenally manifest the soul's engagement in the movement of
concealment, in the withdrawal of things into self-closure and indistinction.

At this point the limit of the fragment begins to come into play, its limitation to
engagement in concealment. This is a limit because in his comportment to things
man's engagement is never solely an engagement in concealment—certainly not
in his waking hours, not even in the night. For, to speak with the Heraclitean
images of Fr. 26, in the night man kindles a light and even in sleep touches upon,
thus lights up, death. The same issue is evident in Fr. 7—provided we attend
carefully to what the fragment says phenomenally. Over against our comport-

ment to concealment, it poses concealment phenomenally as smoke. What we need to notice is very commonplace: Smoke accompanies—*fire!* It is, as Fink says, the "shadow of fire";[26] and yet its concealing power is such that it can even conceal that which it shadows. With smoke there is fire—that is, the one (ἕν), which Heraclitus also thinks as *logos,* as lightning, as sun. But how are they together?

At the limit of the fragment which we have attempted to read, at the point from which it speaks, its beginning—here we come up against the issue from which perhaps all the fragments of Heraclitean thinking ultimately rebound—the issue, to say it phenomenally: How do fire and smoke belong together? We can also ask it mythically: Where lies the joint which joins the domain of the sun to that of Hades, Zeus' lightning to Hades' withdrawal into darkness, revealment to concealment? Where is that joint by which, as Heraclitus himself says (Fr. 15), Hades and Dionysus are held together in the unity of sameness?

This would also be the joint of the soul, the joint which, as *logos* sunk into the depths of the soul, gathers the soul into its limits. The sense of the warning that we heard in Fr. 45 is now clearer: it warns of the rebound from the issue of the togetherness of revealment and concealment. One direction in which the rebound may be sustained is that in which we are carried by taking up Heraclitus' saying in Fr. 32: "The one, alone wise, is not willing and is willing to be called by the name Zeus." Ἕν is Zeus as the highest being, yet Ἕν is not Zeus insofar as it is that which lets every being come forth into presence, be revealed.[27] Must we not say the same of Hades? The nocturnal abyss, set over against the sun's domain (over against the entire domain of ἕν-πάντα) is not willing and is willing to be called by the name "Hades." The abyss is Hades as the lowest (deepest) being yet is not Hades insofar as it is that which withdraws every being back into self-closed absence, into concealment. Or, does the abyss of Hades, as withdrawing things into concealment, perhaps withdraw itself still more sternly from every attempt to call it by name?

In the course of the tradition since Heraclitus, the deepest thinkers have sought nevertheless to name what Heraclitus the obscure names Hades. The task remains—or rather, if we are sufficiently capable of nihilism, it is posed for us with renewed force and clarity, posed as a task that could never be brought straightforwardly to completion without violating precisely that which the name would name, without thus unleashing again the strife between name and the self-closing withdrawal that the name would name. The task is rather to persevere in the difference and to let the strife between name and named be a reenactment of the primordial strife between Zeus and Hades (light and darkness), Dionysus and Hades (life and death). This strife of ἀλήθεια is the strife, the war (πόλεμος) which, in the famous words of Fr. 53, is the father of all things. But it is also a strife which is reflected, duplicated from afar, in the structure of every image, even the simplest—in that dual character by which revealment and concealment are conjoined in every play of images.

5

FIRE AND LOGOS
The Speech of Fire
and Its Contradictions

Ruben Berezdivin

In antiquity, Heraclitus was nicknamed "the obscure." It is his thought that is obscure, which is to say enigmatic, full of riddles. There is the added hindrance, at least for us, that what we have of his writings are only fragments of a book whose form and structure we cannot securely reconstruct. Hence, we do not fulfill those conditions necessary for a secure confrontation with his thought.

I shall not attempt, therefore, to reconstruct his thought in an objective manner. I shall attempt, by projecting back through Plato and Aristotle, to sketch a probable line leading back to what Heraclitus might have thought. We are involved, therefore, in a matter of *possibility*. I shall follow what I would like to call the incline back. Out of the remnants of his thought I shall fashion a pathway leading through the portals wherein philosophy abides. Only through such a methodological screening can I see Heraclitus being of use to us as a thinker. Such an encounter with his possible thought will be risky. Violence with scholarly interpretations may occur. The responsibility cannot be shirked: the most inward matter of thought is at issue.

Heraclitus is famous in the tradition for two major questions, which he was thought to represent: the question of fire as the first principle of things (just as Anaximenes represented the position of air, or Thales water, as the principle); and for contending with a Logos that was contradictory—a matter for which Aristotle rebukes him. Fire and Logos concern Heraclitus from the beginning, in the way his thought touched the tradition. The intertwining of God and Logos in Heraclitus, and of the two with fire, can be seen from the fact that God is thought of as

> ... day night, winter summer, satiety hunger. ... He undergoes alteration in the way fire, when it is mixed with different spices, is named [ὀνομάζεται] according to the scent of each. (Fr. 67)

Fire here 'represents' God as the all—day *and* night, satiety *and* hunger. But the key balance of the fragment depends on the "named," on how each of the different scents of the fire has its own name.

A relationship, pregnant with significance, is intimated, between "naming" and fire. But naming is one of the fundamental structures of human language, which for the Greeks came to be thought of as Logos. Fire and Logos are here correlated in a peculiar way: there is a relationship between fire and Logos, between fire and names. We will see that the relationship concerns the essence (verbal) of Logos—and not just naming. Fire and Logos are essentially intertwined in Heraclitus' thought, much as the body and the mind are intertwined in the modern philosophical tradition. I shall speak more of this when the context is ripe.

We want to consider this peculiar relationship. However, since the question of Logos is methodologically first, I want to begin with a survey of what Logos can mean for us—always in view of its relationship with fire. In this, we shall follow Heidegger, who considers beginning with Logos as fundamental if any headway is to be made in interpreting the fragments. In opposition to Eugen Fink, who begins with lightning in order to retrieve Logos from that dimension, Heidegger suggests that only by beginning with Logos can we avoid losing ourselves in the labyrinth of Heraclitus' fragments. As Heidegger says in the Heraclitus seminar:

> The difficulty, which in the seminar has crept up on us again and again, lies in the methodological set-up [Ansatz], the correctness of which I do not wish to question. So long as one does not have λόγος in view, one does not make it through, one reads Heraclitus with difficulty. Therefore it seems to me that Fr. 1, which stands at the beginning of Heraclitus' writing, should also support the interpretation of Heraclitus as the first fragment.[1]

In agreement with Heidegger's methodological caution, we shall begin, indeed, our interpretation of Heraclitus with Logos, and indeed, with Fr. 1. We follow Heidegger, and we go "from λόγος to fire," instead of going, as Fink does, from "fire to λόγος."[2]

A partial interpretation of the term *Logos* is in order here.[3] Its meaning may be gathered from the fragments in which it appears. Fr. 1, which probably began Heraclitus' work, is reported by Sextus Empiricus in the following way:

> Beginning his book *On Nature* ... offering an indication of sorts about the surrounding [τὸ περιέχον], Heraclitus says: "Of the Logos, which is as I describe it, men always prove uncomprehending [ἀξύνετοι], both before and after they have heard it. For although all things happen in accordance with this Logos, men are like inexperienced people [ἀπείροισιν] even when they experience [πειριόκενοι] such words and deeds as I set forth [διηγεῦμαι], when I distinguish [διαιρέων] each thing according to its constitution [κατὰ φύσιν] and declare [φράζων] how it is [ὅκως ἔχει]; but the rest of men forget [λανθάνει] what they do after they awake, just as they forget [ἐπιλανθάνονται] what they do when asleep." (*Against the Dogmatists*, vii, 132)

In this text, Sextus equates Heraclitus' Logos with his own term *surrounding*, saying that in speaking of the Logos Heraclitus is "offering an indication of sorts about the surrounding.'' This identification we shall keep in mind. The Logos of Heraclitus is a Logos that encompasses us, surrounds us, environs us. Though not obvious (''men always prove uncomprehending''), we are nonetheless in constant touch with it:

> The Logos: though men associate themselves with it constantly, yet they are separated from it; and those things which they encounter daily seem to them strange. (Fr. 72)

Man associates ʿομιλοῦσι, uninterruptedly, διηνεϰῶς, with Logos; ὁμῑλέω, the root verb of ''to associate,'' means in Greek ''to be together with, become or live together, encounter''; of social intercourse, it implies ''to hold converse, live familiarly with, have dealings with, be friends''; of pursuits or business, ''to be conversant with, be engaged in, attend to''; of things, ''to be present at hand.''[4] Manifestly, Heraclitus has some profound type of familiarity in mind in using that word. Man is conversant with the Logos, he lives together with it, attends to it, has it ''present at hand.'' Yet, despite this ''uninterrupted'' familiarity, man is separated from it. Men are always as if ''inexperienced'' with Logos, although by all rights they should be quite experienced, since they encounter it constantly. A strange familiarity indeed!

We men ''forget'' what we are about, even when awake. As Rilke puts it, *''Aus unbegriffenem Schlaf ins unkenntliche Wachsein''* (''from uncomprehended sleep into unaware wakefulness''). We match our nightly ignorance with a good dose of daily stupidity. At night we are forgetful, in ''Lethe,'' oblivion. Every night we are bathed in the waters of Lethe, and as we reemerge into the land of un-covered-ness, ἡ ἀ-λήθ-εια, we continue acting and cognizing as if asleep. But the thinker urges us ''not to act and speak like men asleep'' (Fr. 73); another connected fragment implies something similar:

> Those who sleep . . . are artifacts and coworkers in the events that occur in the cosmos. (Fr. 75)

This implies, I believe, that even those who are when awake AS IF ASLEEP share in the happenings of the cosmos. They also behave according to the Logos (ϰατὰ τὸν λόγον). We have all the data necessary to get it all together and ''follow the common,'' as Fr. 2 urges us to do; yet, unaccountably, we behave for the most part as if in a daze: ''uncomprehendingly.'' Should that be a matter for concern? Fr. 114 suggests, in combination with Fr. 44, to which it is related, a possible answer:

> Those who speak with sense [ξύν νόῳ] must rely on what is common [ξυν ῷ] to all,
> as a city must rely on its law, and with much greater reliance. . . .
> The people should fight for the law as if for their city wall.

From these two fragments we see that to ''rely on what is common'' is as important to those who would ''speak with sense'' as relying on the walls is to a city (the analogy here is from common to law to wall and back). What does it mean to rely on the walls of a city? In fact, to the ancients, this meant a great deal; witness what one scholar says on the matter, one of many similar statements throughout the literature:

> The wall of a city in ancient times was far more than bricks and mortar; it was a kind of magical encirclement, representing and guaranteeing some kind of super-natural protection.[5]

Those who do not want to speak with sense, however, need not rely on what is common. After all, *does* one *have* to speak with sense? Is there some sort of necessity? What happens if we do not? Although a direct answer is not forthcoming, the analogy with the walls of a city makes us wonder: without walls, a city collapses. Perhaps without "speaking . . . sense" something else collapses. What?

> If one does not expect the unexpected (ἀνέλ πιστον), one will not find it; for it is not to be searched out, and it can not be compassed (ἄπορον, impassable). (Fr. 18)

The "unexpected" will indeed not be "found," if it is not "expected." What will be found instead? The all-too-normal, the routine of daily existence, the quotidian. Without the unexpected, things follow their routine ways. But man has in himself the power to compass the impassable, to prepare the appearance of the strange, of the demonic, of the godly: ἦθος ἀνθρώπῳδαίμων (Fr. 119), the way-to-be of the human lies in the encounter with the Daimon, with the godly. Man is himself when he searches out and finds a place for the unexpected, for the amazing, marvelous, for the extraordinary.

> The best choose one thing beyond all else, everlasting fame among mortal men. The many are satisfied like glutted cattle. (Fr. 29)

Only through a compassing of the extraordinary do mortals attain fame "among mortal men." "Everlasting fame" is only for those who make room for the amazing, for the unexpected. In that "room" the godly may appear, the Daimon, the word in Greek denoting the spirit that manifests the divine to humans. "The many," on the other hand, "are satisfied," do not search, do not seek; they are like "glutted cattle" and are "led to pasture with blows." (Fr. 11)

> . . . a man . . . living . . . is in contact with the dead, when asleep . . . and with the sleeper, when awake. (Fr. 26)

When asleep, we touch upon the dead, when awake, with the sleeper. We are thus constantly in touch with both living and dead through our contact with the sleeping and the dead. Sleep, earlier conceived as "forgetfulness," now serves as our way of access to the total forgetfulness that death signifies. But we are unaware, forgetful, of our contact with death, with the dead. The dead touch upon us when we are forgetful, when our power of memory is not functioning. Paradoxically, some of the dead are more awake than we:

> ... they [i.e. the souls in Hades] arise and become watchful guardians of the living and the dead. (Fr. 63)

The guardians are watchful, quite wake-ful, awake. That is where their protection stems from. What is it that they guard? Perhaps our very wakefulness, our intermittent wakefulness. In typical Heraclitean fashion, a circle is here completed. The dead are alive, the living are asleep, the sleeping are dead. Everybody is what he is not. And these unexpected matters are visible only to one who "inquired" of himself (Fr. 101). To some mortals it is granted to harbor the divine in them, to be a dwelling place for daimons. Others, however, the glutted ones, refuse to "speak with sense."

The question of mortality, and its paradoxical double, immortality, pervades the Heraclitean text. In order to obtain the means wherewith to work on this thorny matter, we shall bring in one of the foremost witnesses in the matter of Heraclitus' thought. Sextus Empiricus it is, a "skeptic" compiler who belabored a brief interpretation of Heraclitus in times past. His interpretation seems rather interesting, and for various reasons. We will straightaway attempt to dialogue with Sextus about Heraclitus. (For the convenience of the reader, a translation of Sextus's report on Heraclitus has been appended at the end of this paper.)

For Sextus, Heraclitus' Logos is "common and divine." Participation in the Logos makes men λογικόν, reasonable, akin to the Logos. This Logos, in turn, must be distinguished from others that may not be "common" (in the sense, at least, of universal) or "divine." Here it should be remembered that in Greek *Logos* refers primarily to speech, and to those rules or measures that characterize the nature of speaking with sense, with meaning.[6] It can also mean "doctrine," what someone contends is true. This Logos of Heraclitus, then, according to Sextus, "surrounds" us. "Surrounding," in Greek τὸ περιέχον, from the verb περι-έχω. According to this, the Logos as surrounding us would also press against us, cling to us, urge us on, prod us, in short, beleaguer us. As such, it would be "criterion of truth." One famous scholar, Geoffrey S. Kirk, supposes that by "surrounding" it is "the surrounding aither [that] is meant," "the Logos element in things," which may be envisaged, Kirk suggests, as a "direct offshoot of the pure aitherial fire.'"[7] Among other things, Kirk quotes from a text whose value would consist in the fact that the writer is trying to represent Heraclitean motifs in a Heraclitean—that is to say, archaic—fashion. We reproduce the text here:

> What we call hot seems to me immortal, and to apprehend all things and to see and hear and know all things. ... This ... when all things became confused, went out to the furthermost revolution, and seems to me to be what was called aither by the men of old. (Hippocrates, *De Carnibus*)

However, this text can prove no more than that the outermost revolution sur-rounding us would be aither—not, however, that anything whatever that sur-rounds us is aither. Based on the texts we have, I think that what Sextus means by ''surrounding'' is that which is outside the surface of our bodies, encompassing it, around it; and that it is this meaning that must be taken into account when trying to make use of Sextus' account for a helpful clue into Heraclitus' Logos. And so, we shall do precisely that.

When we go to sleep, we lose touch with our surrounding. Which surround-ing? Certainly not just the aither. We lose touch—except at a kind of ''root-level,'' as Sextus suggests—with the entire encompassing surrounding, that which is around our bodies and outside our selves. Our bodies commune with that outside-us through the pores, or channels of perception, that Sextus men-tions. And yet—has not Sextus begun the report by having Heraclitus thinking of two ways of access to knowledge, αἴσθησις or perception in the most general sense, and λόγος, of which two, the first is unreliable, the second ''criterion of truth''? To support that contention, Sextus quotes Heraclitus' Fr. 107 (cf. appen-dix) and equates it with the proverb that he uses to illustrate its meaning (ibid.). Despite appearances, however, the two are not the same. According to Hera-clitus, and that fragment, the senses give knowledge so long as the soul is not barbaric, so long as the soul understands the language of the senses.[8] As such, the senses are *not* unreliable. But the proverb, on the contrary, implies that the senses are irrational as such, and thus untrustworthy. We take this discrepancy as our clue, and suggest that Sextus is forced despite himself to grant the senses their due when interpreting Heraclitus. Although the reference to the ''channels of perception'' is anachronistic, its basic tenor of recognizing the importance of the senses for knowledge is in accord with profound strata in Heraclitus' text.

Breathing, which is a definite sensual manifestation of our body,[9] is according to Sextus essential in the way Heraclitus conceives our relation to what is exter-nal. Only when our bodies are open to the exterior through the openings of the senses are we open to the ''divine'' Logos. Through the senses, ''the portion of the surrounding which sojourns in our bodies'' is provided sustenance. There is in man a divine spark that Macrobius, an ancient commentator, speaking of Heraclitus, called a ''spark of the stellar essence.'' It is that in us which is akin to the surrounding, our mind (νοῦς), or our soul (ψυχὴ). So long as the mind remains in touch with the surrounding, a human being is sensible, τὸ φρονεέιν. So long as we have full use of our senses, are *in* our senses, we have the ''power of Logos.'' This lasts for as long as the soul feeds on its necessary nutrient, fire. Throughout this metaphor in Sextus' text, the trope that dominates is the one where vision stands for the totality of the intellectual powers of man. The soul is seen as sight. Truth is something *seen*. The mind, ''in the waking state . . . peeps out through a kind of window, and encountering the surrounding, puts on the power of Logos.'' The mind ''peeps out'' through the senses' openings. This image seems, perhaps, a bit too Orphic, or Phythagorean, for us to be sure that it reflects something in Heraclitus. And yet Heraclitean through and through is that part about the mind being unable to "put on" its "power" of Logos except through the nourishment of the senses. It is not through death, sleep, or some kind of disembodied state that we have access to the divine (as we might expect if Sextus were correct in his original dichotomy of perception/Logos); rather, it is precisely through our bodily senses that access to the divine and common is established. This positive relation of the senses to Logos, and hence to truth, emerges clearly out of Sextus' text—and despite him. The senses make us sensible, make us wise, lead us along the path of knowledge.

> . . . in sleep . . . our mind is sundered from its kinship with the surrounding . . . being sundered, it casts off its former power of memory . . .

The power that our mind has when awake is that of "memory." Memory is here taking the place of Logos in the text (cf. appendix). It stands, therefore, for something more than the ability to retain in our mind what happens, as ordinarily it might. Rather, it stands for the ability to put together into a one all that has happened, so that our mind may be *present* to what has happened. Memory is thus the ability to arrange what occurs in such a way that a unique ordering, or cosmos, comes to pass:

> To those who are awake, there is one ordered cosmos common to all, whereas in sleep each man turns away to one of his own. (Fr. 89)

To be "awake" here implies being open to what is manifest to all, to the common. What is common in its totality is the cosmos, the universe. This cosmos may be gathered into a one by our mind—by the power of Logos in our mind—so that an interconnected whole of things may arise out of the otherwise fragmentary disorderliness of chaotic time. For the Greeks, such a gathering into a one pertained to the speaking word, Logos, but also to memory, since in memory all things are ingathered into a world, and a properly structured cosmos is brought to being in its relationship with the dimensions of time.

In fact, the ordering that the mind brings about through its Logos is akin to the one that the Logos induces in things by its very presence. For things are structured according to Logos, and hence are ruled by it. Things behave according to the measure of Logos, according to its formula—a formula that, when formulated in a pertinent manner, Logos is. But the surrounding refers to all that is, since all is ruled by Logos. Hence, the surrounding cannot be simply the aither. It is possible, though, that the aither were understood as that region of the surrounding where the fire can be espied, like a "thunderbolt," "steering all things through all things" (Fr. 64). But this fire would be only one of the many manifestations of fire, another being that which is breathed in by us—air being for Heraclitus a rarefied form of fire. Indeed, it is the fire in the air we breathe in that serves as a spark of the divine while we are asleep and otherwise without contact with the surrounding. Fire, then, is according to Fr. 64 to Fr. 66 φρόνιμον, intelligent;[10] it grants sensibility, intelligence. Breathing, however, is only a "kind of root." When cut off from the surrounding, our mind becomes ἀλό-γον, unlike Logos; when contact is reestablished "through . . . the senses," it becomes of "like nature to the whole," i.e., intelligent, sensible. It is then that we "put on" our "power of Logos," we recover our ability to discern the true. This sensibleness we obtain from the surrounding, which alone deserves the epithet "intelligent," as Sextus tells us (cf. appendix).

> Common to all is to be sensible (σωφρονεῖν) (Fr. 113).

> To all men it pertains to know themselves, and thereby be sense-full, sensible (σωφρονεῖν) (Fr. 116).

> To be sensible is the greatest of virtues (σωφρονεῖν ἀρετὴ μεγίστη) (Fr. 112).

To be sensible is "greatest of virtues" because it pertains to what is common to all. In man it is brought about through "knowing oneself," a wisdom obtained by "agreeing" with the Logos that "all is one," as Fr. 50 puts it. That means that knowing oneself is not what it is in Socrates (which is?), but rather a recognition of the rule of the Logos in all things, a recognition that the Logos gathers the cosmos into a oneness, into a one common to all, a one in which all communes. "When you have listened not to me, but to the Logos, it is wise [σοφόν] to agree [ὁμο-λογεῖν, to become homogeneous with the Logos] that all is one."[11]

What happens, what daily occurs, the τὸ φαινόμενον, has Logos as its criterion of truthfulness. Logos brings the phenomena back into the oneness from which they emerged; it provides the all with a share of oneness. "All is one." But this wisdom requires the proper harmony of the mind and the senses; it requires our body as essential coworker. The body harbors the Logos that abides in us. The "power of Logos" comes to life only with the aid of our sense-pores. A fragment of Heraclitus gathers its motive strength and unique significance from its relation to this problem:

> Those things of which sight and hearing provide μάθησις (learning), those I hold in the highest esteem (προτιμέω) (Fr. 55).

Sight and hearing bring about learning, they provide knowledge insofar as the mind listens and understands the language of the senses. Only those things of which the senses provide information are for Heraclitus *manifest,* and hence honorable as common to all, as truthful. Logos and the body-senses: an intertwining, a togetherness, a chiasmus.

Perhaps a quick rundown on what we have discussed so far is in order at this point. One, Logos is essentially to be thought in its intertwining with the senses, as needing the senses; two, Logos gathered the manifold discreteness of things into a one, a cosmos, common to all; three, fire is intelligent and hence akin to Logos, though not identical to it; four, breathing—that "counterpoise/ wherein I rhythmically happen" (Rilke)[12]—is a form of communion with the surrounding, a way of keeping alive that spark in us while we are asleep. Respiration maintains, through its gathering of fire in the air, our power of Logos. Somehow, fire and Logos are the same:

> This world-order [κόσμος] did none of gods or men bring-forth, but always was and is and shall be—an ever-living fire, kindling in measures, and going out in measures (Fr. 30).

Fire is sensible, φρόνιμον. The cosmos is everliving fire, is itself everlivingly intelligent. Yet: should not the world be *on fire,* if the metaphor here is anything more than mere poetic embellishment? And yet things are not on fire. Fire means, does it not, that event of burning in which everything around is consumed, including itself, until the event ends? How, then, if not as the fire that we know and see, are we to think fire? Fr. 76 begins: "fire lives the death of earth." A gloss on the Fragment, reported by Marcus Aurelius, says along similar lines:

> Because death of earth is to become water, and death of water to become air; and of the air fire, and conversely.

We may couple this with Fr. 36, which offers another clue:

> To souls it is death to become water, to water it is death to become earth. Yet from earth comes water, and from water soul.

Essential to these fragments is death. Fire "lives the death" of earth. It consumes it. Fire lives from the death of other things; its life is constant consumption, constant nutrition from its opposites. Fire relishes contradiction, lives from it. Change, even total change, from one opposite to another, is not extraordinary to fire, it happens all the time. Such dwelling in contradiction, such "living the death" of others, characterizes not only fire, but all of life. Life is a living of death.

> Immortals mortals, mortals immortals, living their death and dying their lives. (Fr. 62)

All things alive, all mortal things, live the death of something immortal. The immortal dies in order to bring forth life, nay, its very death is the life of the mortal. What does Heraclitus mean by the immortal? Perhaps everything that everlastingly returns, endlessly returns, in cycles of being and nonbeing, is immortal. Fire is "everlasting," hence everdying. It lives the death of another, and dies its life. Fire returns everlastingly, endlessly; it consumes itself and what is other to itself. In this respect, fire differs from other things. Water, for example, lives the death of earth, but it does not live its own death. Or rather, its destruction of earth does not appear to be necessary for its own existence. It nourishes itself on earth, but it does not consume it with a passion, greedily. Fire does: whatever it feeds on, it consumes, it needs and it passionately takes. Fire is "everliving" because it needs otherness to nourish itself, to be what it is. Fire is immortal because its life is a constant consumption of itself and its contraries.

But fire is not the only immortal thing. Immortal most of all, in the language of Heraclitus, is the Daimon, the godly; and through kinship with it, the aither, where the godly dwells, and the soul as a spark of the divine. Mortal, however, is all that lives:

> And as the same thing there exists in us living and dead and waking and sleeping and young and old: for these having changed round are those, and those having changed round are these. (Fr. 88)

The living, having changed round, are the dead, and the dead, having changed round, are the living. The living and the dead are "the same thing . . . in us," they are as "changing(s) round" of each other. What is alive, then, is something dead that has changed round and is now alive. Only death grants immortality, a return to life; and therefore, it is perhaps the case that death is merely a going into that "unapparent harmony" of Fr. 54, a way in which what is alive goes into shelter as dead.

Whatever the answer to these riddles, of all things alive, fire is that which most imperiously manifests what life is, how life is a constant consuming of contraries, how what is alive lives only through and in contradiction. Fire is the ἀρχή, the principle of things. So Aristotle reports (*Metaphysics*, bk. A, 984a7–8). All things are fire:

> There is an exchange: all things for fire, and fire for all things, like wares for gold, and gold for wares. (Fr. 90)

All things have, as Professor Harold F. Cherniss reputedly holds, a "fire-value." They all are fire, or can be exchanged for fire. Is fire, then, the primary substance for Heraclitus? The underlying one out of which all things are? All *is* fire. Well and good.

> Fire, having come upon them, and seized all things, will judge them (καταλήψεται). (Fr. 66)

Fire will apprehend all things and judge them. A universal catalepsis. How is such judging to occur? Fire judges by "coming upon" things, by "seizing" them, whether all at once (which would then imply a universal conflagration, a much debated scholarly question), or one by one. The combustion of things, their burning, will be the how of their judgment. When something burns, it is living the death and dying the life of an immortal other. It is alive, and being judged by life. Aristotle reports something quite interesting related to this:

> ... it is said that Heraclitus told some strangers who had come to visit him, and who had stopped when they upon arriving saw that he was warming himself by a stove: "here also there are gods present," inviting them to come in without any fear. (*Parts of Animals,* 645a17 ff.).

When things burn, there are also gods, immortals, present. Immortals dwell in fire, the everliving. Fire is the element of immortality insofar as it lives the death of others in a manifest way. As such, it fulfills the hidden harmony, the Logos of things, fulfills the "back-stretched connection," as in the "bow and the lyre" (Fr. 51).

Fire lives according to the Logos, agrees with it. It is wise, it knows: all is one. To fire all is in *deed* one. "All things for fire, and fire for all things." Fire, the visible and familiar fire we all know, is intelligent; it sees and judges all things. Fire embodies the power of the visible, the apparent, and connects it with the unapparent but more powerful harmony. Fire is an event in which the gods can become present, and where what happens is "back-stretched." Only fire must consume in order to live, must consume *concretely.* Wherever fire is, all is consumed, until the fire itself is destroyed. Fire, the visible, manifest fire, renders manifest through its example that things are πόλεμος, ἔριν (war, strife). Fire is ever at war. But

> War is the father of all and the king of all; and some he shows forth as gods, others as men; some he makes slaves, some free. (Fr. 53)

> It is necessary to know that war is common, and justice is strife, and that things come about by strife and necessity. (Fr. 80)

Fire is strife (ἔριν) and necessity (χρεών). Fire must consume, must judge; namely, that all is one. All goes to smoke, all is burned, all burns. Fire is the visible manifestation of the Logos in Heraclitus. That is why it could be conceived as a first principle by Aristotle, and by Plato, too. "Whether the element through which we think . . . is fire," Socrates asks in the *Phaedo,* in obvious reference to Heraclitus (96b). Indeed, it is only through a catalepsis, through a judgment of fire, that we think. We think *through* fire. Fire is the intelligent par excellence. This being indeed so, how are fire and Logos to be thought rigorously in their interconnectedness? And how is Aristotle's scathing indictment of Heraclitus to be accepted, how is it to be understood? In the light of these questions, I pass over to the final part of this brief paper, to consider fire, Logos, and Aristotle.

> Heraclitus also says that the soul is the first principle . . . and that it is incorporeal to the highest degree, and always flowing, and that what moves is known by what

moves. . . . It seemed to some that the soul was fire, since among the elements it is the subtlest, and . . . besides holds first place among all in moving itself and moving others. (Aristotle, *De Anima*, 405a)

Fire and Logos: a necessary interrelationship. We must look back, and study Aristotle's *Metaphysics*, book Γ, in order to have some sense for what constitutes the real stumbling block in any attempt at an interpretation of Heraclitus. Aristotle speaks, in that book, of the highest form of knowledge:

There exists an επιστήμη that investigates being qua being and what belongs essentially to it. (1003a22)

In the course of reconnoitering the field opened up by such a possibility, Aristotle comes upon the necessity of establishing an absolutely certain principle. That "most certain of all principles" which is the beginning of this first of all sciences is the principle of contradiction:

The same thing cannot at the same time both belong and not belong to the same object and in the same respect. (1005b19-21)

This principle, it turns out, is not just any principle; it is not a hypothesis,

for a principle that one must have if he is to understand [ξυνιεντα] anything at all is not a hypothesis. (ibid., 15-18)

It is rather an a priori principle of intelligibility. Aristotle goes on to demonstrate this by showing that anyone who would oppose it would either have to show both a more certain principle and the source of its certainty—which would mean that the other would be already subject to this Logos, of noncontradiction, since in order to evoke the words he would have to conform to this principle; or he would have to argue that one can speak without this principle—something that can, however, be refuted, since whatever anyone could say, insofar as they would be saying anything with a distinct, determinate meaning, would itself have to obey this most imperious of principles, i.e., he would have to avoid contradiction in the enunciation of his refutation, at the risk of not having said anything definite at all. In that case, what Aristotle calls "demonstration by refutation" will have come about:

What [the opponent] says should at least mean something to himself as well as to another . . . if he grants this, there will already be a demonstration, for there will already be something definite. (1006a21-26)

The one causing the demonstration, however, is not indeed

he who demonstrates, but he who takes a definite stance; for while he denies Logos, he listens to Logos. (ibid., 27-28)

A refutation occurs through the *deeds* of the other, insofar as he shows himself willing to "listen to Logos"; "and to be and not to be will not be the same except by equivocation" (1006b18–19).

It is in this argument of Aristotle, and in the structure it evokes, that we can see what is really at stake in this "principle." For Aristotle, it is precisely Logos that is at stake—Logos here meaning speech in accord with truth, speech that reveals things as they are—beings as being. Onto-logy is here at stake. This principle founds metaphysics as ontology, as the knowledge-type that studies being qua being, and what concerns such being.

For there to be a knowledge of this kind at all, Logos, as the revealer of the structure of what is, must be protected against those who wish to befuddle and obscure issues. The philosophical, wisdom-loving Logos must be protected against the sophistical and rhetorical Logos. In this trial, Logos is defended by Aristotle also against those thinkers whose Logos tends to bring about confusion, and who would leave Logos at the mercy of those sophists and rhetoricians.

> The truth concerning what is manifest . . . came to some thinkers as [being] the same as what shows from sensible things. . . . In general, it is because these thinkers believe thought to be sensation, and sensation alteration [of the body], that they say that what is manifest according to sensation must be true. . . . What results from all this, however, is most distressing. (1009b1–2, 12–15, 33)

It is "most distressing" in that it is a Logos propounded by wisdom-lovers that bites its own tail, cuts off Logos, and destroys it by what should nourish it. According to Aristotle, these earlier thinkers confused thought with sensation, conceived thought as fulfilled through the senses, at those times when our senses are being stimulated with information, when something is becoming manifest to the senses. These as a whole are the physicists, those who see the cosmos as basically sensible. Heraclitus, Parmenides, Empedocles are among them. Aristotle tries to show, in opposition to them, that although sensation is indeed fundamental to knowledge, the ability of the mind to discern the τὸ εἶδος, the form of a being, is still more fundamental.

"Still, it is with respect to the εἶδος that we know" (1010a25). It is not, indeed, with respect to that which cognizes what changes, sensation, but through our ability to perceive the unchanging aspect of things (here understood Platonically as the εἶδος) that we can and do have what is called *knowledge*. It is not the aspect offered the senses, but that offered the νοῦς, the mind, which is true, which is an uncovering of the thing as it is.

> Moreover, observing that all things in nature are in motion, and thinking that nothing is true of that which changes, they came to the belief that nothing may be truly said of that which changes altogether and in every way. Now, it was from this

belief that blossomed the most extreme of the Logoi we have mentioned, namely, that of the followers of Heraclitus. (1010a7-12)

Aristotle is here offering a characterization of Heraclitus' Logos. Its point of departure is change, total and absolute change, "altogether and in every way." But "nothing is true of that which changes": this thought was shared by all Greeks up to and including Plato. What becomes cannot be known, for it is constantly changing; knowledge can only be of the lasting. But as the thinkers in question observed that "all things in nature are in motion," they were led to conclusions that Aristotle is at pains to set aright:

> It is only in the place of the sensible things around us that destructions and genera-tions constantly occur, but this place is, in a manner of speaking, not even a wee bit of the entire cosmos. (1010a29-31)

Around us there is indeed constant change, alteration everywhere, generation and destruction, coming-to-be and passing-away. But farther away things are still, their motion being ever regular, cyclic. The heavens are tranquil. So that, in fact, Aristotle is not only answering the question of change by suggesting that the dimension of change is only the near, the "around us," while in the far, things are otherwise than in motion; but he is suggesting that we can observe such a thing—just look at the sky at night. Our senses can observe areas of nonchange. Against Heraclitus in particular, Aristotle objects that (1) sensation is being granted too large powers, and (2) what is near us is serving as a false guide as to the whole. We might add, to (1), that certain aspects of sensation are granted too much, others not enough. In fact,

> The Logos of Heraclitus, that everything is and is not, seems to make everything true. (1012a25-26)

Heraclitus' Logos, his main doctrine as to how things are, says that all is and is not. But if that Logos is accepted, all things being anything, all Logoi would be true. All discourse being true, there would be no unique truth, since distinction would be impossible. All would be an indeterminate conglomerate, "a pile of dung piled up at random" (Fr. 124), as Heraclitus says.

Heraclitus is here confronted with the consequences of his own Logos: if the Logos is true, so are all other Logoi, and there is therefore no Logos that is uniquely uncovering. Heraclitus' Logos destroys itself; it *is its own death*.

Further, Aristotle argues that even where there is constant change, the change follows in measures and requires an underlying substance that suffers the change:

> When the changing changes, there is some reason for [the Heracliteans] to truly think that the changing thing is not; yet even this is disputable. For even that which

is losing an attribute still retains something of that which is being lost, and some part of that which the changing thing becomes is already there. (1010a16-20)

So, not only is it not the case that everything is changing, as was contended earlier; but even where there is change the change is not total; something must be underlying the change, some substance (οὐσία) must serve as subject (ὑποκεί-μενον) of the change. Aristotle here seems to cut the Logos from under Heraclitus' feet. Can we rescue Heraclitus?

The arguments against his followers seem telling indeed. Are they telling as well for Heraclitus himself? After all, fire is, for him, "contradictory," we had earlier said, "relishing" contradiction, and substanceless, without anything underlying it save change. Fire, for Heraclitus, is not understandable except as total consumption of itself and of everything else. For Aristotle, on the other hand, fire has an "essence"; it is that element which naturally goes up to the outermost region of the cosmos, there to gather itself as a whole as the aither. Does this disagree with Heraclitus? Indeed it does. For him, fire, which has several layers of signification, means not only the fire that we see around us, or the aitherial fire that we notice particularly when there is lightning; there is also the fact that fire as such is not something that moves upward as such—though it may do that. Fire is conceived, is seen, as that which is in eternal strife with everything. Something whose essence is consumption, lack-of-essence. Fire always becomes; it never is. And as such, it serves as a paradigm for the whole cosmos, which is an "everliving fire." Heraclitus would contradict Aristotle and say that the heavens are changing constantly, for strife is everywhere; strife is "necessity." There is indeed "measured" change, but for all that, change. And the true measure of the change is unapparent; it cannot be perceived except by "agreeing with the Logos" that "all is one." Only this is true wisdom, and not ἐπιστήμη. It is preontological, it comes before ontology. How is that possible?

Within the limited horizons of this paper, we can observe only a clash, not a concord, between Aristotle and Heraclitus. There is, in other words, no resolution. And for some type of resolution, we must return to our environment, to the surrounding. Logos is that in us which is akin to our surrounding and which establishes contact with it. We can become more or less like the surrounding, depending on the fieryness in our souls. So long as we remain breathing, warm, we are minimally alive. And we are changing. Our soul is the gathering of the fiery. Through Logos we are one, and through Logos fire is in us, and makes us kindle to life:

Things taken together are whole and not whole, something being brought together and brought apart, something which is in tune and out of tune; out of all things there comes a unity, and out of a unity all things. (Fr. 10)

The gathered-together is both whole and not whole, in tune and out of tune, together and apart—changing, in flux. All things (πάντα ῥεῖ) flow. The Logos brings the unity to completion, it ingathers it. Such a perfection of oneness, unity, comes to pass primordially with human speech, Logos, when it agrees with the divine Logos, the common Logos.

> One thing is alone wise, to know the thought through which all things are steered through all things. (Fr. 41)

Wisdom occurs when our own Logos, our speech, conforms to things in their language—when our Logos is fiery. For fire is that which things truly speak. Fire is ever-other, in flux, ever-changing. The oneness of fire is a scattered and scattering oneness. Its only unity has its source in its power to convert all things to smoke by consuming them, by burning them. Fire makes manifest the perishability of things, their ultimate kinship. The world is, in that sense, a constant conflagration, since all can be converted to smoke, all can be set on fire.

> Fire's turnings: first sea, and of the sea the half is earth, and the half burner . . . [earth] is dispersed as sea, and is measured so as to form the same Logos as existed before it became earth. (Fr. 31)

Fire constantly goes over to something else. It changes in fixed measures, according, that is, to a Logos. So, in fact, does our soul, the fire in us, which consumes the surrounding and lives the death of what surrounds us constantly. It, the soul, no more than fire, has an essence:

> Heraclitus, wishing to show that souls . . . become ever new, compared it with rivers, saying "upon those that step into the same rivers, different and different waters flow. . . ." (Fr. 12)

The soul's oneness, like that of a river, consists in the "different and different" waves that "flow." The soul is ever other, ever "new." "It remains by changing" (Fr. 84a). Our soul provides us with fieryness, with warmth, with life. It is indeed a gathering of fire in us.

Speech and fire: the speech of fire is ever contradictory, it refutes the philosophical Logos, and yet, miraculously, it heeds Logos nonetheless. It heeds the hidden harmony, that harmony which as hidden is the more powerful one. Heraclitus and his Logos cannot preempt the Aristotelian Logos; they come rather before it. Heraclitus' Logos is the forerunner of Aristotle's Logos. The Greek Logos, as thought in Plato and Aristotle, prevails in Western thought to our own time under the form of reason, logic, ground. The Heraclitean Logos, however, is fire, is a mass of contradictions. It is, and it is not, all things. In what respect? Let us leave the last words to Heraclitus, in his appeal to the gods:

> If it were not in honor of Dionysus that they conducted the procession, and sang the phallic hymn, their activity would be completely shameless. But Hades is Dionysus, in whose honor they rave and perform the Bacchic revels. (Fr. 15)

"Hades is Dionysus": they are the same god, the god of death and the god of ecstatic life. For "the bow is called life, but its work is death" (Fr. 48).

Appendix

Sextus Empiricus, Adv. Math. VII, 126ss.

My translations are from the Spanish of Rodolfo Mondolfo, *Héraclito: Textos y Problemas de su Interpretación* (Mexico-Argentina-España: Siglo XXI editores, 1966).

(126) Heraclitus, on the contrary, as he was of the opinion that man was granted two instruments for the recognition of truth, sensation (αἴσθεσις) and reason (λόγος), judged among these sensation unworthy of trust—similar in this to the natural philosophers already mentioned [Parmenides, Empedocles]—and reason, on the other hand, he affirmed criterion [of truth?]. But he refutes sensation, saying textually: "bad witnesses are eyes and ears for those men who have barbaric souls" (Fr. 107), which amounted to the proverb: "it pertains to barbaric souls to lay credence on irrational (αλόγον) sensations."

(127) He shows, on the other hand, that the Logos is judge of truth, but not just any Logos, but the one common to the whole and divine. What that is must be briefly explained, since this natural philosopher is of the opinion that it is precisely what surrounds us (τὸ περυέχον ἡμᾶς), that being imbued with Logos (λογικον) and intelligent.

(128) ....

(129) By drawing in, through breathing, according to Heraclitus, this divine Logos, we become intelligent (γνόεροι), and when asleep, forgetful; but we regain our senses (πάλιν ἔμφρονες) when we wake up again. For in sleep, when the channels of perception (τῶν αἰσθητικῶν πόρων) are shut, our mind (νοῦς) is sundered from its kinship with the surrounding (τὸ περιέχον), and breathing is the only point of attachment to be preserved, like a kind of root; being sundered, it [i.e., our mind] casts off (ἀποβάλλεν) its former power of memory (μνημογικὴν δύναμιν). But in the waking (130) state it again peeps out through the channels of perception as though through a kind of window, and meeting with the surrounding (τῶ περιέχοντι συμβαλών) it puts on its power of Logos (λογικὴν ἐνδύεται δύναμιν). Just as embers, when they're brought near the fire, change and become red-hot, and go out when they're taken from it again, so does the portion of the surrounding which sojourns in our body become αλόγον, without Logos, when it is cut off, and just so does it become of like nature to the whole when contact is established through a majority of the channels.

(131) This common and divine Logos, by participation in which we become λογικόν, endowed with Logos, Heraclitus declares to be criterion of truth. Hence, what manifests itself to all in common, this, he says, is worthy of credibility (since it is perceived by means of the common and divine Logos); while what becomes present to one only, that, he says, is unworthy of credibility for the opposite reason.

(132) ....

(133) By these words, then, having established expressly that everything we do and think is done and thought through participation in the divine Logos, and after having added some other things, he continues: "therefore, it is necessary to follow the common; but although the Logos is common, the many live as though they had a private understanding?" (Fr. 2). Which is nothing other than an explanation of the ordering of the cosmos.

So that, insofar as we participate in the memory of the same, we are in truth, and so far as we come apart from it, we fall into error.

(134) Even in these words, he now shows, then, in the most express manner, that the common Logos is criterion of truth, and says that those things which manifest themselves in common [to all] are worthy of credibility, insofar as they are judged by the common Logos, while those others [which manifest themselves] privately to each one are false.
Ibid., VII, 286

And by the way, Heraclitus expressly (ῥητῶς) says that it is not man who is λογικὸν, endowed with Logos, but rather that only in the surrounding does intelligence (φρενῆρες) prevail.

We might append to this a statement by a compiler of Heraclitus: Diogenes Laertius. IX, 9–10 (DK 22A1):

He [Heraclitus] does not reveal just what precisely the surrounding is.

6

PHYSIS, SOPHIA, PSYCHE*

Daniel Guerrière

Prologue

The aim of this contribution is to outline a comprehensive interpretation of the fragments of Heraclitus in the Heideggerian spirit. Such an interpretation orients itself by the question of Being. What beyond this such a project imports can become clear only in its execution. The aim is not to offer a summary of what Heidegger has said but to do what neither he nor anyone else in his spirit has done: namely, to allow *every* fragment a sense consonant with its philological possibilities and within the framework of the Being-question. This horizon or framework takes on a concreteness peculiar to each thinker. The concrete horizon of the Heraclitean discourse appears historically as one uniquely transitional in character. Or, in terms of the matter (*die Sache*) of the discourse, the historical configuration in which the granting-of-Being concretizes itself is uniquely transitional. For Heraclitus belongs to that remarkable age noticed by those investigators who, like Karl Jaspers and Eric Voegelin, penetrate beneath the surface of events to the history of the soul, or, in a Heideggerian perspective, to the fate-of-Being. He belongs to the axial period—the time when he and Parmenides, Jeremiah and Deutero-Isaiah, the Buddha and Confucius were all roughly contemporaneous. The concrete matter at issue in the text of Heraclitus is *Being in a uniquely transitional configuration*. And the aim of this interpretation is to allow this Fate of Heraclitus to begin to announce itself—first of all to me, but in the same manner to others.

An anticipatory delimitation of the concrete matter at issue will let the interpretation get underway. The matter is *no longer the properly mythic* and *not yet the properly philosophic*. This transitional matter may take on preliminary determinateness for interpretation through a brief consideration of that which 'limits' it on either side—its past and its future. The singular event of Heraclitus culminates the transition that began in Miletus and found its telos in Elea; it bears within itself a reminiscence of Homer and Hesiod and a prevenience of Parmenides and Plato. The name of Heraclitus represents *the final postmythic and prephilosophic event*. In terms of its past and of its future, this event is ambivalent—but by an ambivalence that is not a deficiency but rather a power to gather and to preserve in one-ness elements normally, and by right, asunder. The anticipatory delimitation of what is properly at issue in the fragments—which is the task of this

Prologue—will focus upon three topics: the mythic, the philosophic, and, in these terms, the Heraclitean.[1]

Before it is a discourse, myth names an existence. The structure of this discourse provides a transcendental clue to the structure of the existence that objectifies itself in it. What is peculiar about myth is that it is a *compact* discourse.[2] All those discourses that are for us differentiated—science, literature, politics, liturgy, historiography, economics, and so on—are for mythic man compacted into a single whole. All the levels of discourse that we differentiate—such as explanation, speculation, justification, and evaluation—are for mythic man compacted into a single whole. Compactness imports at least a continuity of elements; not every one of them need be explicit, but none is totally excluded. Myth breaks down with the differentiation of the various elements and their establishment in a quasi-autonomous fashion. The compactness peculiar to myth finds its condition of possibility in an existence likewise compact.

Mythic man exists (transitive) the whole. Any significant word or work of compact man intends (in the phenomenological sense) the whole. The elements of this whole form at least a continuity and become more and more imbricate as the word and work become more and more central to existence. The whole articulates itself primarily into the power (or the sacred) and the cosmos (comprising nature, society, and individual). But this internal articulation is not yet differentiation. Mythic existence breaks down with the differentiation of the sacred, the natural, the social, and the individual. But the whole that mythic man exists is the compactness of the power and the cosmos.

The major elements of this whole—the power and the cosmos—may be characterized as follows. The power is the fundamental origin that *in illo tempore* orders (forms) the cosmos ('order'). The cosmos is in constant degeneration, but this is only a movement into a regeneration; the cosmos, whether on the smallest scale or the largest, reaches its beginning at its end. And this beginning and end is precisely the power. Of course, the origin or the sacred is not outside the cosmos. Although it is other with respect to nature, society, and individual, it is at once the efficacy, the most intense reality, the life, the fixed and enduring in which the cosmos participates to the extent that it is efficacious, real, solid. The cosmos is what it is to the extent that it is a sacred cosmos. The cosmos or world is in some sense formed out of the origin. Even so, it is at once in the process of disintegration, of losing its power, efficacy, endurance. To put the ambivalence in a slightly different way: the power is the preeminently real; insofar as the cosmos is, it is the power; but it is also impotent, more and more disordered, in need of renewal. Or in another way: the sacred makes the world to be the world, and insofar as the world is efficacious and enduring, it is sacred; but it is also nonpermanent, degenerating. The cosmos is fundamentally ambivalent, both manifesting the origin and not manifesting it. The world is thus the symbol of the sacred. Phenomenologically, a symbol is a double-sense, the first of which both hides and reveals a second, which is available only in this way. Ontologically, a symbol is the exteriorization of a phenomenon and hence its ambiguous presence;

the exteriorization is both the revealment and the concealment of the phenomenon (e.g., my body is the symbol of my self). The power exteriorizes itself as a
cosmos; or, reversely, the cosmos is the ambiguous presence of the power.

For mythic existence, the compactness of the power and the cosmos is the
identity-in-difference of the power and the whole and the cosmos. What compact
man exists is *the (power)whole(cosmos)*. The identity-in-difference may be expressed as follows. Within the whole, the power is the fullness, fecundity,
permanence; the cosmos is the opposite (not the contradictory); and the whole
itself is their sameness. They constitute the whole, and the whole articulates itself
into them. As the origin, the power is, in terms of generation, the self-generative.
(This self-generation usually takes the form of the genesis of divinities from
earlier divinities, as, for example, in Hesiod's *Theogony*.) Logically speaking,
within the whole—outside of which there is nothing—there must be a permanent
or self-generative element; otherwise there would be no whole. Within the
whole, the power originates or orders the cosmos: it is the orderedness of the order
(cosmos) that is falling into disorder (i.e., which is not the fullness of orderedness). In these terms, the whole is the orderedness-ordering-order: the ordering.
Thus the power and the whole and the cosmos are identical-in-difference. This is
what compact man concretely exists. Later, when the power and the cosmos
differentiate, the whole becomes abstract for concrete experience. But the matter
of compact existence is the (power)whole(cosmos).

For mythic man the (power)whole(cosmos) is a compact process: the cycle.
The cosmos begins and degenerates to the end out of which it again begins; this
process is that of the self-manifestation, withdrawal, and remanifestation of the
power. In terms of the whole, the process is the whole's renewal of itself, the
whole's cyclic movement. The term *time* is not correct for this cycle; for the
whole encompasses what will later be differentiated as time (cosmos) and eternity (power). The cycle is the compact experiential reconciliation of permanence
and degeneration. Mythic man exists the cycle or the whole.

Mankind decisively broke mythic existence around 500 B.C.—the axial
period. The sites wherein this decisive differentiation took place are Israel and
Hellas. The differentiated existence achieved by the Hebrews may be termed
eschatologic existence; that by the Greeks, philosophic existence.

The event that definitively established philosophic existence bears the name of
Parmenides. In his Poem, the differentiation of the power and the cosmos comes
to expression. The discourse on genuineness (ἀλήθεια) expresses the power in
contradistinction to the cosmos; the discourse on acceptances (δόξαι) expresses
the cosmos in contradistinction to the power. Of course differentiation is not
separation (although it must be noted that interpretation has usually failed to
appreciate the way in which ἀλήθεια and δόξαι—or, on the textual level, the
two parts of the Poem—belong to each other). In mythic terms, the matter of
mythic experience is: the (power)whole(cosmos). And in mythic terms, the matter of philosophic experience is: *the power(whole)cosmos*.

But in philosophic terms, the matter of mythic existence is: (absolute-Being)whole(beings). And in philosophic terms, the matter of philosophic existence is: *absolute-Being(whole)beings*. For the title under which the power first becomes differentiated is "Being" (ἐόν, B4.2, B6.1, B8.13,19,28,33,37,47)— or, equivalently, "is" (ἔστι, B2.3, B8.2) and "to-be" (εἶναι, B6.1; πελέναι, B8.11). "Is," in contrast to the cosmos or beings, is ungenerable and imperishable (thus eternal), unique, without lack and therefore change, and complete (B8.1–49). What must be admitted about Being is this: "it is not possible that it should not be" (B2.3). It is, in a word, "absolute" (πάμπαν, B8.11). In contrast, beings are generable and perishable (thus temporal), multiple and different from one another, changeable, and incomplete. This does not, of course, import that beings stand outside of Being (for only non-Being or absolute nothingness stands outside of Being). The differentiation of Being-absolutely (the power) and beings (the cosmos) only imports that their compactness is no longer the concrete matter of experience. From now on man exists the duality, as it were, of Being and beings. This twofold subsequently comes to expression in many ways: the idea of the good/beauty in contrast to that which both is and is not; the primary οὐσία/ὄν ἢ ὄν/τέλος in contrast to φύσις; the one in contrast to that below it; *esse subsistens* (subsistent being) in contrast to creatures; the infinite in contrast to the finite; and so on. The *(power)whole(cosmos)* has become *absolute-Being (whole)beings*.

But the transition from the one to the other is the achievement of sixth-century Greece, and Heraclitus culminates this transition. The matter of Heraclitean experience is no longer, in mythic terms, the (power)whole(cosmos), or in philosophic terms, (Being)whole(beings); and it is not yet, in mythic terms, the power(whole)cosmos, or in philosophic terms, Being(whole)beings. The proper matter of this transitional experience may be termed, mythically, the power-*as*-cosmos or, philosophically, *Being be-ing beings in such a way that the philosophic sense of this process, though distinguishable, is still united with its scientific, its religious, and its other senses.*[3] This complex matter—in a text always laconic and long since fragmented—both invites and resists analysis.

The positive ambivalence of the matter at issue in the fragments as well as the obscurity of the text pushes every interpretation to the threshold of speculativeness. The interpreter can only endeavor to make his possible speculativeness an accident of enthusiasm rather than the arbitrariness of pride.

Interpretation may now advance to the Heraclitean event in its own right.[4] The attempt to listen to Heraclitus speaking—or more fundamentally, to the matter bespeaking itself in the text—will fall into three parts: (1) The one matter of experience, (2) the correspondence to the matter, and (3) the correlative depth of experience. "Each thinker thinks but a single thought."[5] The one thought of Heraclitus gives itself a multitude of utterances. Some of these focus upon the matter without immediate reference to anything else, and the first part of the interpretation will treat these. Others focus upon the matter in reference to man,

and the second and third parts will treat these. Finally, an Epilogue will venture
to indicate the relation between the concrete matter of Heraclitean thought and
that of Heideggerian thought.

I. The One Matter of Experience

Attention to the fragments themselves may become more precise with the
precision of the one matter at issue in them. Hence the brief characterization at
this point. (Like the anticipatory determination above, this precision is, of
course, heuristic in the order of reading; but it has been a posteriori in the order of
writing.) Above, the one matter appeared as *'Being be-ing beings'* in *distinguishable but inseparable senses*. More precisely, *in its philosophic sense alone:*
on the one side, it is absolute-Being (though not diminished hereby) coming-
forth as beings and, on the other side, beings happening in their what and
how—but both sides experienced as a single event. This singular occurrence is,
in Christian terms, creation (verbally): the primordial event of absolute-Being,
from the far side, laying itself forth as beings, and of beings, on the near side,
congealing into determinateness. This single event is—taking it in its philosophic
sense alone—the be-ing in *Being be-ing beings*, with the middle term understood
to gather into itself the extremes. The one matter may be called the surging,
which, encompassing both that which surges forth (the power, Being) and that
which surges up (the cosmos, beings), is their belonging-together in a single
process. It may further be called presencing, which, implying both the presence
(Being, the power) and the present (beings, the cosmos), is that single event in
which they belong together. This one 'phenomening' comes to expression in the
Heraclitean fragments with extraordinary energy and profusion.

The fragments expressive in a quasi-independent fashion of the one matter will
begin to yield up their substance through the following interpretive division: (a)
the matter in itself, (b) its manifestations, and (c) its hiddenness. Some of the
fragments treated here are *also* expressive of the matter in reference to man and
so will be treated again later.

A. The Matter in Itself

The matter in itself, in all its ambivalence, comes to expression in about
one-third of the fragments. To attend to them is the burden of this section.[6]
Interpretation may begin here:

> 53   War is father of all and king of all:
>   and so some he renders [ἔδειξε] gods, others men,
>   some he makes [ἐποίησε] slaves, others free.

Philological note: the illustrations could continue into another line and beyond:
rich and poor, captain and hoplite, Greek and barbarian. The term "gods"

evidently imports those who, in contrast to most mortals, especially manifest power—a familiar enough image from the epic. The many types in the polis represent the many types in the cosmos.

The Heraclitean matter takes on the name of war. It is the aboriginal discord, the breaking-apart; this action establishes, renders, or decides (ἔδειξε) what is to be. It is, as it were, the primeval explosion from which all things settle into their own place (cf. δειχ-). It is the primordial settling-of-accounts, the fundamental ordering, the primitive bringing-forth (δειχ- and ποι-). This war is the father of all; i.e., it lets the many emerge, it allows them to come forth as what and how they are. It directs them. This father is the king, the one who directs and forges the many into a single realm—a realm in which all stand in harmonious tension. The king keeps the diverse elements together; he makes the realm one.

The next fragment explicates several equivalences:

> 80 It is proper/necessary [χρὴ] to know
> that war is common
> and strife is justice [δίχην]
> and that all (things) come-to-pass according to strife and propriety/necessity
> [χρεών].

Philological note: the terms χρή and χρεών do not import necessity in the sense of external obligation, compulsion, constraint, decree; but rather necessity in the sense of what is right, due, proper, appropriate, fitting, i.e., what should or ought to be.[7]

War or strife settles accounts; it orders or measures things. This strife is *dikê*—justice. The name *dikê* comes from δείνυμι, which imports: to direct, to indicate; hence to show forth, to bring forth or let congeal, to establish, i.e., perforce within limits, thus to establish limits; hence to keep the proper limits or place.[8] Accordingly, *dikê* is the rendering, the bringing-forth, the establishing (within limits): the measuring-out. It measures-out all things unto themselves; it gives them to be what and how they are, no more and no less. It is the judgment, the establishment of order. This is evident in another fragment:

> 94 Helios [Sun] will not transgress his measures:
> otherwise the Erinyes, ministers of justice, will find him out.

The ministers of justice are, of course, justice itself in its operation. The measuring-out is the establishment and maintenance of each thing within its proper bounds. Even the great sun performs its proper work subject to this measure; this subjection is all the more momentous in that Helios is a traditional (symbol for) divinity. If even so powerful a one should overstep his bounds, *Dike* will find him out and will catch, seize, or secure him. The implication is that neither sun nor anything under it in fact transgresses its measures. Justice, the establishing of limits, achieves order and makes things 'right'. Hence it is propriety/necessity: it fits things to their rightful proportions, to their internal limitations; it makes (cf. ποι-) them precisely themselves. According to it or by it, things come to pass as what and how they are. It is the propriety allowing each thing its own proper self; it is internal constraint, measuring each out. This measuring-out or ordering is the inner law according to which all phenomena happen. Like the father, it measures out or sets the limits. This law is common: it is that by and in which all are one. Like the king, it forges all phenomena into a single realm. It is the common, the oneness-of-all.

This one matter has another name:

89   The waking share an order [κόσμον] one and common. . . .

30   This order [κόσμον], the same for all (men),
      neither any one of gods nor of men has brought-forth,
      but it always was and is and shall be. . . .

Philological note: the phrase 'no gods or men' imports 'no one at all.' The term κόσμος imports: 'arrangement' (of parts into a unified whole), 'an order taken concretely,' 'a system in dynamic equilibrium.' Its concrete extension is not only spatial but temporal as well, and so it has an αἰών ('lifetime').[9]

The one matter at stake in the fragments is the order. The term κόσμος must not be taken in the usual sense to mean the world. It is rather the worlding of the world. It is the order—or better: the ordering—that on the far side is the eternal power-of-order and, on the near side, the temporal cosmos (κόσμος in the usual sense). It is the arranging-of-all as one internally balanced realm. This order "neither any one of gods nor of men has brought-forth"; that is to say, it is autonomous, in need of no other power in any sense in order to be itself. It is itself the bringing-forth. And this constitutes a harmonious whole: an order. This bringing-forth, this ordering, "always (ἀεὶ) was and is and shall be." This formula—and later the single word ἀεί ('everlasting')—is, like the very matter that it characterizes, ambivalent; it is both mythic and philosophic and at once neither. Philosophy, in Parmenides and Plato, recognizes the differentiation of eternity and time (although time is nothing other than eternity that is more than time); myth, however, recognizes their compactness in the cycle (the repetition of the same). The idea 'everlasting' combines into one the succession proper to time and the limitlessness proper to eternity. Thus it is an ambivalent idea, compacting the differentiated. And thus it is the perfect characterization of the ambivalent matter of Heraclitean experience: the transitional matter between the mythic and the philosophic. The ordering is the everlasting.

This order—the measuring out of all things and the holding of them in harmonious tension—is itself the great harmony:

51   They [men] do not comprehend how
      what is bringing itself apart comes together with itself:
      a contrary-stretching connection [ἁρμονίη], as with bow and lyre.

At each connecting point of the wood and the string in the instruments, there is a fitting-together that is at once a pulling-away: a dynamic equilibrium. If the ἁρμονία (connection, fitting-together) did not stretch in both directions in a balanced way, the whole would disintegrate. Likewise with the one matter at issue in the fragments. It is the harmonious interconnection-of-all, the harmonizing. What brings itself apart into the many comes together with itself as yet invincibly one: and this process of "Being be-ing beings" is precisely "a contrary-stretching connection." It stretches on the one side to absolute-Being and on the other side to beings. It is the great harmony. The image of the lyre brings the musical sense of ἁρμονία to the fore: attunement, scale, ratio. The one matter is the attunement, the rationing out of all things, the tuning of them (according to a scale or measure), the establishing of proportions. Of course, this harmonizing resolves itself, on the side of the all, into the harmonious cosmos in the usual sense. The harmony in the cosmos is apparent or visible to ordinary comprehension. However:

54   Invisible harmonious-interconnection [ἁρμονίη] is stronger than visible.

The ἁρμονία which is not apparent—ordering, justice, war—is the greater. This attunement or dynamic equilibrium comes to expression in yet another way:

125   The barley-drink disintegrates if it be not stirred.

The drink was made of barley, cheese, and wine; if not stirred, the barley and the cheese sink to the bottom. The tension of the ingredients must be kept if the whole is to remain itself. Likewise with the matter of issue. It is a harmonious tension, a dynamic equilibrium.[10]

This harmonizing or order (κόσμος) is the arranging of things as a proper order. The ordering is aion (αἰών).

52   Aion is a child at play, playing draughts:
       a child has kingly power.

Philological note: the etymological sense of αἰών is "vital force, liquid of life, vitality," which flows (and can thus spill out). Thence it comes to mean "life-duration, lifetime," and even "time" itself.[11] Philosophically it names the same phenomenon as κόσμος, but insofar as process or flow instead of arrangement.

The interplay of all things in succession is not a chaos but an order; this well-ordered movement of the "pieces" takes place in and through the power-of-aion. The one matter is the power of order in development, the processive ordering; this is a kingly power, directing all the "pieces" of the realm according to an "autonomous" will. Aion is the King. Given the original import of the term ("vital force, liquid of life"), aion is the originary inner force of things, the motive power. Aion may ironically be called a child; for a Greek, a child was a vastly inferior species of an adult, a human being proper; but compared to man, this child is vastly superior. The child "playing" is the ordering of all things according to its own intrinsic measure. This matter may be called the playing.

The one matter at issue is the ordering, the common, justice—or the law. Exactly as law orders and founds the polis, so does this law order and found the whole cosmos. The following fragment says this—which is no more than has appeared so far—but it also adds something to what has already appeared.

> 114   Those who would speak with understanding
>   should base themselves upon what is common to all (things),
>   just as a polis (does) upon its law—
>   and much more firmly:
>   for all human [=political] laws nourish themselves
>   upon one, the divine (law);
>   for it prevails as far as it will
>   and is sufficient for all
>   and is still left over.

"What is common to all" is the law that forges all into a single realm. Political law may order the polis, but it prevails only through, and only because it is nourished by, the great law. If human law may be foundational, the divine law is even more so.

But there is more: this divine law not only "prevails" throughout the totality of "all things," but it "is still left over," it superabounds. This feature within the matter at issue has not till now come to the fore. The same feature appears in the epithet "divine." Heraclitus thinks the ordering. But in this fragment, the far side (i.e., the power, Being) of the ordering becomes explicit. The law is indeed the matter at issue. But on its far side (the divine side) it is more than what it is on its near side (the cosmic side). On the far side it is the power of ordering which is not exhausted by the order, though the order, on the near side, is totally based upon it. Starting from the far side, it may be said that in or as the law, the divine law is "common to all." Starting from the law, it may be said that this divine side of it more than suffices for the cosmic side; it is more power than the world needs. This explicitation does not import that the matter at issue is now divinity in contradistinction to things. The matter remains the *one* happening—but it is always the unfolding of the *twofold* (Being and beings) as one. And occasionally the absolute or divine side of this happening comes to the fore.

This single happening is that on account of which the many make up one realm (the cosmos), so that "all are one" (B 50). It is thus the common, the oneness. The next fragment says at least this: all are connected into one. But it may well say more—namely, that the divine side of the oneness is a one out of which all arise.

> 10   Connections:
>   wholes and not wholes [=parts],

> convergent divergent
> consonant dissonant—
> out of all a one,
> and out of a one all.

It is difficult to interpret this gnome in any other way than as saying that out of all a one shows itself, and out of a one all arise. In this case, it, like B 114, explicates the divine one which "does itself" in and as one, interconnected cosmos. The whole process is the matter at issue, of course; but named from the side of the one, it is the showing, and from the side of the all, the arising.

In this happening, the divine one unfolds itself as all the different things:

67 God is
   day night, winter summer,
   war peace, satiety hunger:
   and he alters himself precisely as does fire
   which, when it is mixed with spices,
   is named according to the scent of each of them.

The one, while remaining itself, takes on different appearances; and they are nothing but the one appearing. This process—the appearing—is the matter at issue. It is the self-altering of the divine one into the many opposites: the great happening.

The divine side of the ordering may again come to expression when Heraclitus speaks of

41 . . . the judgment [γνώμην]
   by which all things are steered through all.[12]

Since γνώμη means 'thought, will (intention, purpose), or judgment', it probably imports here the judge (the power of order) rather than the judging (the ordering). In other words, the matter at issue is named here again from its divine side. The judgment pilots, steers, skillfully guides, or shepherds all things. The last phrase of the fragment is ambiguous for us; it may import either "through all ways" or "through all things." If the former: the judgment keeps all things on the right way; it does not wreck or destroy them; it steers them through all possibilities. If the latter: it steers all things through all things, i.e., it harmonizes them, keeps them in order, and makes them constitute an order (a cosmos). In any case, the matter at issue may be called the steering, which implies the steersman (named here the γνώμη) and the steered.

Since the judgment that steers is a wise judgment, it may be called the wise: "the wise is different from all" (B 108). The wise judgment, though it prevails over all, is separate from all, i.e., it is more than sufficient and is beyond the superlative with respect to human wisdom. The far side of the matter at issue is the divine wisdom.

32   One, the alone wise,
     can/wants [ἐθέλει] and can/wants not to be called
     by the name of Zeus.

The wise one or "the alone wise," as the power that originates and directs all, is
divine in this traditional sense. Hence it may be called by us, and itself consents
to be called, "Zeus." However, the connotations of this traditional name are
inappropriate. Evidently inappropriate are: (1) the popular image (not genuine
symbol) of Zeus as a being like any other being and who does not therefore show
himself in or as the many; (2) the popular image of Zeus as not alone divinity;
and (3) the popular image of Zeus as not absolutely wise. Despite the defects,
however, "Zeus" is one of the best traditional names for the divine side of the
steering or ordering, since he can gather into himself all of divinity and indeed
does steer and does order. Hence the gnome:

64   Thunderbolt steers all things.

The thunderbolt or lightning is the traditional weapon of Zeus, by which he
guides the cosmos or establishes justice; by synecdoche, it is Zeus himself. As
the power that steers and guides, he forges the many divergent things into one
harmonious whole.
    Zeus the steersman is implicit in two other fragments. Both of them allude to
the sun to make their point. The first reads:

120 The bounds of dawn and evening
     are the bear and, opposite the bear, the warder
     of bright Zeus.

This difficult fragment may yield up some significance in the present context.[13]
The sun—so important for Ancient Near Eastern man both as a fact and as a
symbol—is, for all its greatness, bounded by law: it is steered by something
greater. Its course stays within measures: one extremity of its course is where it
rises in the summer ("dawn"); the other extremity is where it sets in the winter
("evening"); and it never violates these "bounds." These limits must have been
calculated by a technique unknown to us but evidently based upon the two stars
"Bear" and "Warder."[14] These stars keep the sun within "bounds." They are,
as it were, watchmen of the sun—which is thus subject to something greater than
itself. However, these watchmen themselves only belong to Zeus as his ministers: they are "of bright Zeus." Zeus of the bright sky, i.e., lightning or thunderbolt, appoints guardians to keep even the great sun within its proper limits, to
order it and to establish justice. It is relevant to recall that Justice (Dikê) is
traditionally the offspring of Zeus. He is the origin of measure, he is the ultimate
steersman. The same power may come to expression under another title:

16   Before the never-setting
     how might anyone be concealed?

The old power Helios, the guardian over justice and the judge over wrongdoers, sets every day—not to mention the mere sun. But the Zeus of Heraclitean experience—the judge who dispenses justice and is guardian over it—never goes down (into concealment). His reign never sinks into the abyss, his ordering never disappears, his guidance is never interrupted. To the never-setting, everyone is always subject. The steersman ever reigns.

If the matter at issue (order) may on its divine side be called fiery thunderbolt (power-of-order), then this matter may come to expression under yet another title.

> 30   This order...
>   ... always was and is and shall be:
>   an ever-living fire, kindling itself in measures and quenching itself in
>   measures.

War, father, king, justice, and so on, now take on the name of "fire." This fire is "ever-living," i.e., it "always was and is and shall be." The proper sense of this characteristic was treated above and need not be reiterated here. The happening in and by which things are measured out unto what and how they are is a fire that flares up and goes out "in measures." The dying-out obviously does not import the cessation of fire. Rather the "quenching" and the "kindling" are "the transformations of fire" (B 31a) by which it resolves itself into the elements (and so eventually into concrete phenomena) and they back into it. This whole process is the very matter at issue. The kindling and the quenching *is* the fire-process; the eventual congealment of things, so well measured out, *is* the process of fire. The measured happening of the elements (and so of things) is the near side of fire, just as thunderbolt is the far side of it. The transformations that keep the cosmic elements in balance and thus things within their due proportions is a measuring-out of them: Fire is the measuring-out, or justice.

The transformations come to expression also as an "exchange":

> 90   All things are a precise exchange for fire
>   and fire for all things,
>   as wares are for gold
>   and gold for wares.

It is not as if fire were to cease when things begin. Rather, things are the equivalent of fire, i.e., they *are* it; and fire, on its cosmic side, is the 'equivalent' of things. Of course, on its divine side it is "still left over" (B 114). Fire is what is common to things, as gold is the 'common' for wares. Fire is the common.[15]

The fact that all things are one in and as fire does not militate against their differences among themselves. Fire establishes them each within its own limits, measured out precisely. Hence:

> 7   If all things should become smoke,
>   the nostrils would distinguish them.

By synecdoche, "smoke" imports fire. Though all things are smoke, they are still individually distinguishable. God becomes all the opposites, i.e., he "alters himself precisely as does fire which, when it is mixed with spices, is named according to the scent of each of them" (B 67). This process is the fire or smoke in which all are one yet many.

With the title of "fire" for the matter at issue, the scientific dimension of the text comes to the fore. The ambivalent position of the Heraclitean experience imports that what we differentiate as science, philosophy, religion, ethics, and so on, should, for him, remain unified but distinguishable. (It may be useful to recall that the final differentiation of science and philosophy did not occur until Galileo.) More than twenty fragments advance a "scientific" theory about nature and man. Some of these have an immediate philosophical or ethical dimension; in others, these dimensions are remote, so that, in isolation, the fragments sound only scientific. An exposition of the scientific sense of the matter at issue belongs to the study of Heraclitean thought as a whole; but in subsuming such an exposition, a *philosophical* interpretation would quickly reach the point of diminishing returns. Therefore only an indication of the structure of the scientific world-view operative in the fragments will suffice here.

The basic 'element' in the cosmos is the "ever-living fire, kindling itself in measures and quenching itself in measures" (B 30, above). Thus it is that "all things are a precise exchange for fire and fire for all things" (B 90, above). The congealment of fire into the elements and thence into particular things, and the reverse process, always was and is and shall be. But it is not a process with temporal stages; rather, the "exchange" is always simultaneous, so that a dynamic equilibrium prevails and the cosmos as we know it neither contracts nor augments. In other words, "the way up and the way down is one and the same" (B 60).[16] Given this framework, the basic cosmology may well begin:

31a The transformations of fire:
       first sea,
       and out of sea
       half is earth
       and half is *prêstêr*.

The details continue in B 31b and then (though not in this order) in B 3, 6, 65, 99, 100, 106, 126 and most of the other fragments on the opposites, as well as in A 1 and 10–14.[17] The anthropological extension of this cosmology may well begin in B 36 and continue in B 20, 21, 26, 117 and 118, as well as in A 18–19.[18] The scientific dimension of the Heraclitean discourse centers around the name of "fire."

The matter at issue comes to expression in yet another name: "logos."[19] This title appears in three fragments.

2 Therefore it is necessary to follow the common;
     but while the logos is common. . . .[20]
50 Having listened not to me but to the logos. . . .

And the beginning of the scroll:

1   Although this logos *is*,[21]
    men are ever without comprehension
    both before they listen and when once they have listened.
    For, although all things come-to-pass in accord with this logos,
    they are like the inexperienced while yet experiencing
    such words and works
    as I set forth,
    taking-apart each thing according to its constitution [φύσιν]
    and showing-forth how it holds together. . . .

A paraphrase of B 1 may be helpful. The primary sense of the term "logos" here is "account" or "discourse." However, this sense will be ignored in order to bring to the fore its sense as the matter at issue. Accordingly, the fragment begins: the logos of which I will speak below indeed is, it indeed stands firm. Not everyone affirms it, but it is there (ἐόντος) nonetheless. When there is question of this logos, men are typically unintelligent, stupid, or quite without comprehension. This is so "both before they listen and when once they have listened" to my discourse on it; i.e., they have as little comprehension after as they had before. In other words: men comport themselves as if they do not experience even as they do experience or acquaint themselves with the "words and works" (καὶ ἐπέων καὶ ἔργων) that I set forth; i.e., they are acquainted both with what I say (the "words," ἔπεα) and with what is brought forth or things (the "works," ἔργα), but they act as if everything I say were strange to them.[22] In my discourse, I take apart or analyze each thing properly (κατὰ φύσιν), i.e., according to the way in which it is put together, or its constitution (κατὰ φύσιν). I also show (forth) the result (ὅκως ἔχει), i.e., how it is, or is internally structured (ὅκως ἔχει). In so treating all things, I penetrate to the logos according to which they all happen or come about.

What does the name "logos" say about the matter at issue? What does the term itself import?

The basic sense of λεγ- is "gather." From this, all the other senses derive. They will fall into place as soon as "gathering" be thought of as an ordering. The topology of the word may be schematized as follows:
(1) gathering→ordering→measuring→measure, amount→due measure
(2) gathering→ordering→organization→(a, b, c)
    (a) general principle→law
    (b) proportion→relation→correspondence
    (c) organizing→arguing, reasoning→reason as faculty
(3) gathering→ordering→collecting→(a, b)
    (a) enumerating, counting→number
    (b) laying out→laying forth→letting be manifest→bringing to unconcealedness→calling forth→calling→naming→speaking or saying→(i, ii, iii, iv, v)

   (i) utterance→the saying, the said, word→account, discourse, expla-
       nation→definition (cf. general principle)
  (ii) mention, notice→reputation→fame→esteem→worth
 (iii) conversation→talk with oneself→thinking→considering→consid-
       eration→opinion
 (iv) argument→(α,β)
      (α) reason, cause (cf. due measure)
      (β) logical process→logic
  (v) language→capacity for language

It is evident how apropos the word logos is in naming the matter at issue.

The logos is the ordering, the measuring-out, the Law. It gathers all things unto themselves and into an order; it lays them out and lets them be manifest, i.e., lets them be. It is the gatherative laying-out, the letting-be-manifest-in-ordered-collectedness. The logos is that which accounts for what and how things are; it is, in a later terminology, their cause. The logos is the ordering power in and for all things: they "come-to-pass according to" it. All of them are constituted in and by the logos. To understand things according to this logos is to take them apart (διαιρέων) so that their inside begins to appear, so that their inner constitution or φύσις may be shown forth (φράζων). Things hold together (ἔχει); they have an inner coherence, an "essence" (φύσις). And this φύσις is the logos.

Thence does the gnome speak out:

123   φύσις κρύπτεσθαι φιλεῖ.

A transposition would read: "(The) constitution [of each phenomenon] is wont to hide itself." By attention to each word, interpretation may loosen up the density of this dictum. The root φυ- imports 'be, become, grow.' Hence the φύσις of a thing is its Being, its inner dynamism; the process in which it rises up, by which it surges forth and endures, because of which it emerges as what and how it is; its upsurgence, its presencing. From this basic sense, the derivative senses follow: (inner) constitution→nature, essence→the way a thing is made→organization (= λόγος)→measure→functioning→behavior. The matter at issue is the physis of all things: their Being, their emergence, their presencing. The term κρύπτεσθαι is in the middle voice, indicating not only reflexivity but also self-benefit: φύσις "hides itself for its own benefit"—which is to say, were it not for this self-concealment, φύσις would not be precisely itself. This self-concealment is not imposed upon φύσις from the outside, but is the manner in which φύσις itself "does itself." This further comes to expression in the term φιλεῖ. It imports preference (love) and hence the preferential way (custom); the rendition "is wont to" nicely retains both senses (habitual favoring). Physis loves to hide, i.e., it allows its hiddenness to be, and it does so not in any incidental manner but customarily. Physis—the logos in and as things—is wont, that it might remain itself, to conceal itself. Of course, it not only hides itself but, in and as things, it reveals itself as well. Every fragment so far has implied this. But in its self-revealment, it always conceals itself. The one matter at issue is presencing incognito.

About forty fragments have brought to expression the matter in itself. Its major titles are: war, father, king, strife, measuring-out (δίϰη), propriety/necessity (χρεών), ordering (ϰόσμος), harmonizing, aion, fire, logos, and physis. On its divine side, it is: the law, the one, God, the judgment (γνώμη), the wise, the alone wise, Zeus, thunderbolt, and the never-setting. The self-revelation of the matter is obvious in that it has indeed come to expression; its self-concealment has come to the fore in a few instances. In over twenty-five more fragments the manifestation and the hiddenness of the matter is at issue. These fragments will be the topic for the next sections of this part (The One Matter of Experience). But before treating them, interpretation may attempt a more exact determination of the matter of Heraclitean experience.

Above, in the Prologue, the matter at issue was defined as "Being in a uniquely transitional configuration." It is now possible to make this definition more exact. Two points call for comment: the fact that at stake is "Being," and the fact that at stake is a uniquely transitional configuration of it. (1) Being is the matter at issue. The Western philosophical tradition owes to Parmenides the first explicit name and since him the dominant name for the matter proper to philosophy: Being. In his work, Being appears immediately as absolute-Being or simply the absolute. By this standard, the matter at issue in Heraclitus is, to be sure, Being—but Being in a derivative sense. That is to say, Heraclitus experiences and brings to language the process of *absolute-Being be-ing beings,* the process of beings *emerging* 'out of' the absolute. This single event, i.e., (absolute-) Being-as-*emerging*-as-beings, takes on various names in Heraclitus: physis, logos, fire, aion, and so on. To think this process is to think at once its absolute "side" (Zeus, the alone wise, the one) and its cosmic "side" (all things, beings). *Being in the sense of emergence or physis is the matter of Heraclitean experience.* Of course, Being in *this* sense may be taken as the standard—in which case, Being as the absolute will be the derivative sense. Historically, absolute-Being has prevailed as the standard, while emergence—and not just the emerged, i.e., beings—has sometimes come to expression along with it. But in a few philosophers, e.g., in Heidegger, emergence is the standard—and is even taken in a quasi-autonomous way. The relation of the Heideggerian matter for thought and the Heraclitean will be taken up in the Epilogue. In any case, this characterization of the Heraclitean matter is not yet complete. For, what is it that distinguishes his experience of emergence (Being *be-ing* beings) from that of others? So far, only its philosophic dimension has been noticed. (2) But *emergence also has a mythic sense* in Heraclitus, so that the configuration of Being that he experiences is uniquely transitional. It is transitional in that it is philosophic and mythic at once, and it is uniquely so in that this transition took place decisively (in the West) only once. The mythic character of emergence appears especially in two ways, both in the name of "fire." (a) Emergence, for

Heraclitus, "always was and is and shall be, an ever-living fire" (B 30). The experience of an indefinite extension forward and backward is ambivalently philosophic and mythic. On the one hand, it differentiates eternity (to-be-all-at-once) and time (to be in a less than total way); but on the other hand, it compacts the indefiniteness (indeterminateness) proper to eternity and the extensiveness (successive determinations) proper to time. Thus it is philosophic (in that it differentiates) and at once mythic (in that it compacts). (b) Emergence, for Heraclitus, has a "scientific" (and a "religious") as well as a "philosophic" sense. Though distinguishable by us, the cosmology (and the religion) in the text is inseparable from the philosophy. Hence Heraclitus is mythic. But insofar as the philosophy is distinguishable, he is philosophic. To the extent that dimensions of experience are *distinguishable* in Heraclitus—in contrast to, say, Hesiod—he is no longer mythic; but to the extent that they are *not distinguished by him*—in contrast to us—he is not yet philosophic. He is both at once and so neither: he is ambivalent. It should be more clear now how "Being in a uniquely transitional configuration" is to be understood. The complexity of this matter is a complexity only for us: for him, it was simple.

Interpretation may now turn to the various ways in which this simple matter manifests itself.

B. The Manifestations of the Matter

Although physis is wont to hide itself, it manifests itself in multiple ways. Below, in Part II, it will become clear that physis reveals itself not to everybody but only to those who are attuned to it. Most men do not penetrate beneath the surface of phenomena. In any case, the form in which physis does manifest itself through phenomena is their *oneness*. That is to say, the fragments now in question all suggest a certain oneness in multiple things, a certain *coincidentia oppositorum* (coincidence of opposites). All of them suggest the unity of the cosmos, i.e., the near side of physis; basically, then, they suggest the single cosmos or physis; hence they also suggest the divine one, i.e., the far side of physis. One fragment considered above named the matter at issue from its divine side:

    10   Connections:
          wholes and nonwholes,
          convergent divergent,
          consonant dissonant;
          out of all one,
          and out of one all.[23]

The interconnection or oneness of phenomena is obvious here. But the fragments now in question indicate physis from its cosmic side. The oneness of the cosmos is the one cosmos. The many phenomena, through their peculiar unities, manifest the one matter at issue. Most of the fragments have not only a philosophic dimension but a scientific dimension as well; in the context of contemporaneous cosmology, they advance the theory that there are many genuine opposites in the cosmos, not just the elements, and that even these opposites are one. Of course, the unity of opposite phenomena is never a flat reduction, a collapse of determinateness. The multiplicity and the differences of things are the condition for their possibility to manifest the one physis operative beneath their surface. Physis shows itself in various types of oneness.

Whatever the organization of the scroll, a sixfold division here will help to bring out the significance of each fragment. This division is not rigid; it is fluid and changeable. The opposites are one: (1) in origin, (2) in cognitive coincidence, (3) in evaluative coincidence, (4) in cyclic recurrence, (5) in evaluative correlativity, and (6) in a dialectic of metaphors.

1. Oneness in Origin

Opposites are one in origin, so that the one Origin manifests itself through the *coincidentia oppositorum* (coincidence of opposites). Two fragments convey this. The first:

57   Teacher of most men is Hesiod:
      they feel sure that he knew most things—
      one who did not [even] manage to recognize daylight and night!
      For they are one.

The opposites—here daylight and darkness—are one; they are one insofar as they are brought about by a single agency (the sun). The one sun, by its presence or absence, originates day and night. The sun symbolizes fire or physis. The second fragment:

106   The constitution ($\varphi\acute{\upsilon}\sigma\iota\varsigma$) of every day is one.[24]

Apparently this is a polemic against Hesiod (*Erga* 765 ff.), who accepts that there are lucky and unlucky days. Rather, says Heraclitus, the essence of each day is the same. That which constitutes the different days, that which makes them what they are or originates them, is one—namely the sun, which, as the one physis of each day, symbolizes the physis of all the opposites.

2. Oneness in Cognitive Coincidence

What are opposites for cognitive standpoints may coincide as one concrete phenomenon. Or, reversely: a single phenomenon has, from different standpoints, opposite characteristics. Several fragments are obvious in this regard.

103   Beginning and end in a circle are common.

60   The way up and the way down is one and the same.

59   Of the carding-comb
      the straight way and the crooked
      is one and the same.[25]

However the "way" of the carding-comb or teasel is to be imagined, it is clear
that this one way has opposite characteristics. The one matter shows itself in the
coincidentia oppositorum.

A famous fragment yields up an excellent sense in this context:

12a Upon those who are [in the process of] stepping
      into the same rivers
      different and again different waters flow.[26]

One phenomenon—river waters—is *at once* the "same" or identical (αὐτοῖσιν)
and "different" or other (ἕτερα). The opposites (sameness and difference) are
one; a single phenomenon manifests itself in opposite characteristics (identity
and otherness). The river water symbolizes the one physis.

3. Oneness in Evaluative Coincidence

What are opposites for evaluational standpoints may coincide as one concrete
phenomenon. Or, reversely: a single phenomenon has, from different standpoints, opposite values. The first fragment is obvious:

61   The sea is the most pure and the most polluted water:
      for fish it is drinkable and salutary,
      but for men it is undrinkable and deadly.

The one sea symbolizes the one physis. Another fragment is more subtle:

58   Doctors,
      who amputate and cauterize,
      complain that they receive no worthy fee
      for effecting these things.

Doctors hurt to cure, and the hurting is the curing. The one action (amputation
or, alternatively, cauterization) has opposite values; they are one in the concrete
phenomenon. And in physis the many are one. A further fragment depends upon
a pun to make its point:

48   For the bow (τόξον)
      the name is ΒΙΟΣ
      but the work is death.

Another term for τὸ τόζον is ὁ βιός (ΒΙΟΣ in the unaccented contemporaneous script). And ὁ βίος (ΒΙΟΣ) means "life." The pun was probably common. As ΒΙΟΣ imports life, so it imports death. ΒΙΟΣ has opposite values; in it they are one. Hence the single word ΒΙΟΣ symbolizes the one physis.

Several more fragments are identical in form.

    13   Pigs delight in mire rather than in clean water [as men would].

Here, interpretation must make explicit the second evaluational standpoint. Then the double *coincidentia oppositorum* becomes clear:

    (a) mire is valued as both delightful and not so (by swine and by men); and

    (b) clean water is valued as both delightful and not so (by men and by swine).

In each case, the opposites are one. And the one physis shows itself through all the opposites. The same pattern appears in the following:

    9   Donkeys would choose chaff rather than gold [as men would].

Again the point is double:

    (a) chaff (waste, straw) is highly valued by donkeys (as their normal food), but little valued by men; and

    (b) gold is greatly valued by men, but little valued by donkeys. The one phenomenon—chaff or gold—symbolizes the one physis.[27]

An obscure fragment yields up a plausible sense here:

    11   Every animal is driven to pasture with a blow.

That which has a bad or injurious effect—namely, a blow—is also that which has a good or healthy effect. The good is that the animal gets his food, the bad is that he is hurt. Both result from a single phenomenon (the blow). The coincidence of opposite values in one action allows it to be a symbol of the one physis.

4. Oneness in Cyclic Recurrence

Opposites may be one in their cyclic recurrence: they come around to and replace each other. Whether or not a concrete thing is supposed to be the concrete cyclic unity of opposites (like a stone that heats up and cools down), the opposites would in any case be one as constitutive of a single cycle (like heat-and-cold). The obvious fragment:

    126   Cold phenomena get warm, heat cools down,
            moisture dries up, the parched gets wet.

Through the oneness proper to a cycle, the one physis manifests itself. A more complex fragment:

88   And as the same there is in us
      living [person] and dead [person],
      and awake [person] and sleeping [person],
      and youthful [person] and old/weak [person] (γηραιόν):
      for these having changed round are those,
      and those having changed round are these.

The changing round of wakefulness and sleep in us is clear. But how do the
living and the dead in us, and the youthful and the old in us, change round? Note
that the reference point is "these" (i.e., living, awake, youthful) and that only a
three-term cycle is in question (the reference-point, its negation, the reference
point). Now "dead" imports "nonalive," i.e., *"postalive"* and *"prealive."* In
parallel fashion, "old/weak" imports "nonyouthful," i.e. *"poststrong"* and
"prestrong." And, of course, "sleeping" imports both "postawake" and
"preawake." Hence the reference point (living, awake, youthful) having
changed round is the negation of it (postalive, postawake, poststrong), and the
negation (prealive, preawake, prestrong) having changed round is the reference
point. In this way, the opposites are "the same": they belong to a single phenomenon ("us"). Their oneness symbolizes the one matter at issue: physis.[28]

5. Oneness in Evaluative Correlativity

Opposites may be one in their correlativity: a particular value may be ap-
preciated by man only as correlative to its opposite. For example:

111   It is disease that makes health pleasant and good;
       hunger, satiety; weariness, rest.

The first member of the pair makes the other what it is for man (namely,
"pleasant and good"). The values of health, satiety, and rest are what they are
only in the face of their opposites. Or again:

23   They would not know the name of justice
       if these [injustices] did not exist.

Philological note: the "name of justice" is, of course, justice itself; and the
bracketed "injustice" is clear from the source and the testimonies.[29] Injustice
makes justice what it is for man (namely, godly, good, pleasant); man ap-
preciates justice only in the face of injustice. The opposites form a system of
correlates, a unity. And through this unity the one physis shows itself.

6. Oneness in a Dialectic of Metaphors

The one matter at issue may also manifest itself through a complex oneness
immediately recognizable but difficult to analyze. Metaphors, with or without
their univocal sense also operative, may imbricate so that they form a continuity

of meaning. This continuity is a unity, a unity that symbolizes the one physis. At least, an interpretive framework like this will permit a minimum decipherment of several obscure fragments. Their major sense may well be 'religious' and thus, in their details, beyond the interpretive resources of our age; however, the multidimensionality of the Heraclitean gnome allows them to settle into the present context and yield up a 'philosophical' significance consonant with the other fragments.

The first gnome to be considered is famous:

62   Immortals mortals, mortals immortals,
[a]   living each other's death
[b]   and dying each other's life.

Evidently operative here is the symbol of an existence of man both after life and before life; preliving and postliving existence goes under the title of 'immortality'; and existence in life is, of course, 'mortality'. Whether, beyond this symbol, the further symbol of palingenesis is operative is not clear; fortunately, it makes no difference for interpretation. Each descriptive line ([a] and [b] above) has a double significance in which "life" and "death" take on both their univocal and their metaphoric sense.

(a) What is life for the mortal (= the alive) is death for the immortal (= the preliving), so that the mortal lives the death of the immortal. And what is life for the immortal (= the postliving) is death for the mortal (= the alive), so that the immortal lives the death of the mortal. Hence they live each other's death. Thus immortals become mortals, and mortals immortals.

(b) What is death for the immortal (= the preliving) is life for the mortal (= the living), so that the immortal dies (as) the life of the mortal. And what is death for the mortal (= the living) is life for the immortal (= the postliving), so that the mortal dies (as) the life of the immortal. Hence they die (as) each other's life. Thus immortals become mortals, and mortals immortals.

The metaphors interact in a complex way. And in this complex unity the one matter at issue shows itself.

The next fragment is even more complex:

21   What we see when awake is death,
     and what we see when asleep is real life (ὕπαρ).[30]

Philological note: The term τὸ ὕπαρ means a real phenomenon, seen when awake, as opposed to a mere dream, seen when asleep; and further, a reality as opposed to an illusion. The contrast of ὕπαρ and "death" is clear, so that the term has the figurative sense of "life."

The paradox is obvious. "What we see when awake"—normally speaking, real life—is, paradoxically, death. And "what we see when asleep"—normally speaking, dream (death)—is paradoxically real life. Whatever the immediate "religious" or even "scientific" import of this gnome, it does contain a dialectic

of metaphors such that a certain unity is discernible among them. The symbols
are common enough:

(1) wakefulness is symbolically life;
(2) sleep is symbolically death;
(3) life is symbolically death (cf. B 62 above); and
(4) death is symbolically life (cf. B 62 again).

Given this, the imbrication of sense may be discerned. Start with wakefulness: to
be awake = to be alive (by 1) = to be dead (by 3) = to be asleep (by 2) = to be
dead (by 2) = to be alive (by 4) = to be awake (by 1). The symbols imbricate and
thus form a unity. Through this unity the one physis manifests itself.

The final fragment is the most complex:

26   Man
       in the night
       touches off a light for himself [= sees = dreams],
       though his vision is extinguished;
       though alive,
       he touches the dead,
       [to wit] while sleeping;
       though awake,
       he touches the sleeper.

Once again, the major symbols are sleep for death, and wakefulness for life. The
other metaphors are also familiar. Whatever the "religious" or "scientific"
import of this fragment, its rhetorical coherence gives it a significance that may
be revelatory for the one matter at issue in all the fragments. The following
schema shows the imbrication or 'touching' of sense in the italicized items:

in the *night,* i.e., darkness
though *vision extinguished*
while *sleeping*
touching the *dead*
touching the *sleeper*
touching off a light, i.e., *dreaming or seeing*
though seeing, i.e., *awake*
though *alive*

The sense "night" or "darkness" overlaps, i.e., touches, the sense "vision
extinguished"; which itself overlaps "sleeping"; which itself overlaps "dead";
and so on. In the unity of this dialectic, the one physis manifests itself.

But in this very self-manifestation, the one matter continues to hide itself.

C. The Hiddenness of the Matter

The matter at issue in Heraclitus is, in philosophical terms, absolute-Being
be-ing beings, or again, the absolute *emerging* as the world. This process as a

whole has many names: physis, aion, measuring-out, and so on. On its divine side, it is Zeus, thunderbolt, the alone wise. On its cosmic side, it is all things, the opposites, phenomena. *Physis as a whole or in the full sense* is absolute-Being be-ing beings—i.e., inclusive of Zeus and all things. But it will be useful to develop a nuance: *Physis in the narrow sense.* This would import only the 'be-ing' in 'Being be-ing beings', only emergence—i.e., in abstraction from its two sides. Such a nuance is valid because Zeus is more power than all things need, because absolute-Being *is* more than all beings. Reflection may follow ordinary consciousness and disregard this "more," just as it may conceive the cosmos in a quasi-autonomous fashion. If it makes this double abstraction, then physis appears in the narrow sense. Physis in both senses manifests itself and hides itself.

Through the various *coincidentiae oppositorum* in the quasi-autonomous cosmos and thus in the cosmos as the near side of physis, physis as a whole, and thus its far side, manifests itself. In the same way, the divine one, thus physis as a whole, and thus the cosmos as its near side, hides itself. Primarily it is the divine which both reveals and conceals itself. For, after all, Zeus is the originary origin; *Dikê* is only his daughter, as the cosmos is only her child. *Dikê* or physis in the full sense conceals itself only because its own far side does so all the more. The superabundance of Zeus imports his superlative concealment. Hence the self-concealment of the matter at issue is not due to human inattention. Man may indeed fail to hearken to physis (and, if it be taken in the narrow sense, to Zeus behind it); but even if he were to hearken, it would still be hidden from him (as well as manifested to him). To be sure, the self-concealment (as well as the self-revealment) of physis is always such *for man;* but it can be so only because, antecedently, "physis is wont, in order to be itself, to hide itself" (B 123). That which does not hide itself but is manifestly manifest is things taken in a quasi-autonomous fashion. But the physis of things hides itself, as it manifests itself, in and as them.

Another fragment already treated also brings to expression the fact of hiddenness.

54   Invisible harmonious-interconnection is stronger than visible.

The harmony within the cosmos is beneath the surface of things, hidden, or invisible. The term rendered here by "invisible"—ἀφανής—may also be rendered by "nonmanifest." Likewise in the next fragment:

56   Men are self-deceived in the(ir) knowledge of visible/manifest things
        (φανερῶν),
     sort of like Homer, who came-to-be [considered] wiser than any other Greek;
     for he was deceived by boys killing lice when they said to him:
     "What we have seen and caught, that we leave behind,
     and what we have neither seen nor caught, that we take along."

Philological note: Homer thought that the boys, who had been fishing, were talking of fish, but they were really talking of lice. Thus he was (self)deceived.

In their ordinary knowledge of visible or manifestly manifest things, men see only their obvious surface. They should see through them, as Homer should have seen through the riddle-saying. Of course, it is not as if man were able to make things completely transparent and so make the hidden physis completely manifest. Rather, even as he penetrates their surface, things necessarily retain that surface, just as the saying, even when penetrated, retains its surface meaning. And so does physis, though manifest for man, retain its hiddenness. Phenomena remain riddles: they present the truth but at once veil it. The truth of things—their physis—manifests but at once hides itself.

This fragment (B 56) suggests another name for physis: Truth (ἀλήθεια).[31] Strictly speaking, however, ἀλήθεια means "nonconceal*ed*ness" and not "unconceal*ing*," the state and not the process. It imports the nonconcealedness or open character of something over against a possible or prior unavailability or latency.[32] For example, that woman over there, at first dissembled because of distance, has turned out τὸ ἀληθές to be my mother; or, his speech, whether or not he tried to cover over the fact, and whether or not everybody realized it, was τὸ ἀληθές an attack upon Socrates. From this ordinary sense, ἀλήθεια may, like any other word, take on a philosophical sense, hence share in the connotations of Being, and immediately import beings *as such*. From there, it may, with appropriate caution, be taken to indicate Being-as-emergence: physis in the narrow sense.[33] In that case, physis would be the unconcealing or the manifesting. But what, so to speak, does it manifest? Itself, of course—though such an answer seems to be fruitless, even nonsensical, redundant. However, a nuance is possible. Beyond its manifestation of itself in and as its own near side, i.e., things, what physis as a whole primarily manifests is its own far side, i.e., Zeus. Hence it manifests itself only insofar as it is the manifestation of that which primordially manifests itself. Though revealing himself, Zeus is that which primarily remains (self)concealed in the process and hence may be called the Λήθη in ᾿Αλήθεια (physis). What unconcealing (physis) unconceals is the concealed (Zeus) so that unconcealedness (the cosmos) comes-to-be. The entire complexus: things come-to-be and ipso facto both unconceal and conceal physis in the narrow sense; physis so taken unconceals and at once conceals itself; likewise it both unconceals and conceals Zeus; and Zeus unconceals and at once conceals himself. But the single action of things (coming-to-be) *is* their twofold action (manifesting and hiding), which *is* the fourfold action of physis, which *is* the twofold action of Zeus—all of which is *one* process. And this one process is the matter at issue for Heraclitus.

Finally, the famous gnome:

> 93   The lord whose oracle is the one in Delphi
> neither tells nor hides
> but gives a sign.

The lord here is Apollo. Like the logos of his oracle, he neither totally reveals nor totally conceals—to wit, himself. It is difficult to determine which connotations of the name *Apollo* are to be understood in this context, but, as divine, it is presumably another name for the divine side of the matter at issue. Zeus and Apollo are one: and he is neither fully present nor fully absent in and as the cosmic side but rather hints or gives a sign of himself. Things themselves are that sign. In other words, phenomena *are* the revealment-in-concealment of Apollo, his presence-in-absence. As such they are *symbols*. Zeus symbolizes himself in and as the cosmos; reversely, the cosmos is the symbol—the ambiguous presence—of Zeus.

The primary reference of this fragment is the matter at issue. Like the word λόγος, however, it may well be ambivalent, and therefore express the character of the Heraclitean logos as well as the matter. Just as Apollo, so also the discourse upon him: it gives a *hint,* neither outright exposition nor complete obfuscation. The logos of Heraclitus has the same structure as phenomena. It is a sign. This, of course, is the factual content of the ancient epithet for Heraclitus: "the Obscure." His style is oracular, laconic, gnomic. The sayings have the paradoxical structure of a riddle. One meaning manifests itself through, and hides itself behind, another meaning. His style is the style of things themselves. Or again: Heraclitus does not so much argue as hint. The matter at issue comes upon the searcher in an "unexpected" way (B 18); it is never the expected conclusion of a discursive exposition. Accordingly, the Heraclitean gnome only orients the searcher for discovery: it gives a sign.

In the face of the Heraclitean style or, more fundamentally, in the face of the style of things themselves, men may be adequate or inadequate. They may understand the riddles or they may not. The complex of issues arising herewith and the fragments that move within the ambit of this problematic make up the subject matter of Part II.

II. The Correspondence to the Matter

The matter at issue in Heraclitus is physis. Some of the fragments bring this matter to expression without immediate reference to man, or at least retain their expressive power in abstraction from this reference; and Part I treated these. However, physis (and that means Zeus) both reveals and conceals itself to and from precisely *man*. In other words, any discourse on physis must eventually become a discourse on man as well. The fragments expressive of physis in reference to man or, equivalently, of man in reference to physis, will be the topic for this part and for Part III. This part will thematize the correspondence of man to the matter and the questions connected therewith. This correspondence has the name of wisdom (σοφία). The relevant fragments will begin to yield up their substance through the following interpretive division: (a) the alone wise and wisdom, (b) the lack of wisdom, (c) the polis and wisdom, (d) the wise critique of popular religion, and (e) the destiny of the wise.

A. The Alone Wise and Wisdom

A properly human wisdom measures itself by the divine. The fragments will fall into three sections: (1) Zeus, (2) the inferiority of man, and (3) wisdom in man.

1. Zeus

In physis, the divine law prevails (B 114). This law or judgment steers ordering (B 41, 64). As the power that directs all things into this remarkable order about us, the divine judgment is wise.

> 32   One, the alone wise,
>   can/wants and can/wants not to be called
>   by the name of Zeus.

The term *alone* (μοῦνον) must import not factual but rather essential exclusivity. For man may indeed be wise; but, as will appear, his wisdom comes only after much labor. In contrast, wisdom belongs to the very essence of divinity (cf. B 78 below). Man could never be called simply "the wise" (B 108) or "the alone wise."[34]

2. The Inferiority of Man

The status of man is vastly inferior:

> 78   For human *êthos* has no capacity-to-judge (γνώμας),
>   but divine has.

The term γνῶμαι (plural with singular meaning) probably imports more than just the fact of judging. In view of the name of judgment (γνώμη, B 41) for divinity, it probably imports the power-for-judgments. To have this power or capacity is to dispose of the measure or standard by which the actual judgment is made. In fact, the judgment is *itself* the measure (*Dikê*). The term ἦθος originally meant 'dwelling or customary place,' hence 'world.' But a world is not only given but also constituted. Hence it comes to mean the world that we constitute and bear around within us: our inner world. Accordingly, ἦθος ranges in sense from "character" to "essence." Since this gnome contrasts the human and the divine *êthos*, its sense is probably close to 'essence, nature, self'. The divine *êthos* has the power-for-judgments: in fact, it is *the* Judgment. The human *êthos* is vastly inferior.

Indeed:

> 79   Man is called silly by *daimon*
>   just as a child is by a man.

The Greeks did not recognize children *as* children. They thought of the child as an inferior adult, whose knowledge and judgments are worthless. But in comparison to the wise, man as such is like a child.[35]

3. Wisdom in Man

Nevertheless, man can become wise. An only human wisdom is to penetrate to *the* wise and to base oneself upon it—to follow it or correspond to it.

Human wisdom is a response to the self-manifestation of the one physis in all.

> 50   Having hearkened not to me but to the logos,
>   wise it is to acknowledge (ὁμολογεῖν) that all is one.

Once the logos speaks out as that which is common to all things, man, having listened, can become wise. To be wise would then be *"homologein* that all is one.'' Interpretation must try to experience this term in the way that it must have resounded for a Greek. "To acknowledge" imports "to gather, order, collect, lay out'' (-λογεῖν) "the same'' (ὁμο-). Hence to be wise is to lay out the same (as)—to wit, the same as the gatherative laying-out: to correspond to it. Wisdom occurs in man when man concurs to the logos. Wisdom is to let lie forth the gatherative letting-lie-forth. It is to let be, on the near side, that which, from the far side, the judgment lets be.[36]

To correspond to the logos is to let it *be* (itself). But *this* is to let *oneself* be, inasmuch as all things are the one logos. In terms of fire, the more himself a person is, the more he is wise, the more he is fiery.

> 118   The dry soul is wisest and best.

The soul or self of man, like everything else, is the absent presence of the thunderbolt. To be "dry" or fiery is to be precisely what one essentially is. Opposite, of course, is the "wet" soul (B 117). There are evidently degrees of dryness, and the fully dry soul would be the "most wise" and the "most good" (ἀρίστη, indicating praxis). Concurring to the logos, letting it be, letting it presence more and more as oneself, promoting one's own logos—are all the same: wisdom.

Human wisdom is not merely comprehension but action, as well.

> 2   Therefore it is necessary to follow the common;
>   but while the logos is common,
>   the many live as if they had a discernment (φρόνησιν) of their own.

Wisdom is to follow the logos intellectually and volitionally (ἕπεσθαι). It is to have a φρόνησις that is common, i.e., that follows the common. The root word φρήν imports the "emotional, volitional and intellectual elements in the attitude of a person. But contrary to *noos*, it is always connected with the potential or actual beginning of an action. Contrary to *thymos*, it is never used where a passion or emotion is blind. The intellectual element is always present.''[37] (Heraclitus will call this intellectual element νόος.) Wisdom is the total accord of man with the logos.[38]

The wise are like those awake: in touch with real life, in touch with physis.

> 89   The waking share a cosmos one and common,
>   but the sleeping each turns aside into his own.

The wise are the waking: they participate in the common logos. The nonwise isolate themselves in their private worlds. Wisdom does not split up into many private versions in the relativistic sense. Rather it is one, but in the same sense in which the logos is one—namely, it concretizes itself into many forms while nonetheless common.

At the beginning of his scroll Heraclitus declares that his logos (account) stands firm. He takes apart all things and shows forth how they hold together; he penetrates them and holds them open so that their inner physis shines out. Wisdom is therefore—presuming that his own logos is wise—the penetration through the surface of things to their genuineness, logos, or physis. The Greek word for such penetration is νόος. In Homer all men have this power of penetration; in Xenophanes this power has become the prerogative of the divine. In Heraclitus the term retains its connotation of rarity, although men—a few, to be sure—can have νόος.[39]

> 114   Those who would speak with understanding (νόωι)
>   should base themselves upon what is common to all (things),
>   just as a polis (does) upon its law—
>   and much more firmly [than the polis does upon its law]:
>   for all human laws nourish themselves
>   upon one, the divine (law). . . .

To be wise, to understand (νοεῖν), is to base oneself upon the common logos—which imports eventually upon the one divine law. The rhetoric in this fragment is complex but clear. A polis orders itself upon its law—the common in it, what makes it precisely a polis. And νόος, in order to be precisely νόος, should order itself upon *its* law—namely, *the* law. Even the law which founds the polis is itself founded; and this foundation of the foundation, this law, founds νόος. The wise man penetrates to physis and hence to the divine.

The "few good" men have "understanding and discernment (νόος ἢ φρήν)" (B 104).[40] Wisdom is the orientation—along which praxis may unfold—towards the hidden yet manifest physis, thus Zeus.

Wisdom does not come easy for man. The self-revelation of physis is correlative to a human effort of penetration.

22   Those who quest after gold
      dig much earth
      and find a little [to wit, gold].

The search after physis (including Zeus) is a quest, an endeavor, i.e., it is difficult. As with gold, even a little success requires a lot of hard work. Without hopeful tenacity, physis will not be found.

18   If you do not expect the unexpected, you will not find it;
      for it is difficult to search for and difficult to attain.

Like gold, physis is "the unexpected," i.e., not subject to human dispensation. Yet hopeful expectation must animate the quest, for the gift is hard to reach for and *a fortiori* hard to reach. Nevertheless, it can be won.

To win the treasure and to become wise is not a retreat from the earth.

55   The things of which there is seeing, hearing, and exact knowledge
      (μάθησις)—
      these do I prefer.[41]

Prima facie, this avowal is incompatible with any preference for physis. However, the fragment must be read in the light of all the other ones. Especially relevant are those which castigate the somnolent character of men, their unawareness and vain speculation. What the wise man prefers is the concrete world, *for it is this which manifests physis*. And we do not find physis if we do not engage the wakeful world, if we do not see, hear, or know the concrete. Wisdom is not a flight from but an engagement in the concrete world (as becomes especially clear with respect to the polis). The wise man prefers this.

A properly human wisdom is correspondence to the wise. Most men, however, lack wisdom.

B. The Lack of Wisdom

Although wisdom is possible for humankind, most do not achieve it: ". . . most men are bad, and very few good" (B 104). Not only mankind in general lacks wisdom, but so also do their teachers. The fragments will fall into two sections: (1) the many, and (2) the putatively wise.

1. The Many

The moral tenor of most men is pathetic, if not deplorable. They have no regard for anything but their immediate gratification.

29   . . . the many sate themselves like cattle.

They do not keep within the measure or lay out the same as the measure, and could literally eat themselves to death. For, unfortunately, "it is enjoyment for souls to become wet" (B 77a).[42] The wise soul is dry. Not only do the many eat without measure, but, we may infer, they typically drink in the same way. And their condition is shameful:

117   When a man gets drunk,
      he, staggering, is led (home) by a beardless boy,
      not knowing whither he goes;
      for his soul is wet.

This gnome evidently plays upon a colloquial play on words: getting drunk is getting wet. The drunk man violates the measure for drinking, the logos. He is in a miserable state: an adult led about by a child (who is by definition 'silly'). The wet soul—in basic contrast to the wise or dry—is the one that does not orient itself towards the hidden yet manifest measure of all things. Men ought to resist the impulse to immediate gratification. However:

85   It is hard to fight with passion (θυμῶι):
     so whatever it wants, it buys—at the expense of soul.[43]

The θυμός is the heart as the center of—or is itself—strong emotion, passion or, specifically, blind desire. Though resistance to blind desire is not easy, the stake is high: one's very soul (self). Unmeasured θυμός may get what it wills, but the price it pays is the soul. The more *wet* a man is, the *less* he *is*, i.e., the further he is from fire, the less does fire blaze in and as his very self. To be evil is to lose oneself. Obviously, therefore:

110   It is not better for men
      to become whatever they desire.

To become wet is disastrous. Passion without measure results in a pathetic, not to say deplorable, condition.[44]

The many, prey to inconstant passion, drift about and give no thought to the morrow.

20   Once born,
     they [the many] wish to live
     and to avoid (ἔχειν) their fates (μόρους);
     and they leave behind children
     so that deaths (μόρους) are born.

Philological notes: The term *to live* (ζώειν) may well import here "to enjoy life," i.e., to live out a mundane, pleasurable, and finally dissolute life. The word ὁ μόρος, like ἡ μοῖρα, means: share, portion, appointed lot, fate, destiny, doom, hence death; the fragment plays on its internal richness. Among the senses of ἔχειν are: to bear up against, to resist; to hold in, check, stop; to ward off. These seem to be the most appropriate here.

The many, having been born to life, wish merely to live (perhaps further: to live out a life of mindless desire); and they never attend, in thought and deed, to their imminent fate or death. But of course they do not live forever; ''and they leave children behind.'' Inasmuch as these children, however, are duplicates of themselves, they beget only lives of doom, only ''deaths.'' Hence in the birth of their children only ''deaths happen/come to be/are born (γενέσθαι).'' The many, in their unmeasured, mindless life, try to avoid their death, but only give birth to more death.

They drift about as in a daze.

> 1   Although this Logos is/Although this logos stands firm,
>   men are ever without comprehension. . . .
>   [I myself hearken to and set forth the physis in all.]
>   But for the rest of men,
>   all that they bring-to-pass while awake escapes their notice
>   just as so many things that in sleep they pass over.[45]

Men in general remain as unaware of what they do when they are awake as they are of what they do (i.e. move about) when they are asleep (i.e. dreaming). Their praxis, quite devoid of understanding and discernment, is mindless, like the twitching and turning of the sleeper. They are out of touch with the real world, with physis, with the one.

> 89   The waking share a cosmos one and common,
>   but the sleeping each turns aside into his own.

The many, like those asleep, have private worlds instead of the one cosmos.[46] Likewise, they have a private wisdom.

> 114 Those who would speak with understanding
>   should base themselves upon what is common to all things. . . .

> 2   Therefore it is necessary to follow the common;
>   but while the logos is common,
>   the many live as if they had a discernment of their own.

Genuine wisdom informs neither their words (B 114) nor their deeds (B 2). Hearkening not to the logos, they have a private wisdom—which is none at all. They are like the dreamer: each in his own world, out of touch with the common.

Instead of heeding the logos (discourse) on the logos, instead of placing their trust in the wise man, they learn from the wandering epic rhapsodist or, even worse, from public opinion.

104   What understanding (νόος) or discernment (φρήν) have they?
       They put their trust in the popular minstrels
       and take the mob for their teacher,
       not knowing that "most men are bad and very few good."

In fact, with respect to the wise man, the many behave like dogs.

97   Dogs alone bark at the one whom they do not know.

To bark at one unrecognized or uncomprehended is proper to dogs: but the many
so bark. They bark at the wise. Unaware, asleep, sluggish, foolish, even hostile,
the many do not base themselves upon the firm logos and so have no foundation
for word or deed.

87   A sluggish/foolish man is wont to be in a flutter at every logos.

(The rhetorical contrast between sluggish and fluttery should not be overlooked.)
The many heed not the logos (discourse) on the logos but flit from one opinion or
doctrine to another. With no firm ground on which to stand, they fly off in one
direction or another, according to the latest word from the minstrel or the mob.[47]
They may hear the wise logos but have no comprehension.

34   Fools, (though) hearing,
       are like the deaf;
       of them the saying bears witness:
       "Present, they are absent."

And although the wise man hearkens to the logos in everything, the foolish are
dull to it everywhere.

17   The many do not grasp such things as they come upon,
       nor do they comprehend them in learning (μαθόντες) them;
       but they seem to themselves (to do so).

Whatever they fortuitously encounter or even come to know through long experience, they fail to penetrate. So dull are they that they do not even realize their
own poverty. Although Zeus in physis is close to man in everything and men
thereby associate with him, they are still unaware.

72   With that one
       with whom they have most continuous intercourse
       they are at variance.

The many do not order themselves according to the ordering, according to Zeus,
They lack wisdom.

What is the root of their lethargic, even corrupt, state? By what basic delinquency do they fail to orient themselves towards the hidden yet manifest logos? Heraclitus answers:

86   Through lack of trust (ἀπιστίηι)
      it escapes being recognized/comprehended (γινώσκεσθαι).

The word ἀπιστία belongs to the πείθομαι family, which means: to let oneself be prevailed upon, to let oneself be persuaded. Correlative to this is that which induces, solicits, enlists, persuades, exercises compulsion through attraction. Hence πίστις imports: concord, agreement, avowal, faith, trust, congenial compliance.[48] Physis solicits men. But men do not recognize or comprehend it—because they do not have the attitude of acceptance, concord, availability. Or again:

18   If you do not expect (ἔλπηται) the unexpected, you will not find it. . . .

If he is ever to achieve understanding and discernment, one must expect, stand in readiness for, or be open to the inducement of physis. Of course the only place to find it is where it actually is—namely, in all things. The many do not find the logos in what they see and hear (cf. B 55 above).

107   Bad witnesses are eyes and ears for men
      if they have barbarian souls.

Philological note: although the βάρβαροι are those who do not comprehend the Greek language, the term often carries the same connotation that our word *barbarian* does; and from the connotation to the full metaphor is a short step. Men in general ''have barbarian souls'' and thus do not recognize/comprehend the logos in what they see and hear. The barbarian soul is the one unavailable for the fine solicitations of Zeus in the physis in all.[49]

The many lack wisdom: and their teachers are no better.

2. The Putatively Wise

Whether ancient or recent, the teachers of the Greeks do not teach what really counts. The famous wise men, accepted as such by the many, are not really wise at all.

28a   What views are accepted (δοκέοντα)
      the most accepted man (ὁ δοκιμώτατος)
      knows and maintains.[50]

Philological note: Although δόξα may have a subjective sense (opinion) or an objective sense (appearance), its radical sense is subjective. The verb δοκεῖν means: to seem to someone, upon deliberation; or, to deliberate, to decide a course of action appropriate to the claims of the data; or, to endorse a claim; hence, to let a claim stand; hence, to accept, admit, acknowledge. The word δοκιμώτατος (the man most accepted or acknowledged for something) would normally be a term of approbation, but its irony is evident here. "The most accepted man" among the Greeks must be the one accepted by them as wise. But what the putative wise man has to offer, in his own person or in that of his epigones, is just the "accepted views," the public platitudes which anyone could mouth. The severity of the Heraclitean dismissal of what men accept as wise doctrine is evident from his reversal of the genesis of it: although the common views begin in what the most accepted of men have to say, Heraclitus speaks as if the accepted opinions came first and *they* only accepted them. The most accepted teachers do not penetrate to the physis of all and hence, on its far side, to the divine wisdom which is more than sufficient and thus transcendent to the cosmic side.

> 108   Of all those whose accounts (λόγους) I have heard(about),
>   not one attains to the recognition/comprehension (γινώσκειν)
>   that (the) wise is different from all.

The popular teachers of the Greeks do not reach beyond what the many attain: they, too, lack wisdom. In other fragments Heraclitus assails them by name.
  The poets are fraudulent.

> 42   Homer deserves to be thrown out from the contests and thrashed,
>   and Archilochus likewise.

The contests are the recitations by rhapsodists or minstrels of the epic and lyric poets. But these traditional wise men deserve to be beaten off the stage with a stick. The immediate sense of the fragment may be that it is the reciters who deserve this, but the point is still the same. Traditional wisdom is a fraud, and its authors or purveyors deserve the treatment reserved for frauds. It is indeed reported that Heraclitus called Homer "an astrologer" (ἀστρολόγος) (B 105). The term obviously has a pejorative sense here: Homer pretends to wisdom but tells implausible stories.[51] He was so witless that he could not penetrate what the boys said to him:

> 56   Men are self-deceived in their knowledge of manifest things,
>   sort of like Homer, who came to be [considered] wiser than any other Greek;
>   for he was deceived by boys killing lice when they said to him:
>   "What we have seen and caught, that we leave behind,
>   and what we have neither seen nor caught, that we take along."

The putatively wisest of the Greeks was outwitted by lousy boys. And Hesiod is no better:

57 Teacher of most men is Hesiod:
   they feel sure that he knew most things—
   one who did not [even] manage to recognize daylight and night!
   For they are one.

Accepted by most men as knowledgeable and wise, Hesiod was neither.
   Neither the older nor the newer wise men manage to penetrate beneath the surface of things to physis.

40 Much-knowing (πολυμαθίη) does not teach understanding (νόον);
   otherwise it would have taught Hesiod and Pythagoras,
   and Xenophanes and Hecataeus besides.[52]

The contrast is between, on the one hand, extensive inquiry, knowledge of many particulars, or the wide experience so valued in archaic Greece, and, on the other hand, insight or penetration. Not *much*-knowing but *deep*-knowing is wisdom: not horizontal extension but vertical penetration. And the former does not teach the latter. Just as the soul has a "deep" measure (B 45), so must knowledge be deep. Wisdom, in contrast to wide experience (-μαθίη) with many particulars (πολυ-), is the penetration (νόος) through everything to the one. Extensive inquiry, like private discernment, is a fraudulent wisdom:

129 Pythagoras, son of Mnesarchus,
    practiced inquiry (ίστορίην) beyond all other men
    and, having made a selection of these writings,
    contrived for himself a wisdom of his own—
    a much-knowing, a harmful artifice.[53]

Heraclitus is even supposed to have called Pythagoras the "chief of cheats" (B 81). His teaching is a contrived wisdom; and anyone who follows him, a cheat. Heraclitus dryly remarks the irony of the term "lover of wisdom," invented by Pythagoras and claimed as a title by him and his followers.[54]

35 It befits men who are φιλόσοφοι
   to be inquirers into a great many things.[55]

They only *strive* after wisdom, these much-knowers; unlike the deep-knower, they have not attained it. It is fitting that those who call themselves only "*strivers* after wisdom" should be only *much*-knowers: the name is more appropriate than its claimants would imagine.
   Finally, those responsible for popular wisdom, though they reign supreme now, will not do so forever:

28b Justice will overtake
    the artificers of frauds
    and (their) witnesses.

The artificers are doubtless the original teachers; and the witnesses, those who vouch for their truthfulness, their epigones. Justice will put a stop to their harmful artifices and convict them; just when this will happen is not known, but it surely will. For divinity orders all things, whether men choose to hearken to it or not.[56]

The vigor of the Heraclitean confrontation with the many and with the putatively wise suggests the self-consciousness of a prophet (in the wide sense). In the name of what has overtaken him, he denounces the lack of appreciation of it in others. Indeed, his logos has a dimension not just of philosophical reflection but of religious prophecy as well. This will be taken up in due course. For now, however, interpretation may turn to the political sense of the Heraclitean experience.

C. The Polis and Wisdom

The correspondence to physis has a political significance. First, the wise man knows the ultimate foundation of the polis; second, he should exercise some sort of leadership in it.

Zeus orders the ordering which is the order of the cosmos. Zeus is the ultimate foundation upon which the order of the polis rests.

> 114   . . . a polis (bases itself) upon its law. . . .
>   [But] all human [= political] laws nourish themselves
>   upon one, the divine. . . .

The polis founds itself or relies upon what is common in it—its law. But this law itself feeds upon or bases itself upon *the* law. In other words, what measures the cosmos measures the measure in the polis. Without this founded foundation, the polis would disintegrate:

> 44   It behooves the people to fight for the law indeed,
>   as for the wall.

Just as the polis protects itself from external destruction by fighting for its wall, so it protects itself from internal corruption by fighting for its law—which founds and orders it and is the re-presentation of the divine law in it. The polis would cease to exist were it not to fight for its law, just as it would cease were it not to fight for its wall. The community is to order itself by its law which takes its measure from *the* law. The violation of order, measure, or justice destroys a community more surely than a raging fire does.

> 43   Hubris is to be quenched
>   more than a conflagration.

The term ὕβρις basically means the violation of proper limits, i.e., of justice. Given the prominence of justice (δίκη) and order (κόσμος) in the fragments, the sensitivity of Heraclitus to language, and the primordial intention of his logos, the term probably resounds here in its basic sense. However, it comes to mean an act of individual violence or aggravated personal assault, and this derivative sense may also be operative here. In that case the import of the fragment is this: wanton violence—like civil war—destroys a community even worse than fire. (The details of its contemporaneous allusion are lost for us.) In any case, the people ought to quench ὕβρις with even more energy than they would a conflagration.

In the polis, what is the place of the wise man? After all, wisdom has a social significance; he who penetrates to the oneness of the cosmos and corresponds to the one could hardly ignore his oneness with others and his consequent political import. His role—in the fragments that have come to us—ought to be one of definite influence, if not leadership. But the mediocre many, true to form, reject the wise man. The hometown of Heraclitus is a case in point:

> 121   The Ephesians would do well to hang themselves, every grown man,
>   and leave the polis to the beardless boys,
>   for they have banished Hermodorus, the ablest man among them, saying:
>   "No one shall be the ablest of us;
>   or, if there be such, let him be it elsewhere and among others."

The many cannot endure the one who rises above their level.[57] At any rate, Hermodorus the Able went to another city which welcomed his advice. "To a sensitive witness an event of this kind might well reveal the fundamental foulness of a society and open his eyes to the possibility that one man might be right and the whole people wrong. From such an experience may have sprung the pointed B 39:"[58]

> 39   In Priene lives Bias, son of Teutames,
>   who is of greater account (λόγος) than the rest.

The mediocre multitude makes itself of little account. In fact:

> 49   One is to me ten thousand
>   if he be the best.

If the people as a whole does not base itself and hence the law upon the divine law, then the wise man must protest:

> 33   It is also law to obey the counsel/will of one.

Although a law (νόμος) normally arises by popular consent (νόμος), it is—given, presumably, the inadequacy of this law—"also" law to submit oneself to the will or counsel of only "one" man: the ablest, the best, the wise.

Incidentally, nothing in these political fragments (or any others, for that matter) suggests an aristocratic contempt for a democratic polity. In fact, the "also" (χαί) in B 33 implies a recognition of the normal legitimacy of rule by the *dêmos*. As critique, these fragments show only the disgust, and maybe sadness, of the prophet, the man of vision, in the face of ordinary political realities. Popular religion inspires the same prophetic critique.

D. The Wise Critique of Popular Religion

It is impossible to reconstruct the full response of Heraclitus to popular religion. But the burden of that response is clear enough: on the basis of his experience (of physis and therefore Zeus), he abjures the common ideas and practices. Heraclitean wisdom knows a different standard.

> 14b They are initiated into the mysteries customary among men
>   in no holy manner.[59]

Whatever the mysteries in question, the basic critique is clear: what is commonly taken to be pious is really impious. Implicit here is a standard of the ''holy'' that the wise man follows.

In Heraclitus, interpretation finds the typical critique of compact religion by a more differentiated experience (cf. Xenophanes, B 14–16). That the more compact rites are ridiculous and ineffective, that men do not recognize or comprehend what the accepted powers really are—these are typical depreciations of an experience no longer vital for the critic.

> 5 They vainly purify themselves from blood
>   by staining themselves with blood,
>   as if one who had stepped into mud
>   were to cleanse himself with mud:
>   he would be taken to be mad
>   if any one of [normal] men were to notice him doing so.[60]
>   They pray, moreover, to such images as these
>   —as if one were to talk with houses—
>   knowing not at all what gods and heroes are.

The purification rite is as absurd as cleansing off mud with mud, and the prayers (involved in it?) are as absurd as talking with houses. Men do not recognize that their ''gods and heroes''—in contrast to the one, the wise, the Zeus of Heraclitus—are not at all the powers that count or are not, in the form that men accept, even powers at all. It is typical to absorb the functions of the older powers or even the powers themselves into the newer. The Heraclitean wise man rejects the old on the basis of his new standard.

On the basis of the new penetration to the divine and of well-measured praxis, ''the phallic cult and maenadism of Dionysus are the reverse of holy.''[61] Popular religion harbors not only absurdity but also blasphemy.[62] It is consummate irony that "Dionysus, for whom they go mad and revel," and "Hades," the power of death and destruction, "are the same" (B 15). "The madness and obscenity of Dionysiac worship are after all more appropriate than one would suppose, for . . . the apotheosis of drink and sensuality is in reality the god of death, the *daimôn* of the downward path of the soul to passion, pleasure, and dissolution. It is therefore only fitting to honor the god of destruction with the symbols of debauch."[63]

This whole Heraclitean critique is distinguishable but not separate from his philosophy, his politics, and his science. The religious dimension is neither totally compact with the others nor totally differentiated. The experience that comes to self-consciousness in the logos of Heraclitus is ambivalent. This ambivalence again appears in those fragments that show forth the destiny of the soul.

E. The Destiny of the Wise

The religious dimension of the Heraclitean logos comes to a climax in those fragments expressive of the destiny of the wise soul in contrast to that of the "barbarian" (B 107). Any logos or proclamation on the fate of man in death and on how man in some way determines his own fate is a doctrine of salvation—i.e., a religious doctrine. From the standpoint of philosophy, Heraclitus belongs to the company of philosophers of the Platonic type—e.g., Plotinus, Spinoza, and Jaspers—in whom the properly philosophic and the properly religious are distinguishable but inseparable. Heraclitus is ambivalent. The fragments now in question are difficult to decipher, and the interpretation here will restrict itself to their minimal sense.[64]

The prophetic character of the Heraclitean experience and logos has been noticed above. For the prophet, *all* men need awakening, incitement, even perturbation. Such a necessity takes on proverbial expression from the usages of husbandry:

11   With a blow is every animal driven to pasture.

"Even to do what they do naturally, willingly, and well, they need prodding."[65] And how much more do they need it in the face of "passion" (θυμός, B 85). The prophetic imperative, awakening everyone to what he is doing and should be doing (cf. B 1 *ad finem*), takes on its gravity and urgency as a prophecy on the destiny of man.

This destiny is ultimately his destiny in death. Any other one is not worth the dangers of proclamation for the prophet and, in any case, could hardly be called a destiny if ended by death. By means of symbols, prophecy proclaims that in death the core of man does not cease to be. (Incidentally, interpretation must not invent some death of the body; it is not a body which dies, but *man;* and the question is the fate of *man* in his death.) A gnome already considered in another context would—if the properly Heraclitean in it is more than the *coincidentia oppositorum*—have its major significance here:

> 62   Immortals mortals, mortals immortals,
> living each other's death
> and dying each other's life.

What is life for the mortal (= the living) is death for the immortal (= the preliving) so that the mortal lives the death of the immortal. And what is life for the immortal (= the postliving) is death for the mortal (= the living) so that the immortal lives the death of the mortal. Hence they live each other's death. Furthermore, what is death for the immortal (= the preliving) is life for the mortal (= the living) so that the immortal dies (as) the life of the mortal. And what is death for the mortal (= the living) is life for the immortal (= the postliving) so that the mortal dies (as) the life of the immortal. Hence they die each other's life. Altogether then, immortals are mortals and mortals are immortals. However complex, this fragment at least seems to identify the traditional *daimones* and men.[66] Two other fragments—whatever their specific import—imply that death does not destroy the core of man. The first:

> 98   (These) souls (αἱ ψυχαἱ) smell throughout Hades.

Philological note: the article αἱ is rare in such a construction and may well have demonstrative force ("these"); its exact import is impossible to determine. The sense of the fragment as a whole is likewise unclear: perhaps it alludes to fire; perhaps, more specifically, it imports that the wise soul goes up into the smoky region in death; perhaps, more generally, it alludes to sweet and obnoxious scents given to the good and the bad in death; perhaps something else. In any case, what *is* clear is this: there *are* souls in Hades. The second fragment is even more obscure:

> 96   Corpses are more rejectable than piles of crap.

Beyond "discardable," the adjective ἐκβλητότεροι may well import "despicable"; and the comparison seems to emphasize this. Corpses are better fit to throw away, are sooner to be cast out, and perhaps even are more repugnant than that which no one would hesitate to throw away.[67] What could this mean within the context that the other fragments provide? The following answer tries to avoid speculation. In archaic Greece, the ψυχή is evident only in its absence; i.e., it is that which departs at death and so accounts for the difference between the living and the dead.[68] Add to this the nonhuman character of the corpse, and the implication—actually worked out in the history of the word—is that the psyche is that which makes the human being precisely human. In other words, the psyche is the very core of man, that by virtue of which he *is* man. From the earlier negative psyche, the positive one that appears in the lyric poets and in Heraclitus develops. Now when *that* leaves, nothing human, nothing valuable, remains—so that corpses are worthless and maybe even offensive. On this interpretation, Heraclitus draws the radical conclusion from the positive notion of the psyche. What in the present context is most important in this fragment is what it says on its reverse side: that in and by death what is most to be treasured, the very selfhood of man, departs; and that which departs does not disintegrate, is not what is cast away to disintegrate. Man remains to enter into his destiny.

The immortality of the mortal comes to expression in another fragment whose plenitude is in inverse proportion to its length:

119   *Ethos*—to man—*daimon.*

Interpretation may distinguish two levels of significance. On the first, the soul continues to be in death. A *daimon,* whatever its function and status, is at least a deathless power (cf. B 79 above, and B 63 below). And the term *ethos,* the inner world of a man, may mean (as in B 78) something like essence or essential power (and thus name the same phenomenon as does psyche). In this case, Heraclitus attributes power transcendent to death to the essential power of man: the *ethos* of man is for him a *daimon.* The process of the differentiation of the mythic whole is the separation of that whole or of powers-in-the-whole and their absorption by quasi-independent or differentiated centers of power (e.g., a person, an organ, the rain). The power transcendent to death in the whole is here brought into the essence of man. Heraclitus identifies this power with what is proper to man. "This identification would imply the momentous break with the archaic inseparable connection of immortality with divinity. The soul, in order to be immortal, would not have to be" divine.[69] The soul of man transcends death: he remains to inherit his fate. On the second level of significance, this fate is what man makes for himself. The mythic whole is fate itself, and this fate concretizes or represents itself in the case of each man. The Greeks developed the idea of a personal *daimon* as the mediation of fate itself—a *daimon* which executes the fate, share, or portion of each man. Hence they attributed prosperity or misfortune in life to a *daimon.* But with a little differentiation, the lot of man is no longer a power-in-the-whole, no longer an aspect of fate as a whole. It becomes what a man as a quasi-independent agent makes for himself. What was once attributable to his *daimon* is now attributable to his own praxis. Furthermore: the term *ethos,* the inner world of a man, may mean that which he builds inside himself by what he does—his character. On this second level, then, Heraclitus attributes to character what brings a man his fate: his own *ethos* is for man his *daimon.* But since *daimon* was only the concretization of fate itself, it may now be said that character immediately is fate, that what a man makes *of* himself *is* what he makes *for* himself. Of course this fate or destiny must be a destiny in death; for—quite aside from what other fragments say—it is perfectly obvious that those who make *of* themselves the best and the bad do not certainly take possession in life of what they make *for* themselves. The equivalence is mediated by death.

And while the "barbarians" give way to passion and give no thought to the morrow, a surprise waits in store for them.

> 27   There awaits men having died
>   what [plural] they neither expect nor even imagine (δοκέουσιν).

Just what is it that awaits the bad soul? The answer appears as soon as interpretation remembers that, in contrast to the "dry soul" of the "wisest and best" (B 118), the soul of the bad man is "wet" (B 117). What he makes for himself (his destiny) is precisely what he has made of himself (his character): wetness, moisture, water. In other words, at the death of the barbarians, their souls further die. They become subhuman and so enter the transformations, the conversions, the elements (cf. B 31ab), eventually to be born (γενέσθαι) again as souls:

> 36   To come-to-be water is death for souls,
>   to come-to-be earth is death for water;
>   but then out of earth water comes-to-be (γίνεται),
>   and out of water, soul.[70]

This is the peculiar immortality of the bad soul, this is its fate. It stays within the cycle of elemental transformations.[71] To interpret *this* symbolism is not the present task, which is only to locate the prophetic proclamation within the Heraclitean logos as a whole. Another fragment, already treated, may well belong in the present context (and so have a significance slightly different from that explicated above):

> 20   Once born,
>   they [the many] wish to live [a heedless life?]
>   and to avoid their deaths/fates (μόρους);
>   and they leave children behind [i.e. they die]
>   so that there are born/come-to-be fates/deaths (μόρους γενέσθαι).

The barbarians do not pay heed in word or deed to the common fate *of* death and, further, to their fate *in* death. And when they die, their further death, the fate which *is* their character, is born; their souls come to be water. What they make *for* themselves, a "wet" destiny, is precisely what they have made *of* themselves, a "wet" soul. Their character, Dionysus, is the same as their fate, Hades (B 15). Such a fate is nothing to laugh at:

> 92   The Sibyl with raving mouth uttering mirthless (revelations). . . .[72]

The Sibyl, the ecstatic prophetess, brings to men the truth—usually unpleasant. Perhaps the voice of the Sibyl is a metaphor here for the prophetic logos of

Heraclitus. He is mad by the power of truth, ultimately by Zeus; and what he says to the barbarian souls is what they neither expect nor even imagine: what they would rather not hear.

While the many prefer the immediate gratification of desire, the few wise men prefer that which does not flow away (cf. αέναος = ἀεί-ναος):

> 29 The best choose one thing in place of all others:
> everlasting (ἀέναον) glory (κλέος) in place of mortal things;
> while the many stuff themselves like cattle.[73]

Unrestrained, domestic cattle will eat themselves into a fatal sickness. The barbarian will stuff himself until his soul dies into water; what he makes for himself in death is only death. But the fate of the wise is greater: everlasting glory/honor.

> 25 Greater deaths (μόροι) get greater portions (μοίρας).

The word play in this gnome is remarkable. The greater character and therefore fate or death (μόροι) obtains by fate or lot, has as its share, or takes possession of (λαγχάνουσι) the greater share or portion (μοίρας). And this greater destiny is the glory that never fails.[74]

Finally, what exactly *is* this greater portion of the wise? Heraclitus answers:

> 63 At God's need,
> they rise up and wakefully act as guardians
> of the living and the dead.[75]

Whatever the details import, the major overt sense of this fragment is clear enough: the wise souls come to be or act as (γίνεσθαι) the *daimones* of Hesiod's Golden Race, the vigilant watchmen over mortals, policing their conduct (*Erga*, 121–23, 248–55). The bad have a lesser fate. But *this* is the portion of the wise: their glory.

As with every eschatological or salvational utterance, interpretation must respect the symbolic character of these fragments. The aim here has only been to locate and to release their minimal overt sense within the whole of the Heraclitean logos. Interpretation of prophecy is not necessary for a philosophical appreciation.

Wisdom is the total correspondence of man to the measuring-out. One of the questions connected with this theme is the destiny of the wise. But this question introduces the problematic of the soul (ψυχή). And precisely that is the concern of Part III.

III. The Correlative Depth of Experience

The matter at issue in Heraclitus is physis. The correspondence to the matter is wisdom. And correlative to the matter is a self-experience which is as deep as physis is comprehensive. The experience of physis is an experience of self for two reasons: (1) physis comprehends (encompasses) the self as it does everything else; and (2) the self is the locus where (for the human self) physis comprehends (understands) itself. Human experience is, in terms of physis, the self-experience of physis. Hence any discourse on physis must eventually become a discourse on man. In the Heraclitean experience of physis a peculiar experience of man prevails. Correlative to the penetration to physis is a penetration into the self; the human experience of Physis is at once an experience of the depth of the self.

The differentiation of the compact (power)whole(cosmos) is, among other things, the release of the elements of the cosmos—nature, society, individual—into quasi-autonomous status. Thus the Greeks gradually differentiate the properly human from all other power in the whole, mainly under the title of ψυχή.[76] The differentiation of the mythic whole is the gradual delimitation of the core of man—his selfhood. Hence the greater the differentiation, the greater the experience of inwardness. (It may be useful to compare with the Greek the further, more intense experience of the individual self that defines the Renaissance and that gave to modern philosophy its subjective orientation.) A more intense experience of inwardness, of self-feeling and fascination therewith, appears in the lyric poets; but it is Heraclitus who first brings it to reflective logos.

> 101   I quested after my own self (ἐδιζησάμην ἐμεωυτόν).

Philological note: the verb δίζημαι imports a searching for someone or something already in some way known to be there; a longing as in a relation of love; and a contriving something. The first sense is relevant here. The term connotes an effort to secure the telos, to complete the quest—here, to find the self.[77] Heraclitus searched to find himself. "I sought myself." This is something new in Greek literature.[78]

This gnome is not an autobiographical report on introspection but rather witnesses to the experience of the psyche (self) as newly differentiated. The self as a quasi-independent region of power, as that which has its own peculiar logos or physis, had not been the matter of a reflective exploration among the Greeks. In contrast to *much* experience, Heraclitus searches *into* himself to find the full measure of his soul, to take possession of that inwardness. However:

> 45   You would not, going into (it), find the boundaries of the soul,
>   though you should march down every path—
>   so deep a logos does it have.

The newly differentiated region in experience is an inwardness: it comes to expression in the image of depth, in the image of a psyche with a "deep" logos. The attempt to secure the object of the search fails in principle. For the soul is more than its top layer, i.e., reflection, can master. It can only hint at its measure or constitution, its logos or physis. The psyche has a deep logos because—

whether the scroll gave any hint of this or not—it is the self-experience of physis. So it is that the experience of the psyche and of physis—both genitives in the dual sense—are correlative, are correlatively deep, and call for accounts analogously gnomic.

The logos of the soul or its physis is not only deep but also dynamic:

115   Soul has a logos which augments itself.

The physis of all is dynamism itself; hence the logos of the soul is dynamic. It is impossible to decipher the exact sense of this gnome.[79] Perhaps it is a hint that, in contrast to the negative psyche, which increases from without, the positive psyche is a center of power in its own right and grows deeper or more intense from within. Perhaps it is to be taken subjunctively: tne logos of the soul *in principle* increases, it *may* increase. And the one which *does* increase, i.e., becomes more *itself,* i.e., more *fiery,* i.e., more *dry,* is that of the wise man. Since fire constitutes *all* phenomena, to become more properly human, to augment oneself, is to become (more) dry; so it is that "the dry soul is wisest and best" (B 118). Reversely, the barbarian *diminishes* his soul; he buys whatever passion wants "at the price of soul" (B 85); he becomes *less* human; so it is that *his* soul is finally sublimated into "water" (B 36). In summary, the inwardness of man gathers itself into an order which in principle if not in fact augments itself.

Correlative to physis is the depth of experience, is the experience of a psyche that is deep and self-augmentive. And Heraclitus gives a hint of it.

Epilogue

The matter of Heraclitean experience is Being in a uniquely transitional configuration. In philosophical terms alone, it is absolute-Being be-ing beings—i.e., physis, presencing, upsurgence, Being as emergence. Physis as a whole encompasses the absolute (the "Zeus" of Heraclitus) and beings (the "all" of Heraclitus). Physis in the narrow sense would be physis in abstraction from the absolute and beings, emergence as if it were not precisely the absolute emerging in and as beings and beings in and from the absolute. It is physis as a whole which is at issue in Heraclitus. However, this matter has not only a philosophical sense but a religious, a scientific, and a political sense as well. These senses are neither totally compact (as in Hesiod, for instance) nor totally differentiated (as for us). They are distinguishable though inseparable. For Heraclitus, in other words, Being or physis has a configuration transitional between compactness (the mythic) and differentiation (the philosophic alone, the scientific alone, and so on). This transition decisively occurred in the West only once. Hence, for a philosophical interpretation, the matter at issue in Heraclitus is Being in a uniquely transitional configuration. The present interpretation has sought to explicate the fragments according to an interpretive inner logic; the original organization of the scroll cannot be reconstructed, but its operative poles were evidently physis, sophia, and psyche.[80] This interpretation has developed in the Heideggerian spirit. This means, first, that it oriented itself by the Being-question; and second, that it subsumed a topology of certain basic words, i.e., it attempted to hear them out of their original *topos* and hence in their full expressive power.

If the work of Heidegger has given guidance to this interpretation, then the question may be raised as to the relation between the matter at issue for Heraclitus and that for Heidegger. An answer to this difficult question will serve to delimit the Heraclitean achievement in another way. How does Heidegger "define" himself in relation to Heraclitus?

However named, only one matter was ever at issue for Heidegger: Being, the meaning of Being, disclosure (*Erschlossenheit*), time (*Zeit* or *Temporalität*), the not-a-thing (*Nichts*), the clearing (*Lichtung*), the appropriative event (*Ereignis*), truth or aletheia (*Unverborgenheit, das Wesen der Unverborgenheit, Entbergung*), the process-of-presencing (*Anwesen*), and so on. This matter, he says, though operative, remains "unthought" in the history of philosophy; and so he opposes himself to that historical "forgottenness of Being" and, while "retrieving" what was nonetheless operative in it, seeks to begin anew. According to Heidegger the matter for traditional philosophy is stable or constant presencehood (*Anwesenheit*); constancy of presence (*die Beständigkeit des Anwesens*); mere stability (*Beständung*); the present (*Gegenwart*) as a constant; permanent or static presentness; and so on. This presencehood has the consummate name of the eternal recurrence of the same and, as the matter common to traditional philosophy, both original and epigonic, may be called presence-at-hand (*Vorhandenheit*). But there is more: after the early Greeks, philosophy conceives this constant presencehood (*Anwesenheit*) as just another, even if highest, being, which then serves as the ground for all other beings. In concerning itself with this, tradition forgets the process of presencing (*Anwesen*), the temporal event, the temporality, which first renders possible something like presencehood or the stable present. Only on the basis of presenc*ing* does stable presentness make sense. This presencing process is the process of aletheia or unconcealing (*das Wesen der Unverborgenheit, Entbergung*); with it happens the aletheia or unconcealedness (*Unverborgenheit*) of beings. Traditional philosophy remains oblivious to all this. But even more than that, it remains oblivious to the essential (*das Wesende*)—namely, that aletheia itself comes to pass out of a concealedness (*Verborgenheit*) or concealment (*Verbergung*): out of *lethe*. Not only does the history of philosophy fail to think the region in which something like constancy of presence may congeal (to wit, aletheia or presencing), it more essentially fails to think the *lethe* out of which and within which aletheia eventuates. But this aletheia and this *lethe* is the proper matter for Heideggerian thought.

According to him an active forgottenness is already underway in Plato. But in the early Greeks—Anaximander, Parmenides, and Heraclitus, all of whom he interprets to say the same—evidently only a passive forgottenness prevails. Neither, on the one hand, have they yet reduced presencing (*Anwesen*) to presencehood (*Anwesenheit*), nor, on the other hand, have they yet thought the *lethe* in presencing. It seems that they *experience* the process of presencing or of aletheia, but they do not *think* the *lethe*. Their basic words—Χρεών, Μοῖρα, Λόγος—witness to an experience of presencing which is yet oblivious to it *as* presencing *out of* and *within* the nonpresented, the concealed, the "mystery." In them, the issue hangs in the balance. Thus Heidegger remains ambivalent toward the early Greeks and toward Heraclitus in particular: the matter of *his* thought both is and is not the same as theirs as interpreted by him. For Heidegger, the beginning of philosophy only intimated the matter that must be at issue in the new beginning. Thus, in Heideggerian terms, the matters of Heraclitean thought and of his own are the same insofar as they are both presencing, but are ultimately different insofar as Heraclitus pays no heed to the *lethe* in presencing.

However, interpretation cannot rest content with this. For this is only a report on the Heideggerian text, and not an engagement (*Auseinandersetzung*) with both thinkers or an engagement in the matter for their thought. Interpretation must here make a decision. *Either* we become Heideggerian, i.e., we simply take over his reading of the history of philosophy and proceed from there; *or* we enter into the spirit of Heidegger, i.e., we try to appreciate the whole history of philosophy out of its most primordial matter. It is incumbent upon us to choose the latter. Hence this interpretation of the relation of Heidegger and Heraclitus will differ from Heidegger's own determination. Rather than read the history of philosophy out of Heidegger's "position," it will read Heidegger within that history—or, more modestly, within that history as it presents itself to one who has tried to engage its matter.

Far from having forgotten it, the philosophical tradition has always thought Being—but *Being as the absolute*. What Heidegger calls constancy of presence is, in a sense, a constant presence: it is precisely what has long since been called eternity, i.e., total nowness, the simultaneous and complete self-activity of Being, absolute Being itself. Heidegger recognizes that Being in the traditional sense differs from Being in his sense, but he misapprehends the difference. (That is certainly understandable in great thinkers, who, in giving word to their own unique vision, rarely regard another according to his. The whole question of hermeneutics arises but cannot be pursued here.) But read within the history of philosophy, Heideggerian thought has as its matter not absolute Being but rather the "be-ing" in "absolute Being be-ing beings." What Heidegger thinks is the emerging in "the absolute emerging in and as beings and beings in and from the absolute." Heidegger thinks *Being as emergence* and (with the qualifications noted below) takes it in a quasi-autonomous fashion. That is to say, the matter for Heideggerian thought is, in general, physis in the narrow sense.

The relation of Heidegger to the tradition is complex. He thinks Being as emergence, the presencing process, aletheia, or physis. In his earlier works, Being is always the Being of beings. But in his later works, beings (though never *Dasein*) seem to be suspended in favor of historical experiences with Being. Otherwise put: the later Heidegger thinks presencing or physis in abstraction from the side of beings (the "all" of Heraclitus). Furthermore: whether or not beings be bracketed, presencing is, in traditional terms, finite, or better, it is the very happening of finitude—the Absolute presencing and absencing itself at once. Indeed, Heidegger has written that "Being itself in its essencing is finite."[81] But if he thinks Being as finite, then the traditional absolute is suspended. Otherwise put: Heidegger thinks presencing or physis in abstraction from the side of the Absolute (the "Zeus" of Heraclitus). Nevertheless, he subtly recognizes the traditional Being-absolutely. For presencing (*Anwesen*) is always a presencing out of a concealment (*Verbergung*); *what Heidegger calls lethe, tradition calls Being-as-the-absolute.* And it is indeed *the* mystery. The philosopher of the Black Forest draws nigh to—but draws back from—the traditional absolute. Thus the matter of his thought is, with these qualifications, physis in the narrow sense.

As Heidegger thinks the process of presencing or timing, his characterization of traditional Being as permanent presencehood (*Anwesenheit*) is at once a recognition of its eternality and a depreciation of eternality by the standard of time. *If* the process of time be taken in abstraction from absolute or eternal Being and be made the standard for thinking, *then* the eternal will appear as static, as constant presentness, as stability of presence. But with the activity of eternality as the standard, Time taken concretely appears precisely as this activity present and at once absent, as eternity in its less than total power. In this way, again, the matter for Heideggerian thought is physis with the nuances mentioned above.

The relation of Heidegger and Heraclitus is clear. The matter for Heidegger is the same as that for Heraclitus in its *philosophic* sense alone. Heidegger thinks physis: but in *this* physis the religious, the scientific, and the political senses as well as the ambivalent everlasting character of the physis of Heraclitus are inoperative. Thus the Heideggerian matter and the Heraclitean are the same and not the same.

The ostensibly ready formulae of this epilogue should not deceive. They do not intend to put a stop to philosophizing, whether in the original or in the interpretive mode. But two points, for me, deserve special mention. First, the interpretation here of Heidegger's thought, including his reading of traditional philosophy, gives no hint of its enormous fecundity. Anyone who has engaged Heidegger will know what this means. Second, the word *absolute* and its cognates aim not to arrest questioning but to give a sign—as the word *Lethe* does in Heidegger—of that region which is most worthy of questioning. Anyone who has engaged the tradition will know what this means.

To interpret is, in the end, to appropriate: to let become our own that which the author has, in his generosity, allowed to speak through his text. Like the author, the interpreter and *his* companions must give ear to a voice beyond the subjectivity of all three. We interpret, speaking generously with each other, only insofar as, in our silence, we hearken to that more generous logos.

7

HERACLITUS: FIRE, DREAM, AND ORACLE

Frank A. Capuzzi

How do philosophers regard themselves? As academics, mostly. But also as the spiritual heirs of Socrates. This makes an interesting paradox.

Modern academics take money for what they do. This goes for the very greatest of our teachers. Socrates, our presumed forebear, castigated the Sophists for similar behavior. The Sophists, like their modern counterparts, were often urbane, intelligent, and well-intentioned thinkers. Socrates—forgive the blasphemy—was the town loafer. Even Aristotle, with his reputation as a natty dresser and tutor to emperors, was stamped more in the mold of a Sophist than a Socrates.

As a matter of fact, we philosophers have traditionally derived much of our self-image from old Aristotle. We are gentle, kindly fellows, keepers of the penthouse garden in everyman's ivory tower. Really, what would we do with a character like Socrates? We know about him from Plato's writing. There we get a glimpse into his nature. We discover his ironic humility—certainly not *our* humility—as a subtle form of arrogance. It is not always easy to see how Plato's words quietly reveal Socratic hubris. But then, Plato's love for Socrates is easier to understand than Plato's hatred of Socrates. Perhaps Socrates gave even Plato hives.

But if our self-concept is questionable in its most explicit form, how much more questionable is it with respect to what is unexpressed? Is there anything we have failed to notice in the long history of our argumentative fraternity?

Merleau-Ponty remarks somewhere that philosophy is concerned mostly with philosophy. It is an introspective, not to say narcissistic enterprise. It has been so from the beginning. Practically all the thinkers we call "Presocratic philosophers" exhibit a kind of mystical self-awareness. Their deep sensitivity to their task and to themselves is bound up with what we presumptuously call their philosophy. Happily or unhappily, they are our true spiritual ancestors. They are also, as far as we know, the first real thinkers of the west.

Heraclitus is the worst of the lot. If his writings were any more obscure they would be funny. Heidegger notes that Heraclitus had this reputation almost from the start.[1] So did Heidegger. In fact, modern critics have sometimes hinted that Heidegger and Heraclitus deserve each other.

It is in fact a fortunate combination. Heraclitus' massive arrogance is straightforward. "Heraclitus was proud," Nietzsche remarks, "and when a philosopher exhibits pride, it is a great pride indeed."[2] Heidegger's arrogance, because it always remains tied to what is thought in thinking, is less obtrusive. For the one, Logos is a haughty trademark. For the other, Being of beings is a relentless theme. In both cases, the philosopher is intimately bound into what yields itself up to thinking. This intimacy is the key to Heraclitus' apparent egotism, and the basis for Heidegger's insistence upon philosophy's poetic character. Through the one who thinks, thinking moves forward, is underway. Where is it going? Back to the thinker, as a poem ultimately returns to the poet. There is no progress in thinking. There is only a return to what most properly belongs to the one who thinks. It is too near for words. It is indescribably distant. The journey there is endless, because it is circular. Thinking is a continual departure, out of oneself, and a constant return home, back to oneself. When this journey is reported in words, it sounds arrogant. Perhaps that is the real, rock-bottom definition of philosophy.

The way is the same, but each journey around the circle is different. The thinker is a traveller along this way, but also is the way, and so is different and the same at once. Still, he is not the completing of the way. For Heraclitus, the way is completed in Logos. Logos is not the thinker. It is to-be-thought. But it is nearest the thinker, and describes his journey. This distance between thinker and to-be-thought is infinitesimal, and therefore absolute. Its continual tension generates energy. The boundless energy of this difference impels thought to a leap. The leap of thought is a gesture of hope. But a chasm threatens, and all thinking contains an element of despair. I either think or I do not think. Nobody thinks for me. The chasm, or the difference, defines my singularity as it draws my thought toward it. Its chaotic blackness, impelling my thought, is philosophical imagination. Its hidden expression is mythos. Every thoughtful journey covers the difference over in words, and thus provokes another journey. The description of each separate journey, as the hidden expression of the difference, is mythos. Such descriptions are sometimes emblematic in a philosophy. "Fire" is a Heraclitean mythos that describes the thinker and his thought; "dream" is another mythos by which the thinker locates himself; and "oracle" is Heraclitus' profoundest expression of himself and his destiny. Let us consider them in this order.

I. Fire

Fire is a constant theme for Heraclitus. It appears in his statements on the nature of the universe. It shows up in his frequent references to the sun. It sometimes takes on a personal meaning, as part of an admonition (not to overstep certain limits), or as an element of dream. Heraclitus lets fire assume a variety of specific roles: thunderbolt, boundary, light, and pain. The list is not exhaustive. But nowhere does he explain just how he understands fire. What does become clear, though, is Heraclitus' passion in the use of this image. He is through and through a philosopher of fire. He has been called a "promethean hero of thought (who) brings fire to sleeping mortals."[3] This is not meant to be a passing compliment.

Prometheus, closely associated with the erotic imagery of fire, is himself an erotic hero. Gaston Bachelard says of him that he is "a vigorous lover rather than an intelligent philosopher."[4] We know from Plato that the two traits are not exclusive of each other. Heraclitus is a lover because he is a philosopher. When these two words are spoken basically, as they must be in describing Heraclitus, they are redundant. He is supremely erotic. He is fiery in pursuit of Logos. We find in him an intense light characteristic of the true thinker. Fire is his milieu, from the cosmic to the personal.

Apropos of cosmic fire, Heraclitus speaks out in Fr. B 30. He tells us of a "cosmos" uncreated by either gods or men, an eternal, "ever-living fire" (πῦρ ἀείζωον) that kindles limits and extinguishes them. This cosmos is the same for all, and thus a foundation for the unity of all. That Heraclitus sees room for such a unifying foundation is clear from other remarks he makes (Cf. Fr. B 8, B 10, and B 50). Eugen Fink supports this conclusion when he says:

> Κόσμος, as the beautiful joining of πάντα is that which shines in the fireshine. To this extent, therefore, the first and last halves of the saying (sc. Fr. 30) have a great deal to do with each other. The fire is poetic, productive power. Gods and men are beings who bring to appearance and reveal, but only because there is the fire—toward which they stand in an outstanding relation.[5]

Cosmos is a joining. As a joining it is similar to τὸ χρεών of Anaximander and ἡ Δίκη of Parmenides. These are expressive of the jointure. The jointure can be spoken only in a mythos. For Heraclitus, this mythos is embodied in the words πῦρ ἀείζωον. As Fink says, this eternal fire is a "making" (a *poiesis*) that grounds all subsequent "making," whether human or divine.[6] This truly Promethean insight of Heraclitus' guides the remainder of his thought. Humans (and gods) depend upon the ever-living fire for the *poiesis* proper to them: bringing to appearance and revealing what is. This *poiesis* identifies humanity's poetic power with respect to what is, or what lies before. The lighting of what lies before is called truth. Truth as lighting revelation is at the same time a concealing. The lighting disappears in favor of what is lighted in it. Thus the lighting is concealed in truth. To look directly into the light is to go blind, to see nothing. The limits of lighting are utter darkness, or blindness. In blindness the limits of cosmos come to be. The lighting of the cosmos joins all to all in revealing-concealing. This lighting is the jointure, or the unity of all. As the jointure, it also sets limits. Setting limits and extinguishing them belongs to its character as ever-living fire. This active contradiction is Logos.

Logos is ever-living fire. Ever-living fire fashions the cosmos in a fictive unity of measure, and this signifies the dispensation of limits. The dispensation of limits in light means the onset of darkness. Lighting, which makes vision possible, also contains the negation of vision. Seeing, in its manifold meanings, implicates truth. But truth is a lighting that reveals and conceals. Thought in terms of its limits, absolute seeing is absolute blindness. The one who stands within the dispensation of limits is the Seer, the one who sees. Naturally, the Seer is blind. Even the highest human (and for that matter, divine) *poiesis* cannot escape this pathos. It is the unique and inevitable pathos of truth.

For the Greek, truth is represented by Apollo, the sun. The sun has long been an image of truth. We say that things done openly are done in daylight. We pass bills on honesty in government and call them "sunshine" bills. In Fragment B 6 Heraclitus tells us that the sun is new every day. What does this mean? We can hardly miss its poetic meaning, which indicates that the emptiness of night must be filled anew each day. In the night, we rely upon a promise of the new dawn. Even the fires we light are symbols of this hope. But the dawn is a gift which need not come. This is true for the scientist and for the peasant. The lighting of truth is also a promise which need not be fulfilled. When truth comes, it comes as a gift, and so is new each time. But then, in Fr. B 3, Heraclitus says that the sun is as wide as a human foot. More delicately, we could say that the sun may be covered by a hand. For all its brilliance, for all its real and symbolic power, the sun has very definite limits.

In fact, in Fr. B 94 Heraclitus defines those limits for us: "Sun will not overstep his measures, otherwise the Erinyes, ministers of Justice, will find him out." The Erinyes were spirits of vengeance. They punished disobedience to parents, perjury, inhospitality, and, especially, murder. They were furious, fearful deities, so fearful that people did not dare call them by their real name. They were creatures of the night, whose home was Hades, creatures of the earth, who lived in the blackest depths of Tartarus. As merciless tormentors of the unexpiated, the Erinyes are ministers of Justice (*Dikē*), and are therefore governed by the jointure. Limits are dispensed through the jointure and are guarded by the Erinyes, spirits of darkness. They are outside the limits. To shatter the limits is to invite darkness. As the Greek tragic poets realized, the Erinyes are not easy to control once they have been set loose.

But this warning does not complete Heraclitus' list of warnings. He also has something to say about fire and hubris. In Fr. B 43 he piously tells us to avoid hubris, to avoid it more than burning fire. This strikes us as a piece of effrontery. Who was ever more hubristic than this mocker of great men, this proud critic of human folly? What is hubris, and what is its relation to fire?

Hubris can blind a person to himself. It harbors tragedy because it is the one human passion that conceals totally what ought to be revealed. The aftermath of hubris is utter, stark revelation, sometimes tragic, always difficult. Oedipus, who did not know about his hubris, saw it disappear with the advent of total, unremitting self-knowledge. This light is so brilliant that it blinds. And so Oedipus, in confronting self-knowledge—the fire that blinds—becomes a Seer. Hubris is a concealing that abides in untruth, while self-knowledge is a revealing that blinds. The Seer Heraclitus says: ''I searched myself out.'' His self-searching is also a glimpse into the fire, that is, a glimpse into the cosmos ruled by *Dikē*. For Heraclitus, *Dikē*'s role is superceded by Logos, through which all things are one. The fire into which Heraclitus stares is a mirror, reflecting Logos. It is also Heraclitus himself. This sounds utterly absurd.

Perhaps we are really too far from the essence of fire ever to understand it. For us, fire has a limited array of meanings, and each of these meanings is extrinsic to our contemporary lives. In America, many people yearn nostalgically for a ''fireplace,'' where they can burn logs in winter. This is for romantic effect, not heat. Accidental fire still holds mortal terrors, though it occurs far less frequently than in ages past. Our automobiles run on fire, it is true, and the energy that comes from ''burning'' this or that is a major issue in our lives. But neither of these puts us in a direct relationship with fire, where we have to tend it, and where we can watch its progress. Except on rare occasions such fires are anachronistic. Our Prometheus has stolen electricity from the gods, not fire. The lineage of the arts has been altered. This is intended to be a peaceful reflection on the nature of fire.

But human beings are hardly peaceful. While most fires are anachronistic, unless they serve machines, there are some pure fires that are right up to date. Many of our own contemporaries have seen and felt the fires of conquest. They have learned first hand that no fire is too horrible in time of war. Napalm sticks closely to the flesh it burns, searing to the bone. The nuclear bomb melts the eyes that behold it. Such fire is an unavoidable consequence of war, because war is an utterly human event. Just as some people are capable of speaking poetically about war, so others can speak poetically about napalm and nuclear fireballs. It is doubtful whether such poetry brings insight.

But there are other kinds of fire that are no longer meaningful or up to date. We speak of ''beacons in the night'' or ''guiding lights'', but can no longer understand the signal fire. Radio has replaced it. Another obsolete fire is the watchfire. This is the sort of fire people who are camped far from home gather around for warmth and security. It is the fire shepherds might build, or guards in an encampment. Heidegger calls us the shepherds or guardians of Being. With an effort of imagination, we can extend this image to include the watchfire around which guardians gather in the night. It is a reassuring sign among friends and familiar pastures, but a dangerous sign in the land of enemies. The fire, as a lighting place for guards, opens a space of familiarity in the midst of what is strange, and in this way fosters a being-at-home in the prevailing homelessness. Is there anything similar in modern experience? There is, but only as a dream. This is the dream of a hearthfire. Even the guardians who stand about the watchfire dream of home and being at home. Their fire is an extension of home, derives from the fires of home. It is a sentimental cliché when the guardian who wanders from home exhorts those who remain behind to "keep the home fires burning." We sometimes fail to see the truth in sentimental clichés.

Aristotle himself is the source for a classic piece of sentimentality concerning Heraclitus. The story (taken from *de part. anim.* A 5, 645 a 17) is a simple one. Some tourists come to see the thinker and find him warming himself at a kitchen fire. They are rather embarrassed to see so great a man engaged in so ordinary an occupation, and hurriedly excuse themselves. Heraclitus good-naturedly invites them to stay by assuring them that the gods are present there, too. We aren't told whether the tourists accepted this invitation. Aristotle uses the story to say something about Heraclitus' primitive understanding of nature (that fire has a 'soul', etc.). Heidegger, in his *Letter On Humanism,* uses it to chide superficial curiosity, but also to explain the at-homeness of Heraclitus' being-at-home. According to Heidegger, the visitors must come to learn that this lighting of what is utterly familiar, even banal, also conceals the abode of what is most unfamiliar. The daimonic is present in the familiar. The essence of familiarity is home. The heart of home is the hearthfire, dream of a wakeful, watchful guardian. What is most familiar, the essence of home (ἦθος), is also the most mysterious. One is most at home with himself. The self is the essence of familiarity. But Heraclitus tells us that a man's ethos is his daimon—the essence of what is most familiar is the unfamiliar itself, the divine. He also asserts that he sought himself out, though he fails to tell us just why he did this. We assume he was not searching for the familiar. But that is a gratuitous assumption. When we look inward, we become tourists to ourselves, even though we are most at home with ourselves. We see the ordinary and are dismayed. The essence of our being-at-home is a commonplace reverie before the hearth, where only thought evokes what is uncanny. The tourist departs, demoralized, but the thinker remains to wonder at what is passing strange. The thinker, Heidegger says, is a guardian of Being. His vision of the reveries at home is itself a dream kindled at night around a watch-fire. The guardian, who watches by his fire, must not fall asleep.This is difficult to understand. How are we to describe a nocturnal fire-dream apart from sleep? Much depends upon this question. It contains the whole meaning of Heraclitean self-knowledge.

II. Dream

Heraclitus, it seems, was a splenetic fellow. He was always lodging some complaint or other—against penitents, suppliants, predecessors, contemporaries, and the world in general. But the chief object of his sarcasm was a group of unfortunates he called *anthropoi,* "ordinary men." Ordinary men come in for a special kind of Heraclitean treatment. They are accused of dullness, somnolence, and waywardness of all sorts. Or so it would appear from Fr. B 1, in which the philosopher announces his exasperation.

The fragment talks about Logos, *anthropos,* and the fundamental relationship between them. It also refers to waking and sleeping. Amid this diversity of topics, Heraclitus makes his apparently exaggerated claims.

He first tells us that ordinary men are opaque, dense as it were. They are and remain "uncomprehending" of the Logos, both before *and* after they have heard it. With respect to Logos, ordinary men seem to be basically "uncomprehending." Fr. B 34 says something similar. Both before and after they hear it, ordinary men do not comprehend the Logos. Even after Heraclitus explains how things come to be, and what makes a thing the thing it is, and . . . even after all that, ordinary men *still* fail to comprehend the Logos. Ordinary men, we conclude, are dolts and dullards.

Our conclusion could not be more misleading. The word translated "uncomprehending," which describes *anthropoi*'s relation to Logos, is in Greek ἀξύνετος. It is related to ξυνός, which is simply the adjectival form of σύν, "with." The implication in ξυνός is "together with", "common", "bound into one with". This idea of being together with is, in turn, closely related to ξυνιήμι, "bring together", and is in fact the basic idea underlying the latter. Although Heraclitus time and again emphasizes the unity in opposition and the harmonics of joining (Cf. Fr. B 8, B 10, and B 67, for example), translators fail to note that the same emphasis resounds in the word ἀξύνετος. One can see the consequences of this oversight by examining Fr. B 80. Kirk and Raven's translation says "It is necessary to know that war is common and right is strife and that all things happen by strife and necessity." The Diels-Kranz translation is practically identical. I do not mean to imply that these translations are incorrect. I do mean to imply that they fail to reveal anything significant about Heraclitus' thought.

The fragment refers to war (πόλεμος), discord (ἔρις), and justice (δίκη). It equates discord and justice (according to the fragment, *eris is dikē*). This tallies with what we know about Heraclitus' accent on the joining of what is opposed, or the unity of opposites. Besides, if we examine the writings of Parmenides, we learn that Heidegger's translation of *dikē* as "jointure" is quite correct. The "rightness" implied in *dikē* is the unity implied in the word "with." This concept dominates completely in the Greek word ξυνός. It makes perfect sense for Heraclitus to say that war is ξυνός. War is a kind of discord, maximum discord if you will. Τὸ ξυνόν, like *dikē*, is a joining. Discord and joining are the same, though (as Heidegger points out) not identical. Ξυνός does not mean "common" in the sense of "usual" or even "pertaining to all." Rather, it signifies the bringing together of what is in the jointure of Being. This is what Heraclitus calls Logos. No wonder, then, that Heraclitus substitutes an older idea for *dikē* in the latter part of the fragment. He says that all things come to be through discord (ἔρις) and χρέων. Τὸ χρέων is Anaximander's word for the joining that is *dikē* and Logos.

If we return now to Fr. B 1 and to our consideration of ἀξύνετος, we can say with some confidence that Heraclitus is not nearly so misanthropic as he seems. He is merely trying to tell us something essential about human being. *Anthropoi,* "ordinary men," inevitably and essentially have a certain kind of relation to Logos. That is, they are ἀξύνετοι with respect to Logos. This means that in and of themselves they lack the unity that Logos implies. This is not something they can escape by a simple act of will.

Heraclitus is not raging against the stupidity of other people. After all, being learned is no guarantee against being ἀξύνετος (Cf. Fr. B 40). To accuse others of stupidity, Heraclitus would have to assume that they were unable to hear and understand not only his explanations, but all explanations. He does not make this charge. Even assuming that Heraclitus, when he says "experience", means something similar to our understanding of the word, he still allows that ordinary men act as if they have no experience even after they have experienced his explanatory words and deeds. This curious statement hardly constitutes a blanket charge of stupidity.

Nonetheless, Heraclitus clearly implies that while *anthropoi* are ἀξύνετοι (of the Logos), he himself is ξύνετος—"comprehending." He deserves no praise for this distinction, just as the others deserve no blame for their condition. It is a difference that rests in the thoughtful destiny Heraclitus carries out. He actively takes up this destiny in service to Logos. The thinker simply maintains himself in the right relation to the matter for thought. For Heraclitus, what is to be thought is addressed in Logos. As a thinker, Heraclitus will necessarily be ξύνετος with regard to Logos. In Fr. B 2, Heraclitus affirms that Logos is indeed ξυνός. Logos says the jointure. The thinker hears, and knows it is wise to agree that all things are "one." But the thinker also knows that there is a difference between τὰ πάντα and ὁ Λόγος. Heidegger speaks of it as a difference between Being and beings. It is this difference to which Heraclitus is pointing when he identifies "ordinary men" as ἀξύνετοι and himself as ξύνετος. In Fr. B 1 Heraclitus tries to explain the nature of this difference by a reference to waking, sleeping, and forgetting. The crux of this explanation lies in a proper understanding of its common element: the dream.

The philosopher's function is to pursue truth. Truth has always had an uneasy relationship with dream. Dreams are patently untrue. They are dangerous, wispy stuff. But even a hardened collector of provable propositions is capable of dreaming. He might even dream about truth. In fact, this might be the dream that rules his entire life. It is a dream he has when most awake, most active, and most himself. This has nothing to do with "aspirations" or "life-goals." Everyone knows that philosophers, like poets and other primitives, are "dreamers." Not everyone is willing to admit the truth of this cliché.

The night dream evaporates quicker than morning mist. The underside of every dream is oblivion. Yet we believe that these nightly lantern shows of the psyche are highly significant, so significant that some people expend much time and energy reconstructing them. We fail to notice how far dream qualities enter into our waking lives, and prefer to make a distinction between a diurnal mechanism and a nocturnal mechanism. The one is rational, the other irrational. Sometimes they become confused. This confusion we call neurosis or psychosis.

While we are willing to accept the notion that night dreams and mental illness represent a compromise between these two mechanisms, we are generally unwilling to attribute the activities of our waking, rational life to the same sort of compromise. That we should do so is neither a new nor a startling suggestion.[8]

Our conscious life is structured like a dream. Forgetfulness adheres to it like a heavy fog. Most of life's gestures are dream-gestures that conceal us as they reveal us. Even "seeing the truth" is at times a tenuous, dreamlike process evolved in the twilight hours of relaxation. We are, in short, creatures of the dream. It forms us and shapes our lives. It draws us along in its symbolic destiny. Blinded by the circle of fire we call ourselves, our self-consciousness, we do not see the dream. We merely act upon it. The dream roots out falsehood, determines truth, sings victory hymns, or drives a suicidal knife into our vitals. We die, as we live, victims of the dream.

Of course, Heraclitus was no Freud. But his framing of the question is equally provocative. He says that ordinary men "fail to notice what they do after they wake up just as they forget what they do when asleep." This refers directly to dream and our relation to it.

"Waking up" has nothing to do with hearing clear, scientific explanations of what things are and how they come to be. Rather, it depends upon remembering what has been forgotten. Memory belongs to daylight. It is the active bringing into appearance of what lies concealed. What is concealed is not simply hidden, but has been forgotten. It can be forgotten only because it belongs primordially to memory. It belongs to memory because it can be brought to light. Memory is the creative preservation of this possibility. To remember is to be as one awake, possessing a certain power that one does not possess when asleep. Heraclitus says that ordinary men do not remember what they "do" when they are awake, i.e., they act like sleepers. In Fr. B 73 he says that this is precisely how they should *not* act. Forgetting is an essential part of sleep. What is forgotten? What men "do". What do they do?

Earlier we learned that human *poiesis* derives from the poetic power of πῦρ ἀείζωον. The ever-living fire describes Heraclitus' understanding of Logos. As eternal fire, Logos is the lighting. Lighting, as bringing what is (τὸ ὄν) forward into shining appearance, is most characteristic of human being. What is, in its appearance, obscures the lighting. Lighting—the *poiesis* to which Heraclitus is referring—is therefore forgotten. This forgetfulness too belongs to human being. It resembles the forgetfulness of one asleep. In their daily lives, ordinary men are like the sleeper who, although he has "kindled a light for himself (Fr. 26)," remains essentially in oblivion. But if the lighting belongs to memory as that which makes memory possible, then even the lighting that takes place in sleep is not *only* oblivion. It can be remembered, i.e., brought back into shining appearance. In both cases, the lighting is a dream. Dream is the axis of sleep and wakefulness.

The "lighting" forgotten by those who are awake (though they act like sleepers) is recollected by the thinker. It is a fire kindled in oblivion but remembered by one who is truly awake. Thus the thinker preserves the lighting as the recollection of a dream. This dream is the fire of human *poiesis*. It is Logos. It is πῦϱ ἀείζωον. Ordinary men forget the lighting. The thinker, because he remembers and in remembering cherishes the lighting, is not ordinary. He is extraordinary. Human beings who are extraordinary are called heroes. When heroes die they become daimons, or immortal mortals. Ordinary mortals are like sleepers and sleepers are like corpses. The consequent of finitude is forgetfulness. The forgetfulness of our daily lives reminds us of sleep, and sleep augurs the oblivion of death. A mortal who forgets touches upon death, but a mortal who remembers touches upon immortality. This describes the philosophical hero. Philosophical heroism is found in the thinking that thinks Being.

Heraclitus, the thinker of Logos, numbered himself among these heroes. He speaks of them in Fr. B 62: "Immortal mortals, mortal immortals, living the death of the one, dying the life of the other." By occupying this between, the heroic thinker becomes a daimon, one who belongs neither to heaven nor to earth. His thought is a recollection of a fiery dream. In Fr. B 89 Heraclitus distinguishes between waking and sleeping by saying that sleepers have a private world, while those who are awake share a common "cosmos." If remembrance of the Logos (as πῦϱ ἀείζωον, as τὸ ξυνόν) is the criterion for wakefulness, and if "ordinary men" are like those asleep, then "ordinary men" *must be* ἀξύνετοι τοῦ λόγου. In this privacy, surrounded by what is, ordinary men fail to hear the words of a thinker. They are fiery, dreamlike words. Because they are the thoughtful words of heroic recollection, they never fail to sound oracular. Oracular utterings are notoriously obscure. "Obscure" is the nickname bestowed on Heraclitus by history. If anyone at all ever knew what oracles were all about, Heraclitus must have been the one.

III. Oracle

It has often been noted that Heraclitus got his nickname by commanding an oracular style. He shares the oracle's love for cryptic sayings and obscure riddles. Consequently, when he speaks about oracles, his voice tends to be authoritative. In Fr. B 93, he tells us something about the Lord of Delphi: "The Lord whose oracle is in Delphi neither speaks out nor conceals, but gives a sign." This is fittingly enigmatic. If taken literally, it is also untrue. Can an enigma, or a riddle, be understood as a sign? Does an oracle speak in hints and intimations that are signs of a deeper meaning? Is Heraclitus saying that we can't understand oracles straight off but must first decipher them?

No doubt he is. But over two thousand years of history have conspired to give us this saying, and much has been lost in the process. We today have none of the special regard for oracles that led Heraclitus to make his observation. We no longer know what the words really mean. They go like this:

The Lord [ὁ ἄναξ] whose oracle [τὸ μαντεῖον] is at Delphi, neither speaks out [οὔτε λέγει] nor conceals [οὔτε κρύπτει], but gives a sign [ἀλλὰ σημαίνει].

This fragment is actually concerned with telling us something about the god Apollo. In particular, it speaks about the way in which the god communicates himself, i.e., makes himself known. The vehicle, or medium, of such communication is the oracle at Delphi. The god does not speak out through an oracle, nor does he hide behind an oracular façade. Rather, he becomes present "in a sign." This sign is nonetheless made evident by and through the oracle. Such a distinction would not have been too subtle for the early Christians, but it may be for us. We know too little about how a god is present among those who acknowledge him.

Apollo is a god of sunlight. He *is* the sun. We already know that the sun is bounded by darkness (the Erinyes) and therefore subject to *dikē*. Apollo, who is also truth, must remain within his limits. To set limits (except for himself) is the divine prerogative of Zeus. Zeus derives his power from the thunderbolt that "rules all things (Fr. B 64)." Fink, in *Heraklit,* explicitly relates the thunderbolt's fire to "everliving" fire, to the fire of cosmos.

The sun too belongs in this relationship. But so does the earth—and darkness. The Erinyes are denizens of Tartarus, and therefore belong to the chthonic rule of Hades. Thus Hades too is somehow implicated in this fragment. The tangle becomes even more complex when we consider that Heraclitus himself called Hades by another name; in Fr. B 15 he says that Hades and Dionysus are the same. In Heraclitean thought, πῦρ ἀείζωον seems to involve these three deities in some sort of unity. The fragment directly or indirectly invokes Zeus, Apollo, and Dionysus/Hades. This mysterious unity is also Logos (which alone is wise, according to Heraclitus). This Logos does and does not wish to be called by the name of Zeus (Cf. Fr. B 32).

Ho anax, the Lord, keeps his shrine at Delphi. He is a lord of light, bound within limits, and threatened by night. This lord does not conceal himself. But that is obvious. While "nature" (*physis*) loves to hide, Heraclitus indicates, this lord does not. But the Lord (we assume) is Logos. Logos speaks in a λέγειν (*legein*). *Legein* means to bring forward in speech, to speak out. But most paradoxically, Heraclitus tells us that the Lord does *not* speak out. The Lord at Delphi does not become known as *physis* since he does not love to hide (οὔτε κρύπτει), nor does he reveal himself as Logos since he does not speak out (οὔτε λέγει). The Lord neither reveals nor conceals. He does *both.* The way of his becoming known (the joining of concealing and revealing) is named in σημαίνειν. It takes place through the oracle, τὸ μαντεῖον.

What is the "sign" that the god gives? The word σημαίνειν describes the act of minting coins. In that case, it means something like "stamping out an image and its identifying word on gold for the purpose of commerce." The image and the word are minted on a background of gold, from which they emerge but on which they depend for their import. They are merely a way of *identifying* gold. On the other hand, the gold must disappear into the image-word that defines a coin. The coin is a golden image-word. Still, it is the gold in its luster that shines out to reveal the value of this coin. The gold neither hides nor speaks out. It becomes a coin.

So too must the god "mint a coin." He is πῦρ ἀείζωον, and his fire must be revealed in an image-word so that a true exchange might occur: "There is an exchange of all things for fire and fire for all things, as there is an exchange of goods for gold and gold for goods (Fr. B 90)." For gold and by gold, many commodities are gathered into one. The gold, as coin, comes to "rule over" all those things which have been gathered for its sake. The coin itself has been minted because of a need for an exchange, whereby all goods are joined in a common bond. The goods receive their value, and therefore their commercial truth, on the basis of gold. At this level, commerce is an extension of language. The bringing together makes even opposites "common." If we take the analogy at all seriously, we can see that τὸ ξυνόν, the "common," is πῦρ ἀείζωον, the "ever-living fire". This equation is the whole meaning of Logos. The manner in which Logos comes to presence is told in a mythos. This mythos is concerned with the nature of "oracles," with fire, and with the Lord of the temple.

He is the Lord of fire, of thunderbolt, and of shattered limits. He does and does not wish to be called by the name of Zeus. He is and is not Apollo, god of dreams. He is Hades and Dionysus. This Lord neither reveals nor conceals but "gives a sign." This sign is minted like a coin. The god retreats into this golden image-word, thus concealing himself even as he reveals himself. The coin conceals and reveals the god, i.e., the lighting. The coin is offered in exchange for all things, implying the joining of all in the lighting. The nature of this "coin" is named in the saying: μαντεῖον, the oracle.

The god reveals himself through oracles. He who speaks as an oracle—as a voice of the god—is a Seer. Heidegger, in a long passage, describes the Seer for us:

> The Seer stands in sight of what is present, in its unconcealment, which has at the same time cast light on the concealment of what is absent as being absent. The seer sees inasmuch as he has seen everything as present. . . . The seer, ὁ μάντις, is the μαινόμενος, the madman. But in what does the essence of madness consist? A madman is beside himself, outside himself: he is away. We ask: away? Where to and where from? Away from the sheer oppression of what lies before us, which is only presently present, away to what is absent; and at the same time away to what is presently present insofar as this is always only something that arrives in the course of its coming and going. The seer is outside himself in the solitary region of the presencing of everything that in some way becomes present. Therefore he can find his way back from the "away" of this region, and arrive at what has just presented itself, namely, the raging epidemic. The madness of the seer's being away does not require that he rave, roll his eyes, and toss his limbs; the simple tranquility of bodily composure may accompany the madness of vision.

> All things present and absent are gathered and preserved in *one* presencing for the seer. The seer speaks from the preserve of what is present. He is the sooth-sayer (*Wahr-Sager*).[9]

The god does not conceal, nor does he reveal. Rather, he does *both*. It is the Seer who speaks the lighting in remembrance of the lighting and thus reveals it. But because he is not the lighting which gathers and reveals, he also conceals. Blinded by the fire, he sees. Speaking for the god, he conceals.

The Seer is an image-word stamped from ever-living fire. He is the "coin" given in exchange. The Seer is minted from gold to be the "sign" which the god gives. He is ὁ μάντις, the one who speaks out and conceals his guiding divinity. The Seer *is* the oracle. Heraclitus is not concerned here with the Delphic oracle as such, but with the actualization of πῦρ ἀείζωον. This takes place as oracle (τὸ μαντεῖον) through the utterance of a Seer. The Seer is an image-word who speaks the "truth" in the gathering together and preservation of the present in the light of unconcealment.

If we were awake today, and alive to the duties of a Seer, we might call him a "philosopher." But the light is hidden by him who reveals it, so that most people, even when they have "awakened" from sleep and walk in the sunlight, forget the light they kindle for themselves. That is, they forget both themselves *and* their dreams.

Because the philosopher—at least in the mythos we are using to describe thinking—is a "Seer", one through whom the god speaks, a "sign" that the god gives, he will encounter what is divine only by inquiring into himself. He will recollect the nocturnal flame that underlies all his *poiesis*. Heraclitus takes this task seriously, following the Delphic prescription to "know thyself." Heraclitean "pride" is the philosophical—or better, thoughtful—recognition of mediation. This is the hero role that thinking plays. Heraclitus proclaims himself to be a Hero and a Seer. That is why his style is both heroic *and* oracular. The hubris of his writings is heroic hubris, and defines the fundamental insight of his philosophy. Expropriating one of Nietzsche's remarks into our own frame of reference, we can say: "That dangerous word hubris is indeed the touchstone for every Heraclitean. Here he must show whether he has understood or failed to recognize his master."[10] At the beginning of philosophy—all philosophy—lies hubris. Heraclitus, embodied in his writings, incarnated in himself this hubristic heroic role. He proclaimed himself the heroic Seer of philosophy. What is essential, however, is not simply self-proclamation, but getting underway in thought. In Parmenides, for example, radical and literal self-proclamation is partly abandoned—and partly retained. In Plato's dialogues, where Plato himself does not appear, the roles of Hero and Seer are incarnated and portrayed in Socrates. He recollects and mediates the waking dream, and speaks the truth about lighting. In that sense, he is very much a Heraclitean. As a Hero, Socrates ultimately enacts a tragedy in service to his god. As a Seer, he speaks out what he has beheld—he is ὁ μάντις, the prophet, and μαινόμενος, the madman. The

unity of his life as image-word is mythos. Within the mythos, Logos is recollected and spoken out.

   With Heraclitus philosophy discovers its foundations in arrogance. But it is an
arrogance tempered by innocence, and that, as Nietzsche says, makes it great.
One of the profoundest sayings in the writings of Heraclitus is to be found in the
words that comprise the final portion of Fr. B 56. Our knowledge is truly like
those boys who pick lice while they talk. What they have seen, they leave
behind, what they have not seen, they carry with them. Only the greatest thinker
would compare knowing to lice hunting. Only the very greatest would realize
that what we have grasped we have lost (even thought we have gained thereby),
while what remains concealed determines our present condition. This is the true
nature of the restlessness of thinking. Aristotle might have said that by nature all
men are itching to know. He did not. So for all time we have lost the opportunity
to say that thinking is merely the attempt to scratch.

NOTES

N.B. Page references to the Heidegger and Fink seminar are to the original German edition. The English translation of the work, *Heraclitus Seminar, 1966/67,* translated by Charles Seibert (University, Ala.: The University of Alabama Press, 1979) includes a page guide by Dr. Seibert that will assist readers in locating cited passages in the translation.

INTRODUCTION

1. Martin Heidegger and Eugen Fink, *Heraklit* (Frankfurt am Main: Vittorio Klostermann, 1970). English trans.: *Heraclitus Seminar, 1966/67,* tr. Charles Seibert (University: The University of Alabama Press, 1979). Hereafter "H."

2. "Logos (Heraklit, Fragment 50)" and "Aletheia (Heraklit, Fragment 16)," *Vorträge und Aufsätze* (Pfullingen: Verlag Günther Neske, 1954), pp. 207-29, 257-82. English translation in *Early Greek Thinking,* tr. David Farrell Krell and Frank A. Capuzzi (New York: Harper & Row, 1975).

3. G. S. Kirk, *Heraclitus: The Cosmic Fragments* (Cambridge & London: Cambridge University Press, 1970), pp. 3-13.

4. Ibid., p. 7.

5. *Sein und Zeit,* 9th edition (Tübingen: Max Niemeyer Verlag, 1960). English translation: *Being and Time,* tr. John Macquarrie and Edward Robinson (New York: Harper & Row, 1962). See especially §6 where Heidegger, projecting the course of the existential analytic, indicates that Dasein (the questioner) will eventually get understood in its temporality and, hence, in its historicality; at that point in the analytic there would then be an essential reflection back from Dasein as questioned (and thus exhibited as historical) to Dasein as questioner (as hence also historical); thus, in order that the question be worked out, made genuinely transparent to itself, the historical character of the question would need to be concretely exhibited. The latter is the task which Heidegger projects for Part II (the destruction of the history of ontology).

6. Preface to William J. Richardson, *Heidegger: Through Phenomenology to Thought* (The Hague: Martinus Nijhoff, 1963).

7. See *Being and Time* §7.

8. *Zur Sache des Denkens* (Tübingen: Max Niemeyer, 1969), p. 87. English translation: *On Time and Being,* tr. Joan Stambaugh (New York: Harper & Row, 1972), p. 79.

9. H 100, 138 f., 178, 200-202, 259 f.

10. H 259.

2. Krell

1. Martin Heidegger, *Early Greek Thinking,* trans. D. F. Krell and F. A. Capuzzi (New York: Harper & Row, 1975), p. 14.

2. Fink refers to Hegel's characterization of earth as "the elementary individuality"

into which the dead sink back (91); Heidegger to Hegel's ''dismissal'' or ''release'' (*Entlassung*) of nature (98); Heidegger to Hegel's analysis of the ''now'' in the first part of the *Phenomenology of Spirit* (103); Heidegger to the ''to and fro'' of Hegel's dialectical thought (144); Heidegger to an instance of speculative statement, ''God is Being'' (151); and Fink to the interpenetration of Being and Nothingness in Hegel's *Logic* (251). [Note that the numbers in parentheses here and throughout the text refer to the pagination of the German edition of Martin Heidegger and Eugen Fink, *Heraklit* (Frankfurt am Main: Vittorio Klostermann Verlag, 1970). Readers consulting Charles Seibert's English translation of this work, *Heraclitus Seminar, 1966/67* (University: The University of Alabama Press, 1979), should see the Page Guide provided by the translator.]

    3. See *Heraklit,* 31–32, 41, 46, 111–12, 135, 204. Cf. *Early Greek Thinking,* pp. 19 and 102.

    4. G. W. F. Hegel, *Phänomenologie des Geistes,* edited by Johannes Hoffmeister (Hamburg: Felix Meiner Verlag, vol. 114 of the ''Philosophische Bibliothek,'' 6th ed., 1952), p. 19. Cited in the text as: PG, with page number.

    5. Many authors have discussed this matter. See for example Wilhelm Rehm, *Griechentum und Goethezeit* (3rd ed. Bern, 1952). With special reference to Hegel's ''Hellenic ideal'' see J. Glenn Gray, *Hegel and Greek Thought* (New York: Harper Torchbooks, 1968). These sources provide further bibliographical information. I regret that at the time of this paper's composition the anthology edited by Jacques D'Hondt, *Hegel et la pensée grecque* (Paris: Presses Universitaires de France, 1974), was not available to me.

    6. J. Stenzel, ''Hegels Auffassung der griechischen Philosophie,'' in *Verhandlungen des zweiten Hegelkongresses* (Tübingen, 1932), pp. 168–82, esp. pp. 174 and 182.

    7. Livio Sichirollo, ''Hegel und die griechische Welt,'' *Hegel-Studien,* Supplement 1 (Bonn, 1964), pp. 263–83, especially, p. 264.

    8. G. W. F. Hegel, *Werke in zwanzig Bänden,* vol. XVIII, *Vorlesungen über die Geschichte der Philosophie* (Frankfurt am Main: Suhrkamp Verlag, ''Theorie-Werkausgabe,'' 1971), 289–90. This edition will be cited by volume (in Roman numerals) and page (in Arabic numerals). See also *Early Greek Thinking* for the above quotation, pp. 82–83.

    9. G. W. F. Hegel, *Wissenschaft der Logik,* in the Jubiläumsausgabe (Stuttgart, 1936), IV, 90.

    10. In the Jubiläumsausgabe, VIII, 213–14.

    11. In the Suhrkamp edition, XVIII, 329. Cf. Hegel's *Encyclopedia,* § 258, and Heidegger's confrontation with the same in *Sein und Zeit* (Tübingen: Max Niemeyer Verlag, 12th ed., 1972), § 82a, esp. pp. 432–33 n. 1. Hegel's analysis of time as ''intuited Becoming'' should be compared with SZ § 79, at which point it becomes clear why Heidegger resists Fink's cosmological interpretation of time throughout the Heraclitus seminar. Cf. 98–100, 103, 121 (''Ich verbiete Ihnen jetzt, von Zeit zu sprechen''!), 165 (''weil Herr Professor Heidegger heute nicht unter uns ist, können wir es einmal wagen zu sagen''), and elsewhere. It is in fact the problem of *time* that sparks the interpretive conflict between Fink and Heidegger and that serves as the immediate cause of Heidegger's introducing Hegel's philosophy into the discussion again and again.

    12. See especially Martin Heidegger, *Einführung in die Metaphysik* (Tübingen: Max Niemeyer Verlag, 1953), pp. 87–88, 96–104, and elsewhere. English edition, *An Introduction to Metaphysics,* trans. by R. Manheim (Garden City, N.Y.: Doubleday-Anchor, 1961), pp. 96–97, 106–15, etc. See also *Early Greek Thinking,* pp. 59–78 and 102–23.

13. Martin Heidegger, "Hegels Begriff der Erfahrung," in *Holzwege* (Frankfurt am Main: Vittorio Klostermann Verlag, 1950), pp. 105-92. We refer to this essay in the fourth part of the paper.

14. The first appeared in the *Jahrbuch für Psychologie und Psychotherapie* (Freiburg: Karl Alber Verlag, 1958), VI, 33-41. It is apparently an excerpt from a much larger treatise with the same title to be published in the third division of the *Martin Heidegger Gesamtausgabe*. The excerpt itself, however will appear in volume eleven of the *Gesamt- ausgabe*, in the division of published writings, as part of *Identität und Differenz*. The second appears in the current edition of *Identität und Differenz* (Pfullingen: Günther Neske Verlag, 1957), pp. 31-67. The third, whose importance Heidegger stressed to me in a conversation on 16 May 1975, appears in *Wegmarken* (Frankfurt am Main: Vittorio Klostermann Verlag, 1967), pp. 255-72. During this conversation Heidegger remarked that he thought it was important not to let Hegel stand in isolation and that what he tried to do in this essay was to provide a horizon upon which Hegel's relation to the history of philosophy could be seen.

15. Martin Heidegger, "Die Onto-Theo-Logische Verfassung der Metaphysik," in *Identität und Differenz*, pp. 34-35.

16. I have commented on this problem in "Heidegger, Nietzsche, Hegel: An Essay in Descensional Reflection," in *Nietzsche-Studien*, vol. V (1976).

17. Martin Heidegger, "Hegel und die Griechen," in *Wegmarken*, p. 256. Cited in the text as: (W, with page number).

18. In his *Lectures on the Philosophy of History* (Suhrkamp, XII, 305-06) Hegel defines the "flaw" of Greek religion as the complete absorption of its gods in *Erscheinung*, radiant, beautiful appearance. Since the Greeks do "not yet" know Spirit in its universality, they cling to the beauty = appearance of their gods, molded of marble and fantasy. "Only the inner Spirit that is certain of itself can freely bear to dismiss the side of appearance," Hegel notes, adding, "It no longer needs to project naturalness onto spirituality in order to keep hold of the divine." These essential words follow: "Because *subjectivity* is *not yet* grasped in its depths by the Greek Spirit, true reconciliation is *not yet* at hand in it and the human Spirit *not yet* absolutely justified" (my emphases).

19. For the first phrase see Hegel (Suhrkamp), XVIII, 60; for the second, Heidegger, *Einführung in die Metaphysik*, pp. 11-12.

20. A glance into Hildegard Feick's *Index zu Heideggers 'Sein und Zeit'*, 2nd enlarged edition (Tübingen: Max Niemeyer Verlag, 1968), p. 118, gives external evidence of this: references to Hegel are exceeded in number only by those to Plato, Aristotle, and Kant. For more internal evidence, see *Early Greek Thinking*, pp. 14-15, 33-36 (the reference to Kalchas, ὁ μάντις, *may* have been occasioned by Hegel's analysis in *Lectures on the Philosophy of History*, XII, 289-92), 39 (line 19), 82-83, and 105.

21. See for example Martin Heidegger, *Nietzsche*, 2 vols. (Pfullingen: Günther Neske Verlag, 1961), I, 616-32.

22. Martin Heidegger, *Holzwege*, p. 147.

23. A minimally adequate report, even when limited to the *Phenomenology*, would have to go much further than the present effort. It would have to take into account the identification of death as the initial project of consciousness to be "absolute master" over the other and hence the instrument of his death (PG, 144-48), as a moment in the dialectic of human and divine law, man and woman, state and family (PG, 321-30), as the institutionalization of Terror (PG, 418-22), as the fate of heroes in tragedy (PG, 510) and

of God in revealed religion (PG, 523, 545–46), and as the Golgotha of absolute Spirit (PG, 563–65).

24. Theodor Bodammer, *Hegels Deutung der Sprache* (Hamburg: Felix Meiner Verlag, 1969), p. 238, for this and the following.

25. G. W. F. Hegel, *Vorlesungen über die Philosophie der Religion,* in the Jubiläumsausgabe (Stuttgart, 1928), XVI, 238, 247, and 308. Referred to in the text as: (R, with page number).

26. (R, 299): "so sind alle Bande des menschlichen Zusammenlebens in ihrem Grund angegriffen, erschüttert und aufgelöst."

27. (R, 295). Cf. *Vorlesungen über die Philosophie der Geschichte* (Suhrkamp), XII, 304.

28. See Martin Heidegger, *Nietzsche,* II, 141 ff.

29. (R, 300). Cf. the Suhrkamp edition, XVII, 291.

30. In English:

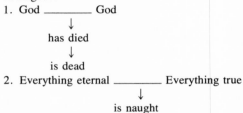

31. In English:

32. What Maurice Blanchot says of the poet after Hölderlin is true also of the thinker: "C'est devant l'absence de Dieu qu'il doit se tenir, c'est cette absence dont il doit s'instituer le gardien.... Aujourd'hui, le poète ne doit plus se tenir entre les dieux et les hommes, et comme leur intermédiaire, mais il lui faut se tenir entre la double infidélité, se maintenir à l'intersection de ce double retournement divin, humain, double et réciproque mouvement par lequel s'ouvre un hiatus, un vide qui doit désormais constituer le rapport essentiel des deux mondes." ("It is in the face of God's absence that he [the poet] must persist; it is this absence he must become the guardian of.... Today, the poet may no longer take his stand between gods and men, as their intermediary, but must persist between the twofold infidelity, maintain his stand at the intersection of this twofold turnabout—divine, human—this twofold and reciprocal movement in which a hiatus opens up, an empty space that from now on must constitute the essential relationship between the two worlds.") Maurice Blanchot, *L'Espace littéraire* (Paris: Gallimard, 1955), pp. 374–75.

33. On the "essence of the nothing" see Martin Heidegger, "Was ist Metaphysik?" in *Wegmarken,* pp. 1–19, and especially Martin Heidegger, *Nietzsche,* II, 49–55.

34. Heraclitus, B 122. See Martin Heidegger, *Gelassenheit* (Pfullingen: Günther Neske Verlag, 1959), pp. 68–71. For the following quotation from Hölderlin's unfinished

hymn, *Griechenland,* see *Early Greek Thinking,* p. 12, and the Beissner-Schmidt edition of the *Hölderlin Werke und Briefe,* 3 vols. (Frankfurt am Main: Insel Verlag, 1969), I, 240.

3. Maly

1. More than characterizing all possibility in Hegel's thinking, this way of saying the issue rather formulates the essential character of the age of modern metaphysics. The greatness of Hegel's work of thinking lies in what emerges there for the first time and is presented to thinking as that which is to be thought. Thus Hegel's thinking goes beyond the subjectivity of modern metaphysics and thus beyond the limits of the thinking of that (our) age. But Hegel's thinking takes place essentially within the age of subjectivity, i.e., of modern metaphysics. It is this aspect that remains, even today, the foremost and central task for thinking.

The same back and forth movement that characterizes Hegel's thinking in general—moving within and beyond subjectivity at the same time—is in play in his interpretations of Heraclitus and of the Greek world: on the one hand he "read into" Heraclitus from out of the perspective of his own authentic thinking; on the other hand he was not unaware of the essential character of the Greek age (cf. H 195).

The following abbreviations are used in this paper:

H   *Heraklit.* Frankfurt am Main: Vittorio Klostermann, 1970.

VA   *Vorträge und Aufsätze.* Pfullingen: Verlag Günther Neske, 1954.

WHD   *Was Heißt Denken?* Tübingen: Max Neimeyer Verlag, 1954.

ZSD   *Zur Sache des Denkens.* Tübingen: Max Niemeyer Verlag, 1969.

2. G. W. F. Hegel, *Differenz des Ficht'schen und Schelling'schen Systems der Philosophie* (Hamburg: Felix Meiner Verlag, 1962), p. 12.

3. Cf. W 269; for an interpretation of Heraclitus in terms of consciousness and rationality see Charles H. Kahn, "A New Look at Heraclitus," *American Philosophical Quarterly* 1:3 (1964): 189–203.

4. Heidegger: "Damit denken Sie schon zu viel" (H 35); "Vielleicht haben Sie damit schon zu viel gesagt" (H 88).

5. Walter Biemel, *Martin Heidegger in Selbstzeugnissen und Bilddokumenten* (Reinbek bei Hamburg: Rowohlt Taschenbuch Verlag, 1973), p. 101.

6. It is perhaps not true to say that this reduction of the meaning of ἀλήθεια takes place only *after* Parmenides and Heraclitus or *after* Plato and Aristotle. Rather already in Homer the word ἀληθής meant true only in opposition to false and usually in connection with verba dicendi. This leads to the question: Is ἀλήθεια (as ἀ-λήθεια, i.e., as derived from with α-privativum) possibly a strange and estranging shape of a word, estrangingly shaped by early Greek thinking in order "to think the most profound issue"? Perhaps the word ἀ-λήθεια is just that "outrageous, unheard of" formulation of the kind that thinking has gathered throughout the history of its thought. Cf., VA 27, I 19 (where the reference is to Heidegger's shaping of the word *Ge-stell*) and SZ 39 (where Heidegger refers to the poverty of ordinary language when thinking is grappling with the one issue for philosophy—how Plato's *Parmenides* and Aristotle's *Metaphysics,* Book VII, are "outrageous, unheard of" when compared to a chapter of Thucydides).

7. The poem of Parmenides could as aptly be entitled Ἀλήθεια as περὶ φύσεος. But the title is not important. What is at issue in the work is the issue for thinking when it is thought in terms of disclosure. And then one could ask: Are Ἀλήθεια and περὶ φύσεος

as titles the names for different issues? Is not the issue named within both "titles" the *one* same issue?

8. Heidegger's attempt to lay out Fr. 16, not as a final correct way of interpretation but as a contribution which offers a question to future thinking, must be read, thought, and re-thought by any thinking whose task is to get at the most fundamental issue for philosophy. This attempt is made in his essay "Aletheia (Heraklit, Fragment 16)," in VA 257–282 (III 53–78); English translation in *Early Greek Thinking*, tr. David Farrell Krell and Frank A. Capuzzi (New York: Harper & Row, 1975), pp. 102–23.

9. In his essay "Aletheia" Heidegger shows how in Homer and the early Greek language λανθάνω and λανθάνομαι and ἐπιλανθάνεσθαι all image—and maintain their essential tie to—their root λαθ- *and* receive their fundamental significance from out of λήθη, remaining hidden.

10. Heidegger says this *one* realm of the λήθη/ἀ-λήθεια most clearly in terms of Lichtung: the *Lichtung* (*das Offene*) is the clearing for light *and* darkness, for sounding *and* fading away, for presencing *and* withdrawal. The task for thinking is not to go further "back" beyond *Lichtung* to something behind it; it is to learn from out of the *Lichtung* itself, i.e. "to let something be said to us . . . from out of it" (ZSD 72).

11. Cf. my paper "Subject, Dasein, and Disclosure," in *Research in Phenomenology* 5 (1975): 191 ff.

12. For an opening up of this difference between Fink's and Heidegger's bearing toward Heraclitus, see F.-W. von Herrmann's contribution in this volume. The issue of world is never really clarified in the seminar itself. For Fink world is the condition for the possibility of what is in the world. Thus world grants what is in it. World in this sense is the ἕν or κεραυνός, which lights up and thus grants what is in the world its place therein. Heidegger's questioning in the seminar tries again and again to show that the *issue* named in Fink's problematic has another issue underlying it: the issue of disclosure. But what is left untouched in the entire discussion is the issue of world as it appears in *Sein und Zeit*, where the issue of world images the issue of *Erschlossenheit* and then of *Sein*. It is important for understanding the seminar to know that Fink is not using the word *world* in the fundamental sense which it has in *Sein und Zeit*.

13. Jacob Klein, "Aristotle, An Introduction," in *Ancients and Moderns. Essays on the Tradition of Political Philosophy in Honor of Leo Strauss*, ed. Joseph Cropsey (New York: Basic Books, 1964), p. 61.

14. G. W. F. Hegel, *Vorlesungen über die Geschichte der Philosophie*, Vol. I, in *Werke* (Frankfurt am Main: Suhrkamp Verlag, 1971), XVIII, 380f.

15. This is in opposition to Kahn's interpretation of Heraclitus. He says: λόγος is "the rational 'account' " (p. 193); Heraclitus relates "the pattern of *nomos* to the rational structure of the *logos* and to reason itself (*nous*)" (p. 198); "rational comprehension is the knowledge of what is common (*xunos*)" (p. 198). Cf. Kahn, op. cit.

16. Klein, op. cit., p. 68.

17. In his large work on Heraclitus Marcovich identifies ἦθος in this fragment with the Greek word ἀρετή. In M. Marcovich, *Heraclitus: Greek Text with a Short Commentary*, Editio maior (Mérida, Venezuela: The Los Andes University Press, 1967), p. 504.

4. Sallis

1. Martin Heidegger and Eugen Fink, *Heraklit* (Frankfurt am Main: Vittorio Klostermann, 1970), p. 259. Hereafter cited as H. The same issue is expressed more problem-

atically by Heidegger in the course of the Heraclitus seminar: Heraclitus' thinking is not yet metaphysical, whereas our thinking is no longer metaphysical. Heidegger grants that the greater difficulty lies in determining the character of the "no longer metaphysical" (H 108, 123–25).

2. Diels-Kranz, *Die Fragmente der Vorsokratiker* (Zurich: Weidmann, 1968), p. 173.

3. John Burnet, *Early Greek Philosophy* (New York: Meridian Books, 1957), p. 136.

4. Kathleen Freeman, *Ancilla to the Pre-Socratic Philosophers* (Oxford: Basil Blackwell, 1956), p. 31.

5. Plutarch, "Concerning the Face which appears in the Orb of the Moon," tr. Harold Cherniss, 28, 943 D–E, in *Moralia*, vol. 12 (Loeb).

6. Cf. Cherniss' Introduction, ibid., esp. p. 24; also ibid., p. 203, note e.

7. Note that the descent to Hades enacted at the beginning of Plato's *Republic* occurs at the festival of Bendis, who is related to or even identical with Hecate, the goddess of the *dark* of the moon; one feature of that festival was to be a torch-race on horseback. Cf. my *Being and Logos: The Way of Platonic Dialogue* (Pittsburgh: Duquesne University Press, 1975), p. 315.

8. Cf. Aristotle, *On Sense and Sensibles* 441 a; *Metaphysics* 980 a.

9. Cf. Karl Reinhardt, *Parmenides und die Geschichte der griechischen Philosophie* (Frankfurt am Main: Vittorio Klostermann, 1959), p. 195; G. S. Kirk and J. E. Raven, *The Presocratic Philosophers* (Cambridge and London: Cambridge University Press, 1957), p. 211.

10. Cf. G. S. Kirk, *Heraclitus: The Cosmic Fragments* (Cambridge and London: Cambridge University Press, 1970), pp. 3–13.

11. E.g., Frr. 1, 2, 17, 34, 51, 56, 72, 104.

12. Cf. *Oxford Classical Dictionary*, p. 484.

13. *Iliad*, XV, 187 ff.

14. H, 64–67, 72–73.

15. After Homer a connection is commonly made between Hades and λήθη. Cf. Simonides 184.6; Plato, *Republic* 621 a.

16. *Odyssey*, XI, 475–76.

17. See the discussion of this fragment in H, 242–46. Note especially Fink's contention regarding the meaning of the final word of the fragment—"dass δοκεῖν hier nicht 'wähnen,' sondern 'vernehmen' bedeutet" ("that δοκειν here signifies not 'believe' but rather 'perceive' ").

18. For review and criticism of the major interpretations, see Kirk, *Heraclitus*, pp. 232–36.

19. Virtually the entire Heraclitus seminar is directed toward clarifying the sense of ἕν and its relation to τὰ πάντα from the various viewpoints from which Heraclitus regards it (as lightning, fire, sun, war, logos). See esp. 11–21, 28–29, 36.

20. Cf. H, 51–54.

21. *On Sense and Sensibles*, 441 a. This is the text, though not the context, in which Aristotle quotes Fr. 7. The quotation comes at 443 a.

22. Cf. Aristotle, *On the Soul*, II, 9.

23. ὅσων ὄψις ἀκοὴ μάθησις, ταῦτα ἐγὼ προτιμέω (Fr. 55). The translation is adapted from Heidegger's, which is defended in H, 224–25.

24. Hesiod, *Theogony*, 756 ff.

25. Diels, 22 A 16.

26. H, 52 f.; cf. Aristotle, *On Sense and Sensibles*, 438 b.

27. Cf. Martin Heidegger, *Early Greek Thinking,* trans. D. F. Krell and F. A. Capuzzi (New York: Harper & Row, 1975), pp. 72–74.

5. Berezdivin

1. Martin Heidegger and Eugen Fink, *Heraklit* (Frankfurt am Main: Klostermann, 1970); English translation by Charles Seibert, *Heraclitus Seminar 1966/67* (University: The University of Alabama Press, 1979).

2. H, 179–80.

3. To fill out the context, the reader may consult the works of Heidegger where he attempts to interpret the Logos. We are heavily indebted to that interpretation and we presuppose it in its entirety here. We shall only make allusions to it.

4. Cf. Liddell and Scott, *Greek-English Lexicon* (Oxford and New York: Oxford University Press, 1966), p. 486.

5. Philip Wheelwright, *Heraclitus* (New York: Atheneum, 1964), p. 88.

6. See Aristotle's arguments about logos in the Metaphysics, about which more later.

7. Geoffrey S. Kirk and John E. Raven, *The Presocratic Philosophers* (Cambridge and New York: Cambridge University Press, 1957), p. 208.

8. Ibid., p. 189.

9. Cf. Rilke, *Sonneten an Orpheus,* Second Part, #1:

   Atmen, du unsichtbares Gedicht!
   Immerfort um das eigne
   Sein rein eingetauschter Weltraum. Gegengewicht,
   in dem ich mich rhythmisch ereigne.

Breathing must be thought along these lines in Heraclitus.

10. H, 41.

11. Cf. Heidegger, *Vorträge und Aufsätze,* vol. III, pp. 3–25.

12. Cf. note 9 above.

6. Guerrière

*A 1975 Summer Grant from the California State University (Long Beach) Foundation facilitated the preparation of this study.

1. The characterization of myth and of philosophy in this prologue will read a lot more dogmatically than self-criticism should allow. However, I would like to plead the usual excuse: a less condensed treatment would unbalance the preliminary and the proper in the interpretation and far exceed its scope.

2. Two excellent articles summarize the work on myth: Percy S. Cohen, "Theories of Myth," *Man,* n.s. 4 (1969): 337–53; and Joseph J. Kockelmans, "On Myth and its Relationship to Hermeneutics," *Cultural Hermeneutics* 1 (1973): 47–86. The resultant definition may be stated as follows: myth is a symbolic exemplary narrative of origins that takes the form of a compact logos (although Kockelmans takes the word in a wider sense, as *Weltanschauung*). For a more extensive essay on myth as a compact logos, and on mythic existence, see Daniel Guerrière, "The Structure of Mythic Existence," *The Personalist* 55 (1974): 261–72. The major influences behind that article and the present analysis are the various works of Mircea Eliade; Paul Ricoeur, *Finitude et culpabilité,* Vol. II: *La symbolique du mal* (Paris: Aubier, 1960); and Eric Voegelin, *Order and History,* Vol. I: *Israel and Revelation* (Baton Rouge: Louisiana State University Press,

1956), and Vol. II: *The World of the Polis* (Baton Rouge: Louisiana State University Press, 1957).

3. The term "be-ing" here is the participle, to be conceived as transitive. Incidentally, the interpreter of Heraclitus need not apologize for the unusual locutions into which he is forced; Heraclitus evidently did not apologize for his.

4. The works decisive in the preparation of this interpretation have been: Martin Heidegger, *Einführung in die Metaphysik* (Tübingen: Niemeyer, 1958), pp. 11-14, 47-48, 54, 77, 87, 95-104, 130-31; "Logos (Heraklit, Fragment 50)" and "Aletheia (Heraklit, Fragment 16)," in *Vorträge und Aufsätze*, Teil III (Pfullingen: Neske, 1954, 1967); and, with Eugen Fink, *Heraklit* (Frankfurt am Main: Klostermann, 1970); also G. S. Kirk, *Heraclitus: The Cosmic Fragments* (Cambridge: Cambridge University Press, 1954, 1962); M. Marcovich, *Heraclitus*, Greek Text with a Short Commentary (Mérida, Venezuela: The Los Andes University Press, 1967); and Eric Voegelin, *Polis*, pp. 220-40. The work by Marcovich is the first complete critical edition of the fragments and will be cited frequently as Marcovich. For a critical edition of the testimonia and imitations, see Rodolfo Mondolfo and Leonardo Tarán, *Eraclito: Testimonianze e Imitazioni*, Introduzione, traduzione e commento (Florence: La Nuova Italia, 1972). In addition to the bibliographies in Kirk, Marcovich, and Mondolfo/Tarán, an extensive, slightly annotated bibliography is provided by Evangelos N. Roussos, *Heraklit-Bibliographie* (Darmstadt: Wissenschlaftliche' Buchgesellschaft, 1971). The notes will not call attention to the debts, whether immediate or remote, that this interpretation owes to the above works, but the reader will recognize them throughout.

5. Martin Heidegger, *Was heßt Denken?* (Tübingen: Niemeyer, 1954), p. 20.

6. The translations will divide the fragments into lines, following Marcovich in all but a few instances. This convention will help to bring out the meaning of the fragments. Besides, the text—with its periodic constructions, paradoxes, and similes—fairly invites stichometry.

7. See Alexander P. D. Mourelatos, *The Route of Parmenides* (New Haven and London: Yale University Press, 1970), pp. 277-78, and the studies cited there.

8. The most sensitive summary of research on the word is Jaap Mansfeld, *Die Offenbarung des Parmenides und die menschliche Welt* (Assen: Van Gorcum, 1964), pp. 262-70; see also Emile Benveniste, *Le vocabulaire des institutions indo-européennes*, Vol. II: *Pouvoir, droit, religion* (Paris: Les Editions de Minuit, 1969), pp. 107-10.

9. On κόσμος, see Hans Diller, "Der vorphilosophische Gebrauch von ΚΟΣΜΟΣ und ΚΟΣΜΕΙΝ," *Festschrift Bruno Snell,* ed. anon. (Munich: C. H. Beck, 1956), pp. 47-60; Jula Kerschensteiner, *Kosmos: Quellenkritische Untersuchungen zu den Vorsokratikern* (Munich: C. H. Beck, 1962), especially pp. 1-114; and Charles H. Kahn, *Anaximander and the Origins of Greek Cosmology* (New York: Columbia University Press, 1960), pp. 188-93 and Appendix One.

10. Another fragment, B 84, may be interpreted within this context: (a) "By changing it rests"; and (b) "Weariness is to toil for and be ruled by the same." These sayings are passed on only by Plotinus and so may be doubtful. If genuine, they may well express dynamic equilibrium. In both, the contrast operative is this: change or rest vs. sameness or weariness. It is restful for it to change, it is wearisome for it to stay (under the dominion of) the same. In change, it is at rest; in fixation, it tires. It—the matter at issue—is a dynamic equilibrium of alteration and repose in self.

11. See Emile Benveniste, "Expression indo-européenne de l'éternité," *Bulletin de la société de linguistique,* 38 (1937), p. 103; R. B. Onians, *The Origins of European*

Thought, 2nd edition (Cambridge: Cambridge University Press, 1954), pp. 200-23, 405-06; and M. L. West, *Early Greek Philosophy and the Orient* (Oxford: Clarendon Press, 1971), p. 158. West's book, important on several counts, will be cited below as West.

12. On this text and its interpretation, see Marcovich, pp. 447-53.

13. The most successful interpretation has been that of Charles H. Kahn, "A New Look at Heraclitus," *American Philosophical Quarterly* 1 (1964): 197. The present attempt appropriates this.

14. "It has apparently not been remarked that the Warder (*ouros*) opposite the Bear (*arktos*) can only be the Bear-Warder (*arktouros*), i.e., Arcturus in Boötes, a well-known star reference as early as Hesiod" (ibid.).

15. Fragment B 66 belongs in the present context: "Fire, having suddenly come upon them, will judge and convict all." I follow Kirk (op. cit., pp. 351, 359 ff.) in rejecting this. For, its content, though reflecting genuine fragments, is incompatible with them. Fire does not "come suddenly upon" anything; it 'constitutes' things. And though indeed judging all in the sense of measuring them out, it does not "convict" all. It *would* seize or convict any which *did* stray from its appointed path (B 94 and 41); but of course nothing *does* stray, for Thunderbolt *in fact* steers all things (B 64).

16. Although this fragment may be an example of the identity of opposites as well, the evidence imports that it belongs in the present context (see West, pp. 121-23).

17. On sixth-century cosmology in general, see Kahn, *Anaximander,* especially pp. 75-165 and 178-93. On the theory of nature in Heraclitus, all the necessary details can be found in Marcovich, pp. 259-349; and in West, pp. 120-23, 129-39, 155-58, 172-76, 190-92. In my opinion, West has given the best possible reading for the difficult B 3 (pp. 175-76; cf. Marcovich, pp. 307-11), B 55 (p. 135), and B 99 (p. 135).

18. On the theory of man in Heraclitus, see Kahn, "A New Look," pp. 198-99; Marcovich, pp. 352-64, 556-59; and West, pp. 147-51, 154-55, 183-88.

19. The term λόγος and the interpretation of it that follows call for some comment. For the range of its sense, see LSJ, s.v. λόγος; and W. K. C. Guthrie, *A History of Greek Philosophy,* Vol. I: *The Earlier Presocratics and the Pythagorians* (Cambridge: Cambridge University Press, 1962), pp. 420-24. On its original sense, see the basic research of Julius Pokorny, *Indogermanisches Etymologisches Wörterbuch* (Bern: Francke, 1959), I, 658; the survey of earlier work in Kirk, op. cit., pp. 37-40; the investigation of Heribert Boeder, "Der frühgriechische Wortgebrauch von Logos und Aletheia," in *Archiv für Begriffsgeschichte* 4 (1959): pp. 82-91 and 101-11; the discussion in E. L. Minar, "The Logos of Heraclitus," *Classical Philology* 34 (1939): 323-41; and the summary by Kahn, "A New Look," pp. 191-92. The question as to whether the term imports the matter at issue or just the account of it is important and strongly disputed. West (pp. 113-29, esp. 124 ff.) offers a very serious challenge to any interpretation that would understand λόγος in B 1, 2, and 50 as other than "account" or "discourse." And it must be admitted that a perfectly coherent and cogent reading of the fragments can be developed if λόγος (and ξύνον: common, public, belonging to all) be understood as the account (given to all by Heraclitus). In fact, such a reading is compatible with the present interpretation; only the title of ξύνον for the matter would have to be withdrawn (not a serious omission) and the following discussion of λόγος left unwritten; nothing essential would change. Perhaps the best defense for taking λόγος as the matter at issue in Heraclitus is offered by Kahn (ibid., pp. 191-93): (1) the word has an "objective" sense in B 31, 45, and 115; (2) a coherent

and cogent reading of B 1, 2, and 50 can be developed if λόγος be understood as *both* the matter and the account; and (3) *given the extensive word-play in Heraclitus, the double sense of the term is quite plausible here* (so that the dispute is fruitless). For a recent, extensive interpretation which accepts λόγος as "objective," see Ewald Kurtz, *Interpretationen zu den Logos-Fragmenten Heraklits* (Hildesheim and New York: Georg Olms, 1971). For a bibliography on λόγος in Heraclitus, see Roussos, op. cit., pp. 56–64. My own interpretation will proceed as if the term meant only the matter at issue, although I think that it means primarily, if not exclusively, the account. The omission of the sense "account" here is not serious (although it must be included in *any* interpretation), since it is easy to develop the reading in which λόγος (and ξύνον) are taken to import 'this public account'. The most profound philosophical interpretation of λόγος as the matter is, I think, that of Heidegger, and my interpretation is in his spirit.

20. The first line is corrupt and is probably not the words of Heraclitus (see West, pp. 118–19).

21. The line reads: τοῦ δὲ λόγου τοῦδ' ἐόντος. I take the genitive as an absolute. Although ἀξύνετον in the next line *may* govern the genitive, the term συνετός means 'intelligent *in* this or that' and often stands alone. Besides, the contrast with the behavior of men is evident, and the genitive absolute here ("Although this" rather than "Of this") better brings out this contrast. The αἰεὶ ("ever") following ἐόντος could modify it instead of ἀξύνετον; but it may well be deliberately ambivalent; the question is not important.

22. This interpretation of ἔπεα and ἔργα is, I think, the best possible (cf. West, p. 117). Heraclitus does not set forth "words and deeds" *as the matter* of his discourse; he rather sets out *all things* (in their unity). Hence "words and deeds," construed in the ordinary restrictive sense, cannot be what he "takes apart" and "shows forth." The term ἔργον should therefore be taken in its basic sense: "what-is-brought-forth"—in this case, all things. In the following two lines, there is evidently a play on words, and the paraphrase here attempts to bring out the double meanings.

23. Needless to stress, this fragment may well name *not* Zeus (the divine side of Physis) but rather Physis as a whole; after all, Physis *is one*. But the ἐξ ("out of") in the last line seems to call for a verb like 'arise' or 'come forth'; and *that* seems to suggest Zeus. In the whole of the present interpretation, the question is not decisive; revision would be simple.

24. Marcovich (pp. 319–21) argues for the authenticity of this fragment. It evidently has a scientific as well as a philosophic dimension.

25. This translation accepts Marcovich's (pp. 162–64) emendation of the MS γραφέων to γνάφων (γνάφος, κνάφος: "carding-comb"). Given the context of the testimony, this must be correct. Nevertheless, the MS version ("of letters/writing") would make no difference in the present interpretation. For a discussion of ancient cloth-fulling, with an illustration of a carding-comb, see R. J. Forbes, *Studies in Ancient Technology*, 2nd edition (Leiden: Brill, 1964), IV, 85–86, 93.

26. For an almost exhaustive discussion of this fragment, and a refutation of the authenticity of B 12b (as well as of B 49 and 91), see Marcovich, pp. 194–214.

27. If authentic, B 4 belongs in this context: "Cattle delight in bitter vetch [rather than in honey, as men would]." Likewise the spurious B 37.

28. A fragment already treated, B 57, may well belong in this context. "Daylight and night" are "one" in cyclic recurrence.

29. Marcovich, pp. 227–30.

30. I accept here Marcovich's (pp. 247–48) emendation of Clement's ὕπνος to ὕπαρ. I also follow his suggestion that the fragment contains an example of the unity of opposites.

31. Evidently Heraclitus did not use the name, but, on one interpretation, the author of the spurious B 112 did: "Discernment . . . is to speak the ἀλήθεα and to act according to φύσιν, paying heed." "Discernment" renders φρόνησις here. This excellent translation I owe to Mr. Paul Schuchman of the New School for Social Research, New York City.

32. The most judicious summary of research is Mourelatos, op. cit., pp. 63–66.

33. Beyond this, ἀλήθεια may be taken to indicate absolute-Being. In fact, this is the case in Parmenides. Though not explicit, this primordial sense remains operative in Plato and Aristotle.

34. This context is as appropriate as any other for the difficult B 102: "To God all things are fair and just, but men have supposed some things unjust and others just." There is some reworking of the original in the source (Kirk, op. cit., pp. 180–81); and it may well be important. Evidently the fragment as quoted imports that the cosmos remains well-measured even while men experience the violations of measure in it. For the essentially Wise, all things are just; but for man, it is not so. What more might this mean?

35. In this context the short B 74 makes sense. Heraclitus is reported to have said that we should not be like "children of our parents." Presumably we should be like 'parents of our children', i.e. like adults; we should, in other words, try to lose our 'silliness' and become wise. Cf. the spurious B 70, 82 and 83.

36. It is apropos to consider B 41 here: 'ἓν τὸ σοφόν: to know the Judgment by which all things are steered through all." Aside from the corrupt text ("by which are steered": see Marcovich, pp. 447–50), there must be something else wrong with this fragment. Probably Diogenes or his source garbled it. For the article in τὸ σοφόν must indicate *the* Wise (as in B 32). The Greek cannot mean: '(human) wisdom is one thing'. Yet the rest of the fragment seems to speak of human wisdom. The original may have read: 'The Wise is one, and it knows [or has or is] that Judgment which [as Thunderbolt] steers everything through all' (cf. West, p. 141).

37. Kurt von Fritz, "Νοῦς, Νοεῖν and their Derivatives in Pre-Socratic Philosophy (Excluding Anaxagoras), Part I: From the Beginnings to Parmenides," *Classical Philology*, 40 (1945): 223–42, as reprinted in *The Pre-Socratics: A Collection of Critical Essays*, ed. Alexander P. D. Mourelatos (Garden City: Anchor Press/Doubleday, 1974), p. 34.

38. Probably spurious is B 113: "The power-for-discernment (τὸ φρονεῖν) is common to all men." That is to say, all men *may* become wise (though few do).

39. Kurt von Fritz, op. cit., pp. 23–43.

40. Probably spurious is B 47: "Let us not conjecture at random about the greatest things" (see Marcovich, p. 572). If authentic, it may be interpreted here: wisdom is νόος and φρόνησις, not conjecture.

41. Referring to the work of Bruno Snell, von Fritz (op. cit., p. 36) writes that "*mathein* and its derivatives originally mean a knowledge, a skill, or also an attitude which is acquired by training, by being brought up in certain ways, or by practical experiences . . . but . . . later they come to designate also the knowledge of specific objects and groups of objects about which very definite and unquestionable knowledge could be obtained."

42. Probably this fragment is spurious (Marcovich, p. 360).

43. Here the γάǫ ("so") must be explicative rather than causative ("for"). For the second line does not give the reason for the first line, though it develops the first line.

44. This may be the context for the doubtful B 95 = 109: "It is better to hide ignorance (ἀμαθίην)." Since the lack of wisdom is shameful, it is better to hide it. However, this dictum may be an ironic attack upon traditional religious practices or upon the traditional teachers of the Greeks. Cf. B 55: that of which there is μάθησις is preferable.

45. The term ἐπιλανθάνονται ("pass-over"), usually rendered as "forget," is unnecessary for the sense of the sentence, but probably added for the word-play on λανθάνει ("escape notice") (Marcovich, p. 10). The translation offered here retains the sense of the original while avoiding the confusion that "forget" may occasion.

46. The doubtful B 73 belongs here: "It is wrong to act and speak like men asleep."

47. Probably spurious, B 46 belongs here: Heraclitus called common opinion or "conceit a sacred disease [=epilepsy]." Men flutter around, agitated; their opinions are epilepsy, i.e., having fits. The many are not only like the epileptic, they are also like the child: their conjectures are "children's toys" (B 70, if genuine).

48. Mourelatos, *Route*, pp. 136-40.

49. This would be the context for the obscure B 124: "The fairest cosmos is but a heap of sweepings piled up at random" (on this text, see Marcovich, pp. 547-50). *For the many,* this is so. They do not see in the cosmos the Ordering and hence Zeus. This is so given *our* world, and would even be so given the *fairest* world—so dull are men in general.

50. On this text, see Marcovich, pp. 78-80; on the proper sense of δοκ- words, reflected in the translation here, see Mourelatos, *Route,* pp. 195-205.

51. It may also be an accurate report that he called Thales, too, an astrologer (B 38).

52. As von Fritz (op. cit., p. 37) says: "What is common to all of them is an unusually broad and detailed knowledge in specific fields: Hecataetus in geography and historical legend, Hesiod also in historical legend and in mythology and earlier mythological speculation, Pythagoras through his interest in various sciences and pseudosciences, and Xenophanes through his travels and as a man who 'saw the cities of many men and came to know their *noos' (Od.* 1.3)."

53. Which "writings" are in question is unknown—and unimportant for a philosophical interpretation.

54. Guthrie, op. cit., pp. 204-05 and 417.

55. The authentic fragment may be less than what is quoted here; see Marcovich, pp. 26-27.

56. The number and trenchancy of the "moral" fragments just surveyed, as well as of the "political" and "religious" fragments to follow, have inspired the interpretive designation of Heraclitus as an "ethical" thinker. This is understandable—and in fact justifiable, so long as the foundation (i.e., Physis, Zeus) for this 'ethical' concern be made explicit. In my opinion, however, such designations come too late for the ambivalent experience of Heraclitus; but they are valuable in bringing to the fore the various dimensions of that experience. For a comprehensive interpretation of Heraclitus as an 'ethical' thinker, see Olof Gigon, *Der Ursprung der griechischen Philosophie,* 2nd edition (Basel and Stuttgart: Schwabe, 1968), pp. 197-243.

57. Here the highly doubtful B 125a may be considered: "May wealth not fail you, men of Ephesus, so that you may be proven to be wicked" (in the usual translation). The text is anachronistic. But Marcovich (pp. 543-45) suggests a corruption from an original

text which may be rendered almost identically: "May wealth not fail the Ephesians, so that they may be exposed as being villainous." Ephesus was a wealthy center of trade, and Heraclitus did not want the city to fail and so to escape by default a judgment as to its character. If genuine, the fragment would have nothing to do with a condemnation of wealth. Rather: sooner or later, the corrupt people, like the fraudulently wise (B 28b, above), will get their confutation.

58. Voegelin, *Polis,* pp. 238–39.

59. For this text, rejecting B 14a, see Marcovich, pp. 464–68.

60. A murderer, to cleanse himself of his blood-guilt, would sacrifice a pig and wash in its blood.

61. Kahn, "A New Look," p. 203.

62. This would be the import of the first part of B 15 if it were to be emended as suggested below. The text now translates: "If they made not a procession to Dionysus and sang not a hymn to shameful parts, then they-behaved [ἔιργασται: "the-conduct-was-conducted"] most shamelessly . . ."; that is, not to perform the rites is shameful. This is a straightforward past *particular* conditional proposition; it is not, as most translations render it, a contrary-to-fact conditional ("were . . . would"). The redundancy of ὕμνεον ᾆισμα (literally "sang a song a song") need not imply a lacuna (*contra* West, p. 145), since the repetition is justifiable as part of a chiastic structure (Marcovich, p. 253). However, there must be something wrong with this proposition. For, as it stands, it does not import a positive rejection of the Dionysiac rites. If we take it to say that their *failure* to perform the rites was *shameful in the estimation of the author,* then it says that Heraclitus implicitly accepts the rites. If we take the proposition to say that their failure was shameful in their *own* estimation, then it says that Heraclitus stands aside as a neutral observer of how some people feel about themselves. It is *these* consequences of the text as it stands that would justify the supposition of a lacuna (cf. West, pp. 145–46). For, given other fragments (B 14b, 5, 29, 117, and 85), given the critical tone of the Heraclitean encounter with other men and their conduct, and given the moderation ("measure") of "wise" praxis for Heraclitus, such neutrality toward Dionysiac rites, not to say acceptance of them, is hardly plausible. Moreover, the second part of the fragment *does* imply a rejection of the rites (as destructive). Therefore, I would accept the hypothesis of a lacuna. Or, alternatively, I would suggest that a scribe or Clement himself (our source) made or inherited a mistake: the negation (μή) in the protasis must be incorrect. In that case, the problems are nicely resolved: "If they made a procession to Dionysus and sang a hymn to (the) shameful parts, then their-conduct-was-conducted most shamelessly; but-even-further (δὲ), Hades and Dionysus—for whom they go mad and revel—are the same."

63. Kahn, "A New Look," p. 203. In a one-word fragment, Heraclitus is reported to have said that the phallic rites are "remedies" (B 68, probably spurious). This would, of course, be an ironic characterization. In the next section it will become clear that the bad man in general suffers "death" and "destruction" of a peculiar kind.

64. West provides the most comprehensive and economical solution for the various interpretive problems concerning the soul and religion, pp. 145–55, 160–63, 183–89, 192.

65. West, pp. 193–94.

66. See the discussion below of B 119. Cf. B 21 and 26 above; these may have something to do with the destiny of the soul.

67. This fragment may further import an exceptional doctrine for a Greek, namely, that corpses are *only* to be thrown away, i.e., *not* buried or cremated. "This treatment would involve maltreatment by dogs and birds, and would be repulsive to ordinary Greek

sentiment'' (West, pp. 183-84). In that case, the point of the fragment as interpreted here would be even stronger.

68. Onians, op. cit., pp. 93-122, 200-08; West, p. 149; and Bruno Snell, *Die Entdeckung des Geistes,* 4th edition (Göttingen: Vandenhoeck & Ruprecht, 1975), Chap. I (cf. Chap. VIII).

69. Voegelin, *Polis,* p. 224.

70. Of course, this fragment also has a scientific dimension.

71. I owe this interpretation to West, pp. 186-88. Cf. Kahn, ''A New Look,'' p. 199, who calls attention to the curse of Menelaus upon the Greek heroes in a moment of cowardice: ''May you all become water and earth!'' (*Il.* 7.99).

72. For this text, see Marcovich, pp. 403-06. The longer text preferred by some scholars does not say anything more.

73. For line two, see Marcovich, pp. 507-08.

74. Antiquity associated this fragment with B 24: ''Gods and men honor those slain in battle.'' It is difficult to interpret the Heraclitean sense of this popular sentiment. If ''gods and men'' imports ''everybody'' (cf. B 30) and ''those slain in battle'' is synecdochic for ''exemplars of civic virtue,'' i.e., the best, then the saying is inconsistent with the direction of Heraclitean thought as a whole, for it is certainly not true that everybody honors the wise man. Perhaps the saying was ironic for Heraclitus and had a complement, explicit or not, that gave it the following sense: ''While men in general honor the soldier who falls in battle, no one [or: only the few] honors the wise—but wait! For he will have his own honor.''

75. For the corrupt opening phrase I accept the emendation by West (p. 153): ἐν θεοῦ δέοντι. The interplay of symbolic and univocal sense is not to be overlooked: the wise are in death as they were in life, i.e., ''awake,'' i.e., ''alive''; just as (cf. B 36) the bad are in death as they were in life, i.e., ''asleep,'' i.e., ''dead.''

76. What is called here the differentiation of the psyche has been investigated under various rubrics. See the citations in footnote 68, as well as Voegelin, *Polis,* passim; and Hermann Fränkel, *Early Greek Poetry and Philosophy* [*=Dichtung und Philosophie des frühen Griechentums,* 3rd edition], trans. by Moses Hadas and James Willis (New York: Harcourt Brace Jovanovich, 1975), pp. 272-73, 298.

77. On the proper sense of the δίζησις family, see Mourelatos, *Route,* pp. 67-68.

78. Cf. Kahn, ''A New Look,'' p. 201.

79. It may be spurious; see Marcovich, p. 569.

80. This interpretation has accounted for every genuine fragment except B 122, which is only a report that Heraclitus somewhere used the word αγχιβασίη (''drawing nigh to''?)—which is impossible to interpret. All the other fragments not mentioned are spurious (see Marcovich, *ad fr.*): B 8, 19, 69, 71, 73, 75, 76, 82, 83, 91, 116, 126, 127, 128, 130 ff.

81. ''Sein und Nichts gehören zusammen, aber nicht weil sie beide—vom Hegelschen Begriff des Denkens aus gesehen—in ihrer Unbestimmtheit und Unmittelbarkeit übereinkommen, sondern weil das Sein selbst im Wesen endlich ist . . .'' (''Was ist Metaphysik?'' [1929], in *Wegmarken* [Frankfurt am Main: Klostermann, 1967], p. 17). Nearly forty years after this lecture, in October 1968, Heidegger said to an interlocutor: ''I make use of this word *Brauch* also to express my thesis about the finiteness [*Endlichkeit*] of Being, to say that Being is no Absolute'' (Zygmunt Adamczewski, ''On the Way to Being (Reflecting on Conversations with Martin Heidegger), in *Heidegger and the Path of Thinking,* edited by John Sallis [Pittsburgh: Duquesne University Press, 1970], p. 34). These few

remarks, however, do not compare to that pervasive expression of the thesis of the finitude of Being—namely, the "necessity" of there-being (*Dasein*) in the Being-process, the "appropriation" of finite there-being by the event-of-presencing.

7. Capuzzi

1. Martin Heidegger, "Aletheia," *Early Greek Thinking,* translated by David Ferrell Krell and Frank A. Capuzzi (New York: Harper & Row, 1975), p. 102.

2. Friedrich Nietzsche, *Philosophy in the Tragic Age of the Greeks,* translated with an Introduction by Marianne Cowan (Chicago: Henry Regnery, 1962), p. 65.

3. Kostas Axelos, *Héraclite et la Philosophie* (Paris: Les Editions de Minuit, 1962), p. 65.

4. Gaston Bachelard, *The Psychoanalysis of Fire,* translated by Alan C. M. Ross, with a preface by Northrop Frye (Boston: Beacon Press, 1968), p. 24.

5. Martin Heidegger and Eugen Fink, *Heraklit* (Frankfurt am Main: Vittorio Klostermann, 1970), p. 62.

6. Ibid., p. 108.

7. Translation of Kirk and Raven.

8. Freud himself did as much with *Jokes and Their Relation to the Unconscious* and the *Psychopathology of Everyday Life*. They are closest in spirit to his masterpiece, *The Interpretation of Dreams*.

9. *Early Greek Thinking,* "Anaximander," pp. 35–36.

10. Nietzsche, op. cit., p. 61.

GLOSSARY

This glossary contains the Greek words that occur in the studies in this volume except for those whose English equivalents are immediately given in the text itself. The listings present (1) the Greek word, (2) a transliteration, and (3) the traditional English translation.

ἀείζωον (from ἀείζωος). *aeizōon:* everlasting.

ἀθάνατος. *athanatos:* immortal.

ἀλήθεια. *alētheia:* truth.

ἀληθης. *alēthēs:* true, unconcealed.

ἀξύνετος. *axunetos:* uncomprehending.

ἁρμονία, ἡ. *harmonia:* a fitting, joining together, proportion, decree (order), harmony.

ἀτρεμός. *atremos:* unwavering.

βάρβαρος, ὁ. *barbaros:* foreigner.

δίκη, ἡ. *dikē:* justice, rule of justice.

δόξα, ἡ. *doxa:* opinion.

εἶδος, τό. *eidos:* form, shape, figure.

εἰρήνη, ἡ. *eirēnē:* peace.

ἕν, τὸ. *hen:* the one.

ἐνέργεια, ἡ. *energeia:* action, operation, energy.

ἐπιστήμη, ἡ. *epistēmē:* knowledge.

ἔρις, ἡ. *eris:* strife, discord.

ἑρπετόν, ὁ. *herpeton:* reptile, snake.

θεός, ὁ. *theos:* god.

θνητός. *thnētos:* mortal.

ἰδέα, ἡ. *idea:* form, appearance.

κεραυνός, ὁ. *keraunos:* thunderbolt.

κόσμος, ὁ. *kosmos:* order, the universe.

λάθοι (from λανθάνω). *lathoi:* I escape notice, am unseen.

λέγειν. *legein:* to lay, gather, arrange.

λήθη, ἡ. *lēthē:* forgetting, forgetfulness, concealment.

λόγος, ὁ. *logos:* saying, word, reason, account.

μάθησις, ἡ. *mathēsis:* learning.

μάντις, ὁ. *mantis:* seer, prophet.

μοῖρα, τό. *moira:* fate.

νοεῖν. *noein:* to perceive, notice, think.

νόος, ὁ. *noos:* mind, judgment, thought.

νοῦς, ὁ. *nous:* intellect.

ξυνός. *xunos:* common, public.

ὄν, τό. *on:* Being, beings.

οὐσία, ἡ. *ousia:* what is one's own, substance, essence.

πᾶν (neuter of πᾶς). *pan:* everything, the whole.

πάντα, τά. *panta:* all, everything.
πίστις, ἡ. *pistis:* faith, assurance, reliability.
πόλεμος, ὁ. *polemos:* battle, war.
πῦρ, τό. *pyr:* fire, fever.
σῆμα, τό. *sēma:* sign.
σοφός. *sophos:* wise, skillful.
σῶμα, τό. *sōma:* body.
τέλος, τό. *telos:* end, accomplishment.
ὕβρις, ἡ. *hybris:* wanton violence, outrage.
φαινόμενον, τό. *phainomenon:* appearance, manifestation.
φρόνιμος. *phronimos:* understanding, thoughtful, discerning.
φύσις, ἡ. *physis:* nature, constitution, origin.
χρεών, τό. *chreōn:* fate, necessity.

SELECT BIBLIOGRAPHY

The following select bibliography may be supplemented by reference to the comprehensive listing given by Evangelos N. Roussos, *Heraklit-Bibliographie*. Darmstadt: Wissenschaftliche Buchgesellschaft, 1971.

Text Editions

Bywater, Ioannes. *Heracliti Ephesii Reliquiae*. Oxford: Clarendon, 1877.

Diels, Hermann, and Kranz, Walther. *Die Fragmente der Vorsokratiker*. 3 vols., pp. 139-90, 491-95. Berlin: Weidmann, 1954.

Heraklit. *Fragmente*. Edited by Bruno Snell. 5th ed. München: Heimeran Verlag, 1965.

Kirk, G. S. *Heraclitus: The Cosmic Fragments*. Cambridge and London: Cambridge University Press, 1970.

Lassalle, F. *Die Philosophie Herakleitos' des Dunklen von Ephesos*. 2 vols. Berlin: Duncker, 1858. [Hildesheim: Olms, 1970]

Marcovich, M. *Heraclitus: Greek Text with a Short Commentary*. Editio maior. Mérida, Venezuela: The Los Andes University Press, 1967.

Mondolfo, Rodolfo. *Heráclito: Textos y problemas de su interpretación*. Mexico: Siglo XXI Editores, 1966.

Mondolfo, Rodolfo, and Tarán, Leonardo. *Eraclito: Testimonianze e Imitazioni*, Introduzione, traduzione e commento. Firenze: La Nuova Italia, 1972.

Schleiermacher, Friedrich. *Herakleitos der dunkle, von Ephesos, dargestellt aus den Trümmern seines Werkes und den Zeugnissen der Alten*. In *Museum der Alterthums-Wissenschaft*. Edited by F. A. Wolf and P. Buttmann. Vol. I, pp. 315-533. Berlin: Realschulbuchhandlung, 1807. [Sämtliche Werke, Abt. III, 2, pp. 1-146. Berlin: Reimer, 1838]

Walzer, Ricardo. *Eraclito. Raccolta dei frammenti e traduzione italiana*. Hildesheim: Olms, 1964.

Studies

Axelos, Kostas. *Héraclite et la philosophie*. Paris: Les Editions de Minuit, 1962.

Beaufret, Jean. *Dialogue avec Heidegger*. Vol. I: *Philosophie grecque*. Paris: Les Editions de Minuit, 1973.

Binswanger, Ludwig. "Heraklits Auffassung des Menschen," in *Ausgewählte Vorträge und Aufsätze*, pp. 98-131. Bern: Francke Verlag, 1947.

Boeder, Heribert. *Grund und Gegenwart als Frageziel der frühgriechischen Philosophie*, pp. 73-117. The Hague: Martinus Nijhoff, 1962.

———. "Der Frühgriechische Wortgebrauch von Logos und Aletheia," *Archiv für Begriffsgeschichte* 4 (1959): 82-112.

Brieger, A. "Die Grundzüge der heraklitischen Physik," *Hermes* 39 (1904): 182-223.

———. "Heraklit der Dunkle," *Neue Jahrbücher für das klassische Altertum* 13 (1904): 686-704.

Bröcker, Walter. "Heraklit zitiert Anaximander," *Hermes* 84 (1956): 382-84.

———. *Die Geschichte der Philosophie vor Sokrates*, pp. 25-47. Frankfurt am Main: Vittorio Klostermann, 1965.

Brun, Jean. *Héraclite ou le philosophe de l'Eternel Retour*. Paris: Editions Seghers, 1965.

Burnet, John. *Early Greek Philosophy*. New York: Meridian Books, 1957.

Cherniss, H. F. *Aristotle's Criticism of Presocratic Philosophy*. Baltimore: Johns Hopkins University Press, 1935.

———. "The Characteristics and Effects of Presocratic Philosophy," *Journal of the History of Ideas* 12 (1951): 319-45, esp. 332-38.

Cleve, F. *The Giants of Pre-Socratic Greek Philosophy*, pp. 31-129. The Hague: Martinus Nijhoff, 1965.

Deichgräber, K. *Rhythmische Elemente im Logos des Heraklits*, pp. 1-76. Wiesbaden: Steiner, 1963.

———. "Bemerkungen zu Diogenes' Bericht über Heraklit," *Philologus* 93 (1938): 12-30.

Diller, Hans. "Der vorphilosophische Gebrauch von ΚΟΣΜΟΣ und ΚΟΣΜΕΙΝ," in *Festschrift Bruno Snell*, pp. 47-60. München: C. H. Beck, 1956.

———. "Weltbild und Sprache im Heraklitismus." In *Das Neue Bild der Antike*, edited by H. Breve. Vol. I, pp. 303-16. Leipzig: Köhler & Amelang, 1942.

Fink, Eugen. *Spiel als Weltsymbol*. Stuttgart: Kohlhammer, 1960.

Freeman, Kathleen. *Ancilla to the Pre-Socratic Philosophers*. Oxford: Basil Blackwell, 1956.

Fränkel, H. *Dichtung und Philosophie des Frühen Griechentums. Eine Geschichte der griechischen Literatur von Homer bis Pindar*. 3rd ed., pp. 422-53. München: C. H. Beck, 1969.

Fritz, Kurt von. "Νοῦς, Νοεῖν and their Derivatives in Pre-Socratic Philosophy (Excluding Anaxagoras), Part I: From the Beginnings to Parmenides." In *The Pre-Socratics: A Collection of Critical Essays*, edited by Alexander P. D. Mourelatos. Garden City: Anchor/Doubleday, 1974.

Gadamer, H. G., ed. *Um die Begriffswelt der Vorsokratiker*. Darmstadt: Wissenschaftliche Buchgesellschaft, 1968.

Gigon, Olof. *Untersuchungen zu Heraklit*. Leipzig: Dieterich, 1935.

———. *Der Ursprung der Griechischen Philosophie. Von Hesiod bis Parmenides*. 2nd ed., pp. 197-243. Basel and Stuttgart: Schwabe, 1968.

Gladigow, Burkhard. *Sophia und Kosmos. Untersuchungen zur Frühgeschichte von σοφός und σοφίν*, pp. 75-124, 133-38. Hildesheim: Olms, 1965.

Guthrie, W. K. C. *A History of Greek Philosophy*. Vol. I: *The Earlier Presocratics and the Pythagorians*, pp. 403-92. Cambridge and London: Cambridge University Press, 1962.

Hegel, G. W. F. *Vorlesungen über die Geschichte der Philosophie*. In *Werke*, XVIII, pp. 319-43. Frankfurt am Main: Suhrkamp Verlag, 1971.

Heidegger, Martin. *Einführung in die Metaphysik*. 3rd ed., pp. 11-14, 47-48, 95-104, 130-31. Tübingen: Max Niemeyer Verlag, 1966.

———. "Aletheia (Heraklit, Fragment 16)," in *Vorträge und Aufsätze*, pp. 257-82. Pfullingen: Verlag Günther Neske, 1954. [3rd. ed., 1967, vol. III, pp. 53-78]

————. *Early Greek Thinking.* Translated by David Farrell Krell and Frank A. Capuzzi. New York: Harper & Row, 1975.

————. "Brief über den 'Humanismus,'" in *Wegmarken,* pp. 145-94, esp. 184-87. Frankfurt am Main: Vittorio Klostermann, 1967.

————. "Hegel und die Griechen," in *Wegmarken,* pp. 255-72, esp. 262-64. Frankfurt am Main: Vittorio Klostermann, 1967.

————. "Logos (Heraklit, Fragment 50)," in *Vorträge und Aufsätze,* pp. 207-29. Pfullingen: Verlag Günther Neske, 1954. [3rd ed., 1967, vol. III, pp. 3-25]

————. "Der Spruch des Anaximander," in *Holzwege,* pp. 296-343. Frankfurt am Main: Vittorio Klostermann, 1972.

————. "Vom Wesen und Begriff der Aristoteles' Physik B,1," in *Wegmarken,* pp. 309-71, esp. 370-71. Frankfurt am Main: Vittorio Klostermann, 1967.

Heidegger, Martin, and Fink, Eugen. *Heraklit.* Frankfurt am Main: Vittorio Klostermann, 1970. English translation: *Heraclitus Seminar, 1966/67,* tr. Charles Seibert. University, Ala.: The University of Alabama Press, 1979.

Heinze, M. *Die Lehre vom Logos in der griechischen Philosophie.* Aalen: Scientia-Verlag, 1961.

Heitsch, Ernst. "Die nicht-philosophische ΑΛΗΘΕΙΑ," *Hermes, Zeitschrift für klassiche Philologie* 90 (1962): 24-33.

Held, Klaus. "Der Logos-Gedanke des Heraklits," in *Durchblicke. Martin Heidegger zum 80. Geburtstag,* pp. 162-206. Frankfurt am Main: Vittorio Klostermann, 1970.

Hölscher, Uvo. *Anfängliches Fragen,* in *Studien zur frühen griechischen Philosophie,* pp. 130-72. Göttingen: Vandenhoeck & Ruprecht, 1968.

————. "Der Logos bei Heraklit," in *Varia Variorum. Festgabe für Karl Reinhardt,* pp. 69-81. Münster/Köln: Böhlau, 1952.

Kahn, Charles H. *Anaximander and the Origins of the Greek Cosmology.* 2nd ed., pp. 224-27. New York: Columbia University Press, 1964.

————. "A New Look at Heraclitus," *American Philosophical Quarterly* 1:3 (July 1964): 189-203.

Kirk, G. S. "Heraclitus' Contribution to the Development of a Language for Philosophy," *Archiv für Begriffsgeschichte* 9 (1964): 73-77.

Kirk, G. S., and Raven, J. E. *The Presocratic Philosophers. A Critical History with a Selection of Texts,* pp. 182-215. Cambridge: Cambridge University Press, 1957.

Kojeve, Alexandre. *Essai d'une raisonnee de la philosophie paienne.* Vol. I: *Les Presocratiques.* Paris: Gallimard, 1968.

Kurtz, Ewald. *Interpretationen zu den Logos-Fragmenten Heraklits.* Hildesheim: Olms, 1970.

Lilja, S. "On the Style of the Earliest Greek Prose," *Commentationes Humanarum Litterarum* 41:3 (1968): 1-150.

Marcovich, M. "On Heraclitus," *Phronesis* 11 (1966): 19-30.

————. "Herakleitos," in Pauly-Wissowa, *Real-Encyclopädie der classischen Altertumswissenschaft,* Suppl. Vol. 10 (1965), pp. 246-320.

Minar, E. L. "The Logos of Heraclitus," *Classical Philology* 34 (1939): 323-41.

Mourelatos, Alexander P. D. "Heraclitus, Parmenides, and the Naïve Metaphysics of Things." In *Exegesis and Argument,* edited by E. N. Lee, et al., pp. 16-48. Athens: Van Gorcum, 1974.

————. *The Route of Parmenides.* New Haven and London: Yale University Press, 1970.

Nietzsche, Friedrich. *Die Philosophie im tragischen Zeitalter der Griechen*. In *Werke*, edited by Karl Schlechta. Vol. III, pp. 349–413. München: Carl Hanser Verlag, 1966.

Ramnoux, C. *Héraclite ou l'homme entre les choses et les mots*. Paris: Les Belles Lettres, 1959.

Reinhardt, Karl. *Vermächtnis der Antike*. "Heraklits Lehre vom Feuer," pp. 41–71. "Heraclitea," pp. 72–97. "Κοπίδων ἀρχηγός," pp. 98–100. Göttingen: Vandenhoeck & Ruprecht, 1966.

————. *Parmenides und die Geschichte der griechischen Philosophie*, pp. 155–230. Frankfurt am Main: Vittorio Klostermann, 1959.

Robinson, J. M. *An Introduction to Early Greek Philosophy*, pp. 87–105. Boston: Houghton Mifflin, 1968.

Snell, Bruno. *Die Entdeckung des Geistes*. 4th ed., chapters 1 and 8. Göttingen: Vandenhoeck & Ruprecht, 1975.

————. "Die Sprache Heraklits," *Hermes* 61 (1926): 353–81.

————. *Die Ausdrücke für den Begriff des Wissens in der vorplatonischen Philosophie* (σοφία, γνώμη, σύνεσις, ἱστορία, μάθημα, ἐπιστήμη), pp. 1–100. Berlin: Weidmann, 1924.

Vlastos, G. "On Heraclitus," *American Journal of Philosophy* 76 (1955): 337–68.

————. "On Heraclitus." In *Studies in Presocratic Philosophy*, edited by D. J. Furley and R. E. Allen. Vol. I, pp. 413–29. London: Routledge & Kegan Paul, 1970.

————. "Theology and Philosophy in Early Greek Thought," ibid., pp. 92–129.

————. "Equality and justice in Early Greek Cosmologies," ibid., pp. 67–73.

Voegelin, Eric. *The World of the Polis*, pp. 220–40. Baton Rouge: Louisiana State University Press, 1957.

Wheelwright, P. *Heraclitus*. Princeton: Princeton University Press, 1959.

Zeller, E. *Die Philosophie der Griechen in ihrer geschichtlichen Entwicklung*, pp. 783–939. Darmstadt: Wissenschaftliche Buchgesellschaft, 1963.

Zoubos, A. N. "Die metaphysische Bedeutung des Wortes Ἅιδης bei Heraklit," *Actes du XIeme Congress international de philosophie* 12 (1953): 54–55.

INDEX